Plagiarism and Literary Property in the Romantic Period

Plagiarism and Literary Property in the Romantic Period

Tilar J. Mazzeo

PENN

University of Pennsylvania Press
Philadelphia

10   9   8   7   6   5   4   3   2   1

Published by
University of Pennsylvania Press
Philadelphia, Pennsylvania 19104-4112

Library of Congress Cataloging-in-Publication Data

Mazzeo, Tilar J.
   Plagiarism and literary property in the Romantic period / Tilar J. Mazzeo.
      p. cm. — (Material texts)
   Includes bibliographical references and index.
   ISBN-13: 978-0-8122-3967-6
   ISBN-10: 0-8122-3967-9 (acid-free paper)
      1. English poetry—19th century—History and criticism.   2. Romanticism—Great Britain.
3. Plagiarism—Great Britain—History—19th century.   4. Plagiarism—Great
Britain—History—18th century.   5. Intellectual property—Great Britain—History—19th
century.   6. Intellectual property—Great Britain—History—18th century.   7. Coleridge,
Samuel Taylor, 1772–1834—Criticism and interpretation.   8. Wordsworth, William,
1770–1850—Criticism and interpretation.   9. Shelley, Percy Bysshe, 1792–1822—Criticism
and interpretation.   10. Byron, George Gordon Byron, Baron, 1788–1824—Criticism and
interpretation.   I. Title.   II. Series.

PR590.M39   2006
821'.709145—dc22   *2006042194*

Contents

Abbreviations

BLJ	*Byron's Letters and Journals*. Ed. Leslie A. Marchand. 12 vols. Cambridge, Mass.: Harvard University Press, 1974.
CLSTC	*The Collected Letters of Samuel Taylor Coleridge*. Ed. E. L. Griggs. 4 vols. Oxford: Oxford University Press, 1959.
LBCPW	*Lord Byron: The Complete Poetical Works*. Ed. Jerome J. McGann. 7 vols. Oxford: Clarendon Press, 1980.
LPBS	*Letters of Percy Bysshe Shelley*. Ed. Frederick L. Jones. 2 vols. Oxford: Oxford University Press, 1964.
LWDW	*Letters of William and Dorothy Wordsworth*. Ed. Ernest DeSelincourt. Rev. Mary Moore and Alan G. Hill. 7 vols. Oxford: Clarendon Press, 1970.
NMS	*Novels and Selected Works of Mary Shelley*. Gen. ed. Nora Crook. 8 vols. London: Pickering and Chatto, 1996.
NSTC	*Notebooks of Samuel Taylor Coleridge*. Ed. Kathleen Coburn. 5 double vols. New York: Bollinger Foundation, 1957.
Poetical WW	*Poetical Works of William Wordsworth*. Ed. Ernest DeSelincourt and Helen Darbishire. 5 vols. Oxford: Clarendon Press, 1949.
PWS	*Poetical Works of Percy Bysshe Shelley*. Ed. Mary Shelley. London: Edward Moxon, 1839.
PWWW	*Prose Works of William Wordsworth*. Ed. W. J. B. Owen and Jane Worthington Smyser. 3 vols. Oxford: Clarendon Press, 1974.
SPP	*Shelley's Poetry and Prose*. Ed. Donald H. Reiman and Sharon B. Powers. New York: W.W. Norton, 1977.
STC	*[The Selected Works of] Samuel Taylor Coleridge*. Ed. H. J. Jackson. Oxford: Oxford University Press, 1985.
TM	Thomas DeQuincey. "Samuel Taylor Coleridge: By the English Opium Eater." *Tait's Magazine* (September, October, and November 1834 and January 1835). Rpt. *The Collected Writings of Thomas DeQuincey*. Ed. David Mason. 2 vols. Edinburgh: Adam and Charles Black, 1854.

WW   *[The Selected Works of] William Wordsworth*. Ed. Stephen Gill. Oxford: Oxford University Press, 1984.

WWSL   *The Complete Works of Walter Savage Landor*. Ed. Stephen Wheeler. 16 vols. London: Chapman and Hall, 1936.

Preface

This book reconsiders allegations that the Romantic poets were plagiarists. In many ways, the subject is a treacherous one. Even after some two hundred years, more or less, these charges of plagiarism evoke strong responses. My objective here, however, is not to reignite a familiar controversy, and it is not to defend or to indict either an individual poet or a literary movement. This is not a book about guilt or innocence, although those have been the terms of the plagiarism debate almost since its inception.

Rather, this study sets out to answer what turns out to be a deceptively simple question: What constituted plagiarism in Britain during the late eighteenth and early nineteenth centuries? From this central historical question, a series of other questions inevitably develop, and these become the topics that give shape to the chapters that constitute this book. For if plagiarism did, indeed, mean something different in Georgian Britain—and how could it not, in a period where the relationship to literary property was legally, culturally, and historically distinctive—then what was at stake when Romantic-period writers levied these charges against each other? How was the articulation of acceptable literary appropriation framed within British culture? To what extent did the rhetoric of plagiarism intersect with the other eighteenth- and nineteenth-century discourses of inheritance, legitimacy, miscegenation, colonialism, consciousness, gender, class, improvement, and enclosure? Was the relationship between commercial print culture and literary culture, between reviewer and poet, constitutive? Perhaps most importantly, has Romanticism's almost exclusive critical association with the values of self-legislating originality helped to obscure the degree to which these writers were concerned with issues of borrowing, textual assimilation, and narrative mastery over another?

The first chapter of this book begins by considering the critical tradition that has privileged Romantic ideas of the autogenous author to the exclusion of models of coterie or collaborative authorship, and it explains why this tradition has focused so intently on the plagiarisms of a single poet, Samuel Taylor Coleridge, as ideologically and culturally aberrant. Within this context, I historicize Romantic plagiarism and its immediate eighteenth-century precursors by distinguishing these borrowings from familiar textual strategies such as imitation and satire. The following chapters take up the alleged plagiarisms of a range of Romantic-period authors, beginning in Chapter 2 with Coleridge's literary obligations and with the conventions of plagiarism outlined by his first accuser, Thomas DeQuincey. My particular interest here is in the critical description of Coleridge's borrowings as psychologically motivated, and, by rereading Romantic-period models of the unconscious, I consider how plagiarism was linked to habit and inhabitation for the poet. Chapter 3 examines the problem of coterie and oral circulation and issues of plagiarism as they emerged primarily in the Wordsworth and Shelley households, and the argument addresses the ways in which private ownership was complicated by both gender and genre, especially for cultural materials located at the margins of literary print culture. Chapter 4 focuses on charges of aesthetic plagiarism levied against Lord Byron, particularly by William Wordsworth and his supporter Henry Taylor, while Chapter 5 rereads Percy Bysshe Shelley's "A Defence of Poetry" and *Alastor* in light of the poet's anxieties about his literary obligations. Finally, Chapter 6 explores Wordsworth's concern regarding the appropriation of his style and voice and examines the charges of plagiarism brought against him in *The Excursion* in relation to the larger legal discourse of enclosure. Wordsworth's rhetorical investment in class metaphors is contrasted with the accusations of plagiarism brought against "peasant" poets such as Ann Yearsley and John Clare in the periodical press.

This study is an avowedly historicist project, and part of my larger objective here has been to interrogate the limits of historical imagination. Put another way, the theoretical ground that this book attempts to negotiate is this: What would it mean to attempt to judge the literary obligations of Romantic-era writers by the standards of their own national moment? In the most obvious sense, of course, this is an impossible project, but the effort has shaped my critical methodology. For me, in this work, that project began with an effort to forestall interpretation and to listen intently to what Romantic-period writers and critics said about the problem of plagiarism, even when that evidence had nothing to recommend it as obviously momentous or contentious. These initially unpromising researches led to unexpectedly interesting places. For, through an accretive process, I came to realize that these writers were in agreement about something that I could not claim to understand: they *knew* what constituted plagiarism in the late eighteenth and early nineteenth centuries, when the term applied, and what the stakes were. In some respects, it was a matter of getting out of the way and letting the historical evidence speak, and my goal as literary interpreter has been to position these voices in relation to the critical tradition of "Romantic" studies and to literary texts from the period, in order to provide a new way of understanding both the perennial question of plagiarism and the specific aesthetic contests that it masks.

Any historicist methodology is, of course, indebted to theoretical paradigms that are broadly familiar to scholars of the Romantic period. In some important respects, this book is a belated response to Jerome McGann's succinct observation in *The Romantic Ideology: A Critical Investigation* that we have tended to accept the self-representations of Romantic-period writers.[1] Insofar as the most familiar of those self-representations have emphasized the "Romantic" ideologies of the solitary genius, originality, and invention to the exclusion collaboration, assimilation, and narrative dominance, this project is an extension of McGann's thesis. However, there are ways in which it represents a revision: one of the central premises of my argument is the contention that there are other equally motivated self-representations that have been overlooked by the critical tradition and which are necessarily integral to any historical understanding of the period. This study demonstrates that early nineteenth-century British writers consistently privileged strategies of textual appropriation even as they emphasized the value of originality. The almost exclusive association of Romanticism with self-origination is largely a belated critical invention.

Moreover, although this project is informed by and sympathetic to the objectives of New Historicism and other recent scholarship deconstructing Romanticism as a disciplinary category and "self-perpetuating model," there is also at least one important respect in which this study does not participate in that critical endeavor: I have not been particularly focused on reading at the margins of Romantic-period culture and have not engaged consciously in "recovery" research, except in relation to the specific category of plagiarism.[2] The early nineteenth-century discourse surrounding plagiarism, however much in need of being historicized at present, was very much part of the mainstream and dominant culture of the period. In many ways it is part of the history that produced the inheritance that we designate the Romantic period. While this book considers several "non-canonical" figures and argues for their relationship to both plagiarism and more familiar literary texts of the early nineteenth century, this is essentially a study of the Romantic "canon" and of the ways in which its formation was connected to the critical debate surrounding plagiarism, influence, and the tradition. I focus primarily on the textual appropriations of Wordsworth, Byron, and Coleridge for no other reason than that these writers were the ones who were accused of plagiarism both in the early nineteenth century and in the subsequent scholarly tradition.

I have used the term *historical imagination* to describe what I consider to be the central methodological goal of this project, and what I mean by that term is perhaps best articulated by Charles Altieri, whose essay "Can We Be Historical Ever? Some Hopes for a Dialectical Model of Historical Self-Consciousness" engages directly the problem of historical impossibility in criticism.[3] In the face of our inevitable failure to view the past as the past viewed itself, Altieri proposes that we might be able to

account for the historical process out of which one finds oneself locating the terms for one's own historical work . . . [by casting] [h]istorical interpretation . . . as responding to a call from the past—not some mystical appeal but a concrete sense of what is incomplete within it that has claims on the present. . . . This makes historical analysis the work of self-consciously taking on the burden of completing or resisting what we show we inherit. (229–32)

This book is an effort at just such an historical relation. In concrete ways, Romanticism and its ideological effects on poetry are the inheritance this study takes up, and plagiarism is one of the claims that early nineteenth-century history makes upon the present. In the course of this study, I use the terms *Romanticism* and *Romantic* deliberately, understanding that these are not neutral categories and that both words invoke a particular critical and aesthetic tradition that has privileged certain values, authors, and forms of subjectivity. The intention in allowing these terms to operate as unmarked signs is not to reify the Romantic ideology but only to reflect the critical inheritance that "Romanticism" necessarily represents for a literary scholar trained as a specialist and professional in that field. If the use of the term *Romantic* is a way of denoting what we inherit in all its complexity and with all its limitations, then I propose that Romanticism's relationship to plagiarism represents one of the claims for incompleteness that this particular history makes on the present. Early nineteenth-century British writers and readers talked about plagiarism. They debated particular instances and its aesthetic implications in both private correspondence and public print media. The critical tradition, however, has analyzed the topic without considering how the historical deployment of the term has evolved. One of the specific ways in which the picture of British Romanticism remains incomplete is in respect to the question of plagiarism—a question that shaped not only how these writers responded to each other but also how the critical tradition of scholarship, from the nineteenth century until the present, has constructed its literary past.

This study challenges that assumption that we know what "Romanticism" was. The characterization of the period and its ideological effects as centered on autogenous originality and models of solitary genius does not square with how early nineteenth-century British writers described or enacted their relationship to appropriation, borrowing, or plagiarism. However, while this book is primarily about Romantic-period literature and its related historical and critical contexts, readers interested in other historical periods and disciplinary approaches will recognize the ways in which the "inheritance" of Romantic authorship continues to shape contemporary analyses of intellectual property. Roland Barthes's famous observations in "The Death of the Author" locate the origins of authorship as an ideological function in the Romantic period, and, of course, many of the "myths" of authorship that he identifies can be located as emergent in late eighteenth-century British culture. In *The Death and Return of the Author: Criticism and Subjectivity in Barthes, Foucault, and Derrida*, Séan Burke demonstrates how persistent the connection between Romanticism and the rise of the author has been in poststructuralism, while the legal historian Fiona Macmillan argues for the "inherent" connection "between the romantic figure of the author, literary theory, and copyright law."[4] However, Romanticism's own commitment to models of autogenous originality and solitary genius is largely rhetorical, as engagement with plagiarism in the period reveals.

Most recently, the mythology of Romantic authorship has been at the heart of critical investigations into the rise of plagiarism in the academy. It is a contemporary truism that plagiarism has reached epidemic proportions in classrooms across America and that this crisis is connected to Internet technologies and to the disruption in print-culture ownership that they represent. In recent years, composition specialists have focused with particular intensity on deconstructing the myth of the singular, autonomous author, and the foundational works in this criticism have identified this myth as an authentically Romantic one. In an important early essay, for example, James Porter argued for two "poles" of authorship, one intertextual and collaborative and the other autonomous and "Romantic," and advocated for the displacement of Romantic models in pedagogical theory. Rebecca Moore Howard advances a similar argument in her influential study *Stand-*

ing in the Shadow of Giants: Plagiarists, Authors, Collaborators, proposing that "by the dawn of the Romantic era, it was no longer acceptable to stand on the shoulders of predecessors" and that, "in the nineteenth century, originality gains the textual prominence that we know today, and with its emergence comes the notion of morality as an attribute of true authorship."[5] While this is a conventional view of Romanticism, historical evidence does not support this characterization of plagiarism in the early nineteenth century. During the Romantic period, plagiarism was primarily concerned neither with textual parallels nor with moral failure. In fact, writers of the period were as concerned with strategies of collaboration and assimilation as they were with the category of originality—values that were not seen as mutually exclusive in the nineteenth century.

This book considers, then, the disjunction between how Romantic-period writers engaged with issues of literary borrowing and how history has come to mythologize them. My thesis proposes that early nineteenth-century British writers understood plagiarism according to criteria that were distinct from twenty-first-century constructions of the charge. Indeed, while modern plagiarism is increasingly critiqued for the "Romantic" values that it privileges, this Romanticism has little in common with the actual ways in which writers in Georgian Britain defined their own relationship to either authorship or appropriation. This history of Romantic-period plagiarism and the aesthetic contests that were central to the contemporary debate are the topics of the chapters that follow.

Chapter 1
Romantic Plagiarism and the Critical Inheritance

[T]he concept of "plagiarism" cannot stand the stress of historical examination.
—*Thomas McFarland,* Coleridge and the Pantheist Tradition *(1969)*

Asking what defined plagiarism in the late eighteenth and early nineteenth centuries in Britain is another way of asking what defined Romanticism. The central claim of this study is that the relationship was constitutive. The stakes in Romantic-period charges of plagiarism were aesthetic, and the contemporary debates regarding the legitimacy or illegitimacy of particular literary obligations masked a larger contest about how to come to critical judgment. But what did plagiarism mean for readers and writers in Georgian Britain? And what defined the success or failure of a literary work in the period that we have come to call Romanticism? As a determination of aesthetic failure, plagiarism and the critical discourse that surrounded it offer a sustained account of the cultural negotiations that shaped the literary expectations of early nineteenth-century readers and writers. This chapter provides an overview of the standards required to "prove" a charge of plagiarism in the Romantic period and focuses particularly on the ways in which the conventions of literary appropriation were historically distinct from both earlier eighteenth-century and current modern/postmodern constructions.

The Elements of Romantic Plagiarism

The basic parameters of plagiarism in the Romantic period were remarkably stable, although there were interpretive disagreements regarding the

precise applications of the standards. The charge and its nuances are explored throughout the course of this study, in chapters dealing with the
particular alleged plagiarisms of writers ranging from Wordsworth and
Coleridge to Byron, Clare, and Shelley. However, by way of introduction
and summary, it will be useful to know that, in early nineteenth-century
Britain, there was, in general, a distinction between two forms of plagiarism, one commonly designated "culpable" plagiarism and the other commonly designated "poetical" plagiarism. Only culpable plagiarism
represented a moral indictment of an author, and it was almost impossible
to demonstrate conclusively during the period. The difficulty stemmed
from the complex circumstances that were required to show that plagiarism
of this sort had occurred. In the period, culpable plagiarism was defined as
borrowings that were *simultaneously* unacknowledged, unimproved, unfamiliar, and conscious. In the absence of any one of these elements, culpable
plagiarism could not be said to have occurred.

In contrast, a writer could be persuasively charged with poetical plagiarism if borrowings were simply unacknowledged and unimproved. Plagiarisms of this sort were not culpable and, therefore, did not carry with
them moral implications. Rather, the charges conveyed an aesthetic violation of the conventional norms by which "literature" was evaluated as distinct from other forms of expression, and authors found guilty of poetical
plagiarisms were simultaneously guilty of writing badly. Plagiarism signaled
a failure to achieve the minimum aesthetic objectives that constituted a successful work of Romantic-period literature, and to be charged with poetical
plagiarism was to face a serious critical attack that focused primarily on
questions of voice, persona, and narrative or lyric mastery. The question of
improvement was central to this charge. Authors who acknowledged their
borrowings and failed to improve upon them, of course, were not typically
charged with plagiarism, although they were frequently derided as con-
temptible writers by reviewers. On the other hand, writers who did not acknowledge their borrowings, even implicitly (and implicit avowal was one
category of acknowledgment), were not considered plagiarists, no matter
how extensive the correspondences, if they had improved upon their borrowed materials. Where improvement existed, acknowledgment was irrelevant because improvement was understood as a de facto transformation of
the borrowed materials.

Particular instances of early nineteenth-century plagiarism can be understood more clearly if we can appreciate the complex ways in which these
categories of acknowledgment, improvement, familiarity, and conscious-

ness operated in relation to each other. In the context of nineteenth-century critical discourse, each of these terms had a particular historically and culturally determined set of associations, and their relationship to charges of plagiarism, extrapolated here from a range of Romantic-period texts on the subject that I discuss in the course of this study, were often the subject of interpretive but not general disagreement.[1]

Acknowledgment: Apart from the obvious strategies of citation, a work could be considered implicitly acknowledged or "avowed" if a "well-versed" reader could be expected to recognize the original. Ironically, the more extensive the borrowing the more likely it was to have been considered acknowledged. The reemployment of texts that were familiar or should be familiar was considered sufficient acknowledgment, and, unlike some of the other, more particularized elements of Romantic-period plagiarism, this was generally true throughout the eighteenth and nineteenth centuries. As A. C. Bradley argued early in the twentieth century regarding Alfred, Lord Tennyson's borrowings from Percy Bysshe Shelley's *Prometheus Unbound* in the 1830s and 1840s, "Sometimes a writer adopts the phrase of an earlier writer . . . with the intention that the reader should recognize it. . . . and if the reader fails to recognize it, he does not fully appreciate the passage."[2] However, the reemployment of borrowed material for the purposes of satire during the Romantic period, even where those intentions were explicit and the sources were acknowledged, could be considered plagiarism because satire was often understood by early nineteenth-century writers and readers to have violated the standard of improvement.

Improvement: By far the most important element of any Romantic-period charge of plagiarism, a successful improvement justified any borrowing, regardless of extent, and no other elements were necessary to defend an author from allegations of illegitimate borrowing. By the same token, in the absence of improvement, no other elements were necessary to indict an author on charges of poetical plagiarism either. Improvement did not necessitate an author making any change to the phrasing or wording of another author's text; it was sufficient to alter the context of the borrowed work, which could include extending the idea, adding new examples or "illustrations," or seamlessly integrating the borrowed text into the voice or style of one's own production. Most often, discussions of improvement rested upon this matter of "seamlessness," and unimproved texts were frequently described as monstrous, patchwork, or unassimilated, suggesting that the evaluation of literary works depended upon precise definitions of textual unity. Unity of style was paramount, and seamlessness depended more upon stylistic qualities of voice and tone than upon other narrative elements. This critical emphasis was supported in eighteenth- and early nineteenth-century law, which recognized style as an element of literary property. Improvement represents one of the clear ways in which Romantic-period assessments of plagiarism rested upon aesthetic judgments, and the discourse surrounding it illustrates how invested early nineteenth-century writers were in appropriation, textual mastery, and the control of voice within a literary work.

Familiarity: The category of familiarity was subject to contemporary disagreement, and the debate concerning which texts constituted part of the common literary inheritance was related to other discussions on the establishment of national literature and on the relationship between "high" and "low" genres. The most conservative position considered as familiar only those major texts that were regularly taught as part of the national curriculum. Shakespeare and Milton were almost universally considered familiar texts, reflecting the nineteenth-century reevaluation of the status of both writers. The most inclusive position considered as familiar a far broader range of texts and included in that category works written in popular genres by contemporary authors. Although not precisely a matter of familiarity, it is worth noting that the protections of literary property only applied without contest to works that were, as the term suggests, identified as literary. Historical and scientific texts, which included travel narratives and folklore, were considered by many in the period as forms of knowledge or learning rather than invention and were treated by some writers as implicitly authorless texts available for general reemployment.

Unconsciousness: Psychological philosophy in the Romantic period was distinct from Freudian and post-Freudian constructions of the unconscious, and contemporary discussions of an author's consciousness of an obligation cannot be easily understood in Freudian terms. The term *unconscious* was in regular use by the turn of the nineteenth century, and it was generally accepted that all writers would borrow unconsciously from time to time. Charges of culpable plagiarism were frequently dismissed on these grounds, and the standard was generous. Often even very extensive borrowings could be considered legitimately unconscious, in part because the knowledge of the act did not always preclude it having been performed unconsciously.

The term *coincidence* is frequently used to describe unconscious plagiarisms and had particular philosophical associations.

The combination of these elements and the emphasis on improvement in particular suggests how deeply invested late eighteenth- and early nineteenth-century writers were in textual strategies of assimilation, absorption, and appropriation. While Romanticism has been traditionally associated with the values of autogenous originality and invention, the cultural conventions of Georgian Britain privileged as literary achievements those novels, dramas, and especially poems that demonstrated mastery over a range of sources, and writers were given broad license to borrow from the works of other authors so long as those appropriations satisfied particular aesthetic objectives and norms.

Modern/Postmodern Plagiarism and the Critical Inheritance

It should also be apparent that these standards of plagiarism are distinct from modern twentieth- and twenty-first-century constructions of the term in clear ways. Perhaps most importantly, questions of improvement and ownership of tone and style no longer operate either legally or rhetorically in the same manner. Because plagiarism represents a statutory violation of property only insofar as it is related to the infringement of copyright or moral tort law, the legal definition of the term is inferred rather than explicit. However, as Stuart Green argues in "Plagiarism, Norms, and the Limits of Theft Law," plagiarism can be defined as the failure to acknowledge the "source of facts, ideas, or specific language" and functions most commonly within the terms set out by the Berne Convention for the Protection of Literary and Artistic Rights as a violation of the "European doctrine of moral rights . . . [particularly] the right of attribution."[3] This definition differs from Romantic-period constructions of plagiarism in several distinct respects, particularly in its exclusive focus on the appropriation of specific language. In other recent court decisions, including *Napolitano v. Trustees of Princeton University* (1982), specific language has been understood to include the verbatim repetition of particular phrases or sentences, the use of paraphrase, and the reemployment of ideas or facts that cannot be considered generally known.[4] Sub-semiotic similarities in voice, tone, or sentiment are notably excluded from this catalogue, and the appropriation of style or "spirit," as early nineteenth-century writers understood those terms, no longer clearly constitutes plagiarism.[5] As a result, modern cultural conventions likewise do not recognize the "improvements" created by textual mastery, which in the Romantic period meant that an author had infused the borrowed materials with her or his own subjectivity to the extent that it became "new" property even when verbatim parallels persisted.

Modern controversies surrounding plagiarism also emphasize the moral elements of the charge to a far greater extent than did the Romantics, who distinguished between culpable and poetical appropriations. In light of the current legal statutes (which have precedent in late nineteenth-century international law) that allow writers to prosecute plagiarism as a violation of moral rights, this investment is not surprising, and, as Green and other scholars have observed, the debate that surrounds plagiarism at the beginning of the twenty-first century is largely figured as a contest between the postmodernists and their detractors, traditionalists of a sort, who dismiss postmodernism as an exercise in moral relativism.[6] The postmodern position, following from the early work of Barthes and Foucault, reads authorship as a cultural function with an institutional history and in its most extreme articulations proposes that plagiarism is a charge used in a market economy to discipline authors and to perpetuate "Romantic" ideas of solitary genius by obscuring the extent to which all writing is necessarily collaborative and intertextual.[7] The traditionalists respond by arguing that this is a transparent effort to excuse plagiarism and the literary theft that it represents by casting it as a deconstructive activity. Both positions are fundamentally concerned with the moral elements of the charge. Scholars such as Rebecca Moore Howard and others working particularly in rhetoric and composition studies understand the recent and apparently epidemic rise of plagiarism on college campuses as the result of a rupture caused by Internet technologies in the structure of authorship, and they propose that student plagiarism often does not reflect an intention to defraud but rather an emergent collaborative relationship to literary property that needs to be explored.[8] Traditionalists dismiss these claims as ridiculous, asserting that plagiarism has always been and remains a transgression against the property of another writer that merits moral condemnation.

Christopher Ricks, one of the most venerable of these traditionalists, has recently been at the center of a particularly acrimonious debate centered on the question of historicizing plagiarism. He has argued both in a 1997 British Academy lecture and in his *Allusion to the Poets* that plagiarism functions as a transhistorical category, and he indicts those who seek to historicize either it or the construction of literary property as apologists engaged in a pernicious moral relativism.[9] Ricks's response indicates how powerfully the moral elements of plagiarism continue to resonate in Anglo-American culture. As Paulina Kewes and the other contributors who respond to Ricks in her collection of essays *Plagiarism in Early Modern England* argue, understanding how plagiarism operated culturally in Renaissance and eighteenth-century Britain is a descriptive position rather than a proscriptive one. Indeed, the same can be said of the Romantic period.[10] Ricks's conflation of historicism with the destruction/deconstruction of moral and literary values is unfortunate because it defines our engagement with the past in a particularly narrow manner, but his outrage is a sign of how important the morality of plagiarism remains in current cultural contexts, postmodern or otherwise.

Authors in early nineteenth-century Britain, however, were neither postmodern nor traditionalist, and they did not understand plagiarism primarily in moral terms. As I have suggested, the "culpable" element was nearly impossible to prove, and few writers in the early nineteenth century were charged persuasively with it. The current debates surrounding plagiarism and our twenty-first-century investment in the morality of authorship cannot accurately explain literary appropriation in the Romantic period. Yet, Romanticism is part of the modern controversy. It is "Romantic" authorship that postmodern scholars hope to deconstruct in the process of theorizing plagiarism and that the traditionalists are seen as defending.[11] This definition of the "Romantic" is particularly unsatisfying because it bears so little historical relation to the complexities of plagiarism in Georgian Britain, and, at the same time, it is part of the critical inheritance of the field. The plagiarisms of the Romantic poets and of Coleridge, in particular, were debated vigorously throughout the twentieth century, but their appropriations have been read in relation to the modern or postmodern conventions of intellectual property. While investigations of this sort tell us a great deal about how we read the Romantics and about our imaginative relationship to our literary past, they tell us much less about how early nineteenth-century writers understood themselves, their poetic objectives, or their use of tradition.

The almost exclusive critical emphasis on the plagiarisms of Coleridge is one way of understanding the distortion that can be produced by applying twentieth- or twenty-first-century standards to late eighteenth- or early nineteenth-century texts. Coleridge's plagiarisms have been scrutinized in a half-dozen different book-length studies, and he has become the literary curiosity of the period in large part because his borrowings contradict the logic of Romanticism: he is the brilliant and innovative poet who claimed imaginative origins for his works but who borrowed covertly from the texts of other writers.[12] The plagiarisms have generated sustained critical interest, I suspect, because Coleridge seems to represent the failure of Romanticism. Casting him as a damaged individual, consumed by private neuroses, twentieth-century scholarship treated both Coleridge's personality and his plagiarisms as exceptional. Yet, Coleridge was not a nineteenth-century anomaly. The tension between originality and appropriation that his plagiarisms embody is the tension that defined the aesthetic objectives of literary Romanticism for the poets writing in the period. At the same time, the singular attention given to his borrowing is clearly disproportionate when we consider that William Wordsworth, Lord Byron, Ann Yearsley, John Clare, Hannah More, Walter Savage Landor, and Matthew Lewis were all publicly accused of plagiarism in the periodical press.[13] The celebrated plagiarisms of Byron, in particular, were the topic of a controversy that was far more extensive than any contemporary attention given to Coleridge's borrowings, yet the critical tradition is largely silent on the matter. Why? The reason has to do, I think, with the assumption that plagiarism meant the same thing in the Romantic period that it meant in the twentieth century. Byron's plagiarisms involved the appropriation of voice, style, and tone, elements that were legally and culturally recognized as elements of literary property in Georgian Britain. In the twentieth century, however, those particular protections no longer operated so powerfully, and Byron's plagiarisms no longer obviously looked like plagiarism at all. Coleridge's borrowings, on the other hand, demonstrated extensive verbatim correspondences, at the same time that his self-defense emphasized a model of unconscious appropriation that was familiar to his contemporaries but did not resonate with modern readers.

The "New" Aesthetics: Imitation and Originality

While modern constructions of plagiarism emphasize the moral elements of the charge and focus particularly on similarities in phrasing, Romantic-era constructions were primarily concerned with aesthetic and stylistic concerns, and, despite some interpretive disagreement, the definitions of culpable and poetical plagiarism went largely uncontested in the period. Late eighteenth- and early nineteenth-century writers and their reviewers by and large agreed that allegations of plagiarism could be settled according to rubrics I have outlined. More importantly, both writers and reviewers understood the charge and its complexities to center on questions of literary judgment. Charges of plagiarism in the Romantic period were an occasion for a sustained critical assessment of a work, and this assessment was typically conducted as a public or semi-public dialogue between the writers and their reviewers—or, as in the case of Wordsworth and Byron and, later, Wordsworth and Landor, a dialogue between two writers in which one or both used the reviewers as mouthpieces. It is not difficult to find instances in which prominent writers of the period were accused of plagiarism, and, seen in aggregate, the pattern suggests that the literary climate was often ruthlessly competitive. Françoise Meltzer and Marilyn Randall have argued that power and dominance are frequently at the heart of allegations of plagiarism, and this is perhaps particularly true in the Romantic period.[14] Conscious of their own involvement in creating "new" poetry, these authors were also keenly aware of the personal and professional stakes involved in failing to articulate the standards by which those works were to be judged. Wordsworth made precisely this point in the "Essay Supplementary to the Preface" (1815) of *The Lyrical Ballads* when he distinguished "new" literature from the simply "novel" or "popular," writing that "genius is the introduction of a new element into the intellectual universe" and that "every author, as far as he is great and at the same time *original*, has had the task of *creating* the taste by which he is to be enjoyed."[15] Coleridge likewise wrote of the "new school of poetry" instantiated by Southey and later Wordsworth, and in some respects the *Biographia Literaria* represents a sustained critical effort to recuperate the aesthetics of the new from the denigration associated with novelty in the eighteenth century.[16] In this context, accusing one's literary competitors of plagiarism—a charge implying precisely the opposite of "new"—offered the occasion simultaneously to dismiss the efforts of another writer as not part of the current literary scene and to demonstrate that exclusion through the exercise and often extended articulation of the aesthetic judgments one considered most valuable.

The sense that the Romantic poets shared that they were engaged in reinventing or reinvigorating English verse is, of course, directly related to the concept of originality that they have been credited with developing. *Originality*, however, is a difficult term, because during the late eighteenth and early nineteenth centuries it did not exclude the possibility of imitation. While the "original" is sometimes understood to imply ex nihilo invention and a solipsistic expressivism, it was employed during the British Romantic period to signify a form of imitation that was transformative because it was individual. In many cases, originality was a function of style rather than content. The earliest articulation of the original as an aesthetic category designating *superior imitation* is generally credited to Edward Young's pre-Romantic *Conjectures on Original Composition* (1759), in which he defined as original the imitation of nature or of the universal rules presented by another author, as opposed to the imitation of his or her particular textual identity.[17] Young argued that imitations from the universal, by which he meant the natural, the true, or the common cultural elements of another writer's text, were original compositions, so long as the appropriation did not extend to personal characteristics, which included style and tone as well as a broader range of localized eccentricities and opinions.[18] In Young's formulation, the potentially "noble Contagion" (94) of plagiarism rested upon a clearly aesthetic judgment: had an author imitated the universal or the particular? In "The Defence of Poetry" (1821), Percy Shelley made a similar point when arguing for the originality of Virgil. It was, Shelley wrote, "with a modesty that ill became his genius [that Virgil] affected the fame of an imitator, even whilst he created anew all that he copied; and none among the flock of mock-birds . . . have sought even to fulfil a single condition of epic truth."[19] Shelley's argument was that, by copying the truth, Virgil had simultaneously borrowed from his predecessors and "created anew," while his imitators—"mock-birds" such as Nonnus, Lucan, and Statius—had failed to write the highest form of poetry because they followed Virgil in the particulars. Thus, when we speak of the ways in which writers of the British Romantic period valorized the original, we need to incorporate into that model an acknowledgment of their simultaneous investment in imitation and assimilation.

Copyright, Satire, and the Ownership of Literary Style

While the discussions surrounding plagiarism in Georgian Britain functioned as a crucible in which the literary values of Romanticism were contested and articulated by writers and their readers, that debate was inevitably shaped by the broader legal and cultural contexts surrounding issues of intellectual property. Unlike copyright infringement, piracy, or forgery, plagiarism was not a charge with direct legal consequences, but it was informed by many of the same concerns, and, although the history of copyright and its influence on eighteenth- and early nineteenth-century publishing is not the subject of this book, there are several significant parallels. The development of a Romantic attitude toward plagiarism that is distinct from earlier eighteenth-century or neoclassical conventions can be traced to the 1760s and becomes culturally dominant by the 1790s, and this emergence mirrors the contemporary legal debates concerning copyright, intellectual property, and the commodification of authorship. Historians such as Mark Rose, Brad Sherman, Lionel Bently, Peter Jaszi, and Martha Woodmansee have documented the complex arguments that shaped copyright law and its related "battle of the booksellers" in eighteenth-century Britain, and they demonstrate that, in the period bracketed by the repeal of the Licensing Act in 1694 and the decision of *Donaldson v. Beckett* in 1774, the conflict was between two competing models of intellectual property, which Rose characterizes as "natural" versus "proprietary" or "artificial."[20] The natural argument extended the position outlined by John Locke in the second of his *Two Treatises of Government* (1690), in which he argued that, through the investment of labor into an otherwise unclaimed property in the state of nature or disuse, an individual could claim a natural and implicitly permanent right of possession over property either real or intellectual.[21] The proprietary argument held that intellectual property could only be owned by social convention and in a limited manner, in order to protect the expansion of knowledge and learning, which needed to circulate freely in order to ensure the progressive civilization of culture. This proprietary argument was privileged in the Statute of Anne in the first decade of the eighteenth century, but the copyright restrictions it created were prevented from enactment until the 1770s. The legal history of copyright during the first three-quarters of the century swung from one pole to the other. The proponents of the natural law argument were vindicated in *Webb v. Rose* (1732) but undermined by the Society for the Encouragement of Learning Act (1736); they won a decisive victory with *Millar v. Taylor* (1769) but were finally reversed by *Donaldson v. Beckett* (1774), which confirmed original limitations to copyright (fourteen years, plus an additional fourteen years if the author were still living) proposed in the Statute of Anne.[22] This interesting history is primarily relevant for understanding Romantic-period attitudes toward plagiarism because it explains one of the central metaphors employed by writers in bringing charges of illegitimate appropriation: the metaphor of the literary estate. Wordsworth was particularly invested in comparing literary borrowing to the trespass upon a figurative "manor," and his commitment to seeing literary property as a natural right comparable to the ownership of real estate placed him in conflict with writers such as Byron and even Coleridge who tended to view the possession of texts as less restricted. In some respect, then, the Romantic poets continued to play out the debate between natural law and proprietary models, as indeed did early nineteenth-century culture more generally.

I have said that distinctively Romantic attitudes toward plagiarism began to emerge in the 1760s and operated coherently in British culture by the 1790s. One sign of this was the renewed interest in charges of plagiarism that began in the decade following *Donaldson v. Beckett.* Despite the notable celebrity of the attacks on Milton at midcentury, early eighteenth-century writers were less invested in charges of plagiarism than their Romantic successors were. Although writers were, of course, accused of plagiarism in eighteenth-century Britain, Augustan literature privileged displays of erudition, imitation, and satire that Romanticism subsequently deemphasized in favor of originality. Because an author's engagement with learning and tradition was a crucial component of his or her ability to "instruct and delight," extended allusions to and unacknowledged borrowings (both particular and universal) from classical and contemporary literary sources were routine in the eighteenth century. A writer could rely upon "well-versed" readers to recognize and to appreciate the complexities of the imitation being presented; or, as Richard Steele described it: "Poetry being imitation, and . . . that imitation being the best which deceives most easily, it follows that we must take up the customs which are most familiar or universally known, since no man can be deceived or delighted with the imitation of what he is ignorant."[23] Because they were more concerned with erudition than with uniqueness, earlier eighteenth-century writers did not need to negotiate the complex tension between originality and imitation that in many respects defines literary Romanticism. Plagiarism represents a critical effort to negotiate that tension, and the interest in charges of illegitimate appropriation during the 1780s and 1790s indicates how central the issue was to the evaluation of literary texts in the Romantic period.

Precisely what constituted plagiarism in the pre-Romantic period has been explicated by Richard Terry in his essay " 'In Pleasing Memory of All He Stole': Plagiarism and Literary Detraction, 1747–1785."[24] Examining attitudes toward plagiarism at midcentury and in the context of the Lauder controversy, in which Milton was posthumously charged with (and vindicated from) plagiarism, Terry argues that neoclassical writers were particularly and often exclusively concerned with verbatim parallels.[25] Indeed, "it is perhaps only at this time," he writes, "that those parts of a literary work over which it was felt that an author could exercise a proprietorial role shrink down so severely to the merely phraseological" (193–94), and he cites as evidence Richard Hurd's 1751 testimony that plagiarism is confined to "the same arrangement of the same words."[26] Terry suggests that this perspective on plagiarism reflects a broader eighteenth-century belief in the "inseparability of invention and imitation" (188), and the perception that an author could borrow from other texts in the process of composing an original work is one that Romantic-period writers shared to a considerable extent with their immediate predecessors. However, the neoclassical emphasis on plagiarism as the reemployment of word-for-word particulars gave way by the last quarter of the eighteenth century to conventions that also characterized the appropriation of stylistic and tonal elements as a literary transgression, and this evolution was related to the increased privileging of both textual originality and identity from the 1770s onward.

Put another way, the aesthetic problem faced by writers at the end of the eighteenth century was how to be simultaneously original—in the more complicated sense of that term articulated by proto-Romantics such as Young—and free to appropriate from the literary tradition, and the solution to this problem lay in the privileging of authorial subjectivity. In his definition of originality at midcentury, Young had distinguished between the particular and universal elements of an imitation and had proposed that originality only precluded the imitation of the *particular* elements of another writer's text. This distinction was codified as a matter of law in the 1760s and 1770s by a series of legal decisions that defined authorial style, sentiment, and tone as elements of literary property. While authors had advocated for the protection of sentiment, in particular, as early as William Warburton's 1747 essay *A Letter from an Author to a Member of Parliament Concerning Literary Property*, the decision in *Tonson v. Collins* (1760) formalized this nascent discourse by finding that, while style could be considered a factor in determining a charge of literary appropriation, it could not be the sole element of the charge, because "only some few may be known by their style . . . the generality are not known at all."[27] The decision concerned charges of plagiarism alleged in *The Spectator*, and the rhetorical effect of this limitation on the extent to which style alone could constitute literary property was to associate distinctive style with the highest literary achievements. By the mid-1770s, style was considered an important element in the evaluation of a text, and it was generally recognized as part of the literary property an author possessed. W. Enfield argued, for example, in his essay *Observations on Literary Property* (1774) that "the style or mode of expression the author used to express their sentiments [was] the exclusive domain of literary property," and this aesthetic valuation of the personal or particular elements of a text as original property was reiterated by Francis Hargrave, who proposed in his *Argument in Defence of Literary Property* (1774) that, "a literary work *really* original, like the human face, will always have some singularities . . . to characterize it and to fix and establish its identity."[28] In the 1770s a legal discourse emerged that increasingly located property rights in the identity of the author and defined originality in terms that recognized a distinction between the imitation of the universal and the particular. While particular borrowings included, of course, the unacknowledged or wrongful appropriation of verbatim expression, of idea, or of narrative "machinery," it also extended to similarities in style, tone, and "spirit."

Romanticism in its various articulations emerges directly out of this context and contributes to establishing these ideas as culturally dominant by the end of the eighteenth century. Because the central tension concerned the negotiation between originality and imitation rather than the exclusive valuation of originality as autogenous invention, writers of this period were centrally concerned with strategies of appropriation and assimilation. One of the results was an intense reemergence of public interest in charges of plagiarism in British print culture from circa 1790–1840. The reevaluation of the role of "particular" imitations in literature also affected the critical reception of certain literary genres. The denigration of satire in the 1780s and 1790s reflects the change inaugurated by new attitudes toward plagiarism. During the first three-quarters of the eighteenth century, satirical imitation was distinguished from plagiarism, and there was the tacit understanding that appropriation for the purpose of satire could rise to the standard of instructive wit. The rise of the English novel depended upon the same conventions of self-imitation, approximation, and mimicry that characterized the Age of Satire generally; Alexander Pope did not trouble himself unduly about adopting Horace's *Satires* for his comic purposes, and Henry Fielding was not charged with plagiarism of Samuel Richardson's *Pamela* (1740) upon the publication of his directly imitative *Shamela* (1741), although Tobias Smollett later accused him of plagiarism for covert and less extensive borrowings from *Roderick Random* (1748) in *Tom Jones* (1749).[29] By the end of 1780s, however, a satirical author could no longer be certain of his or her license to borrow with impunity, and the Romantics, it seems, lost something of the sense of humor their predecessors possessed. As Thomas Lockwood argues in *Post-Augustan Satire*, the late eighteenth century saw the decline of verse satires in particular, and the Romantics often viewed the genre with hostility rather than appreciation.[30] More recently,

Stephen Jones and Gary Dyer have documented this same critical devaluation, although each argues for the continued presence of satire in the Romantic period.[31] This relative decline in the status of satire is related to the pursuit of plagiarism that accelerated during the 1780s and into the 1790s. Authors who had not been charged with plagiarism for satirical works published in the 1750s and 1760s found themselves facing belated charges of plagiarism by the end of the century.

Thomas Mallon has discussed the most celebrated instance in *Stolen Words: Forays into the Origins and Ravages of Plagiarism*, where he details the charges made against Laurence Sterne's *The Life and Opinions of Tristram Shandy, Gent.* (1759–67). Sterne's novel was first published serially just after midcentury without controversy, although contemporary readers could not have failed to recognize his use of source materials. Indeed, early reviewers such as Edmund Burke emphasized that the "story is in reality nothing more than a vehicle for satire."[32] By the 1790s, however, Sterne was being accused of plagiarism from sources that ranged from sermons to Shakespeare, and these charges persisted until at least as late as 1821, when Walter Scott derided Sterne as an "unhesitating plagiarist."[33] Although many of the charges brought by his chief antagonist of the 1790s, John C. Ferriar, were dismissed, the incident demonstrates the interest in debating questions of plagiarism in the periodical reviews that developed at the end of the century and the change in cultural assumptions about what constituted legitimate appropriation.

The charge of plagiarism that Wordsworth brought in 1804 against the satirical poet Peter Bayley reflects this same shift in sensibilities, and it highlights how closely plagiarism was connected to questions of style and to the particularities of literary property.[34] In his complaint, Wordsworth alleged that Bayley simultaneously plagiarized from *The Lyrical Ballads* and satirized them through "ridicule" and "parody."[35] Although Wordsworth recognized that his texts had been reemployed in order to exaggerate and to ridicule them, he insisted that these appropriations constituted plagiarism, and his perspective can be understood more clearly if we reflect that satire necessarily focused on the imitation of particular rather than universal elements of a literary production. The humor of satire depends upon the mimicry of individual characteristics and authorial eccentricities—but particular appropriations were not elements of an original text. As a result, satires were particularly prone to charges of plagiarism, and often those charges centered on the imitation of style.[36] Wordsworth had characterized Bayley's plagiarisms as "absolutely by wholesale" (1: 455), despite the fact that there are no extended word-for-word correspondences between the two volumes. The similarities that grieved Wordsworth were similarities in tone, sentiment, and spirit, textual features that he regarded as elements of his literary property.

This example is among the particular instances of early nineteenth-century literary appropriation that this book sets out to explore more fully, and, like so many other allegations of plagiarism in the Romantic period, Wordsworth's indictment of Bayley demonstrates how historically distinct the discourse was that shaped attitudes toward the charge in Georgian Britain. Over the course of this study, I consider how the rhetoric of plagiarism was used in concrete instances to articulate these and other aesthetic judgments in order to privilege particular literary values. Then, as now, plagiarism mobilized a broad set of cultural expectations regarding ownership, authority, imitation, originality, and legitimacy, but each of these terms operated in a context that was informed for early nineteenth-century writers by the awareness of their own inheritance, one that necessarily did not yet include them or the mythology of the "Romantic" author. The Romantics could not have known that they were Romantic, and their understanding of plagiarism did not and could not reflect the emphasis on autogenous originality only later ascribed to them in nineteenth- and twentieth-century scholarship. Inflected by contemporary legal conditions and marking an internalization of the values of imitation and assimilation that dominated literary culture during the eighteenth century, the public controversies surrounding plagiarism became one of the critical occasions upon which early nineteenth-century British writers and their readers contested, considered, and finally defined the aesthetic objectives of the new literature that they were in the process of imagining.

Chapter 2

Coleridge, Plagiarism, and Narrative Mastery

The critical tradition surrounding Romantic-period plagiarism has been almost exclusively focused on the transgressions of a single poet, Samuel Taylor Coleridge, and one of the claims of this book is the contention that such silent literary appropriations were far more widespread and common among writers of the period and were viewed according to historically distinct standards of intellectual property. However, it is worth considering at the outset why Coleridge's particular borrowings have sparked such controversy and sustained interest. That Coleridge's debts to other writers are substantial is undeniable. They were catalogued piecemeal for readers as early as the nineteenth century, and Norman Fruman's monumental work, *Coleridge: The Damaged Archangel*, effectively settled the questions of whether the poet had unacknowledged sources and what they were. However, had the critical tradition simply documented Coleridge's borrowings, the case would be less interesting. Instead, Coleridge himself—his motivations, his evasions, his character—has frequently become the real subject of analysis. To observe this is not a criticism of the scholars who have shaped this tradition: the trajectory was, in a sense, inevitable. Coleridge himself cast his plagiarisms in terms of the unconscious, and Thomas DeQuincey, in his infamous 1834 serial exposé of the poet, characterized Coleridge's most culpable intellectual debts as a personal neurosis. The psychological analysis of Coleridge's plagiarisms, then, began almost from the moment the borrowings were publicly noted, and since the nineteenth century the question of consciousness has continued to shape some of the most important works of Coleridgean criticism, with the poet's defenders evoking his prodigious powers of memory or eccentric work habits and with his critics documenting the extent of his obligations and deceptions. However, while Coleridge's debts have been extensively catalogued, neither the constructions of plagiarism nor of the unconscious, as Coleridge and his Romantic contemporaries might have understood those terms, have been scrutinized. As we have seen, intellectual property was an evolving legal category during the Romantic period, and plagiarism was often articulated as an aesthetic judgment rather than as a moral one. Likewise, notions of the unconscious and of psychological philosophy were emerging as modern discourses during the eighteenth century, but they cannot be understood in the familiar Freudian terms that were current only at the beginning of the twentieth century. Perhaps most importantly, the particular relationship between questions of consciousness and intellectual property in the Romantic period deserves much closer attention. For, if we are to understand the nature of Coleridge's borrowings and, by extension, the nature of his art, we must understand what he might have intended by claiming his plagiarisms were unconscious—and what his contemporary critics might have imagined was at stake by claiming that they were not.

Thomas DeQuincey and the Principles of Romantic Plagiarism

The public debate surrounding Coleridge's plagiarisms began in 1834, with Thomas DeQuincey's publication in *Tait's Magazine* of four articles on the poet, in which his literary debts were catalogued for the reading public.[1] Although DeQuincey's claim to have been the first to call attention to Coleridge's intellectual obligations was not strictly accurate (they had been noted by Coleridge himself as early as 1796), the *Tait's Magazine* articles inaugurated the controversy and, in doing so, articulated some of the complexities that informed Romantic-period attitudes toward literary property.[2] In *Tait's Magazine*, DeQuincey calls to public attention four potential instances of plagiarism in Coleridge's work: his debt to the German poet Friederike Brun in the "Hymn before Sun-rise" (1802), his borrowings from Milton in "France: An Ode" (1798), his reliance on George Shevlocke's travel narrative *A Voyage around the World* (1726) in *The Rime of the Ancient Mariner* (1797–98), and his appropriations from the philosophical works of Friedrich W. J. von Schelling in the *Biographia Literaria* (1815–17) (*TM* 143–46). In three of the four instances, DeQuincey argues that the charges are overstated. In respect to the last—the appropriations from Schelling—he constructs an account that contemporary readers would have understood as a glancing but devastating critique of the *Biographia Literaria* and its author.

DeQuincey's essays offer one of the most extensive contemporary discussions available to us of what constituted plagiarism in the Romantic period. In these articles, DeQuincey outlines three possible circumstances in which the appropriation from the text of another writer cannot be said to constitute culpable plagiarism: (1) when the author has improved upon the original work; (2) when the author has borrowed from a work so well known that a well-versed reader may be expected to credit the original source; and (3) when the borrowing has been unconscious. The first two circumstances address the nature of the particular textual relationship and rely upon aesthetic judgments, while the last circumstance addresses the problem of intention and relies upon psychological evaluation. On the basis of this definition, DeQuincey analyzes each case of literary borrowing, and he begins by dismissing the debt to Friederike Brun on the grounds that Coleridge has improved upon her work. In DeQuincey's words, there can be no plagiarism, despite the extensive and often word-for-word correspondences, because "by a judicious amplification of some topics, and by its far deeper tone of lyrical enthusiasm, the dry bones of the German outline have been awakened by Coleridge into the fulness of life" (*TM* 143–44). DeQuincey asserts that Coleridge has not paraphrased the poem but has entirely recast the work from an original, despite the obvious verbal parallels between the two texts. Although the obligations to Brun and the degree to which such judgments of improvement were influenced by gender merit further critical attention and are discussed in detail in Chapter 3 of this study, the borrowing was permissible by contemporary standards. By the standards of the time, there was no plagiarism from Brun. Likewise, Coleridge's appropriations from Milton's *Samson Agonistes* (1671) in his poem "France: An Ode" are cast as an example of a poet's legitimate use of literature understood to be part of the public intellectual tradition, on account of its familiarity to readers. On this occasion, DeQuincey argues that

to take a phrase or an inspiriting line from the great fathers of poetry, even though no quotation marks should be added, carries with it no charge of plagiarism. Milton is justly presumed to be as familiar to the ear as nature is to the eye; and to steal from him as impossible as to appropriate, or sequester to a private use, some "bright particular star[.]" (*TM* 144)[3]

Milton's celebrity (figuratively his "star" status) as a poet effectively naturalizes his work and transforms it into a species of property not limited to exclusive or "private use." Implicitly, DeQuincey draws a distinction here between two categories of borrowing: public appropriation and plagiarism. Works in the literary tradition, like the landscape (and perhaps most nearly like the rural village common of the eighteenth century), represent a class of multiple-use property subject to the rights of public domain and forage. As property of value to the entire community, such a work cannot be reserved for exclusive use, even by its author; rather, all authors are free to appropriate from it. Thus, while appropriation can represent a legitimate exercise of common property rights, plagiarism implies the illegitimate violation of rightful exclusivity. Neither the extent of the borrowings nor the absence of attribution is relevant. At stake is simply the class of property itself, and an author had no exclusive rights to a work that had become part of the familiar tradition. In short, DeQuincey tells us that a Romantic-period author could not be charged with plagiarism, irrespective of the extent of a literary obligation, provided the original work either had been improved upon or was part of the common tradition.

In dismissing these types of borrowing from the category of plagiarism, DeQuincey and his Romantic contemporaries were, of course, reflecting the attitude toward intellectual property that had predominated during the eighteenth century. However, unlike his neoclassical predecessors, DeQuincey brings the question of consciousness to bear in his analysis of literary appropriation, and, in doing so, he goes on to propose two additional instances of borrowing that he maintains represent possible instances of plagiarism on Coleridge's part. The question of consciousness as it applied to plagiarism was complex; for, as DeQuincey demonstrates, not all instances of plagiarism were equally censurable. In the *Tait's Magazine* essays, he distinguishes between two categories of plagiarism: "conscious" or culpable plagiarism and "unconscious" or merely aesthetic plagiarism. While both cases imply a species of literary failure within a text, only conscious plagiarism merits a moral condemnation of the author. In the instance of Coleridge's debt to Shevlocke's travel narrative, DeQuincey does not minimize the extent of the borrowings, but he argues instead that the appropriations may be presumed to be *legitimately* unconscious. In the instance of the debt to Schelling, DeQuincey is less generous.

According to DeQuincey, Coleridge had borrowed when writing *The Rime of the Ancient Mariner* from Shevlocke's travel narrative, *A Voyage around the World*, in which the author recounted the story of an unfortunate and superstitious mariner who killed an albatross following his benighted vessel (*TM* 145). Although the textual parallels here are far less extensive than those between the "Hymn before Sun-rise" and Brun's poem, DeQuincey identifies this debt as a clear instance of illegitimate borrowing, which may be justified only because it was unconsciously performed. By turning to the question of consciousness at all, the implication is that Coleridge's borrowings from Shevlocke's text cannot be accounted for as a matter of either familiarity or improvement, and it is not difficult to understand DeQuincey's reluctance to view this otherwise undistinguished travel narrative as part of the common national literary tradition. However, the question of improvement is somewhat more difficult because Coleridge's obligations in this instance are largely narrative rather than word-for-word and because the changes to the context are apparent. While the standard of improvement in respect to the particulars of expression was quite generous in the eighteenth and early nineteenth centuries, the standard in respect to the borrowing of plot or what the Romantics called "machinery" or "situation" was remarkably rigorous. The best evidence of the risks an author took when appropriating narrative elements of another text is Coleridge's own indictment (discussed at greater length below) of Matthew Lewis, whom he charged with "patchwork" plagiarisms of precisely this sort in *Castle Spectre* (1797). Likewise, what Ellen Donkin has characterized as the periodical "paper war" between Hannah More and Hannah Cowley centered on charges of plagiarism that arose from similarities in "essential circumstance[s] in the Plot, and Character" (Cowley iv) of their respective dramas, *Albina* (1779) and *Percy* (1779)—a matter deeply complicated by the fact that *Percy* was an acknowledged translation of a French tragedy and that both plays bear more than a passing resemblance to the unquestionably "familiar" *Othello*.[4] In other words, critics in the period considered it particularly difficult to assimilate or to improve upon "machinery" successfully, and, in DeQuincey's estimation, Coleridge clearly failed to meet the necessary standard of improvement when borrowing narrative elements of his poem from Shevlocke.

In the absence of either familiarity or improvement, the question of consciousness became central in determining the degree of authorial culpability, and DeQuincey was convinced that Coleridge borrowed unconsciously in this instance because, when confronted with the correspondences, the poet denied the debt. This led DeQuincey to believe that Coleridge may have been unconscious of his own actions. To confirm the unwitting nature of the debt, DeQuincey turned to the testimony of William Wordsworth, and Wordsworth, while confirming Shevlocke as Coleridge's source, proposed that "it [was] very possible . . . that, before meeting a fable in which to embody his ideas, he [Coleridge] had meditated a poem on delirium, confounding its own dream-scenery with external things" (*TM* 145). DeQuincey argues that Coleridge's associations and, subsequently, his borrowings were unconscious, to the degree that they were unknown to the author himself. Such unconscious borrowings were considered aesthetically treacherous because the author's ability to exercise mastery over the materials (and, therefore, to write good poetry) was jeopardized by the unwitting nature of the appropriation, but they carried with them no moral censure at all. They were potentially a matter of bad verse but not bad faith. Indeed, unconscious plagiarism was not considered unusual in the least; according to DeQuincey, "An author can hardly have written much and rapidly who does not sometimes detect himself, and perhaps, therefore, sometimes fail to detect himself, in appropriating the thoughts, images, or striking expressions of others" (*TM* 226). As one of the conditions of authorship, unconscious plagiarism, although perhaps regrettable, ultimately became a legitimate form of appropriation—in other words, hardly a plagiarism at all.

In the matter of Coleridge's borrowings from Schelling, however, DeQuincey could find no such justifications, and he begins by arguing that the other legitimizing principles do not apply to this instance. There is, he asserts, neither improvement nor familiarity. In respect to the standard of improvement, DeQuincey finds that "the entire essay, from the first word to the last, is a verbatim translation from Schelling, with no attempt . . . to appropriate the paper by developing the arguments or by diversifying the illustrations" (*TM* 146). Had Coleridge improved upon Schelling, which might have been as simple as adding to this extended transcription a few of his own examples, DeQuincey acknowledges that the threshold for improvement would have been met. Indeed, so long as improvement existed, verbatim borrowings and unacknowledged sources were irrelevant. For modern readers, this is a striking implication. While the twenty-first century values linguistic uniqueness and proper citation, the Romantics—despite having been associated almost exclusively with values of autogenous originality—placed a great deal of importance on models of appropriation. Furthermore, in respect to the question of familiarity, DeQuincey observes that this was also a plagiarism that Coleridge "could in prudence have . . . risked only by relying too much on the slight knowledge of German literature in this country" (*TM* 146). Had Schelling been better known to Coleridge's contemporaries, there would have been no indiscretion. The implication here for modern readers is, perhaps, no less striking: had Coleridge filled the *Biographia* with transcriptions from the works of Milton, Shakespeare, or perhaps even Ann Radcliffe, his borrowings would have been irreproachable.

Having dispensed with the issues of improvement and familiarity, De-Quincey returns to questions of consciousness, the only remaining legitimizing principle on which plagiarism could be justified, and he argues that there are limits to plausibility. Addressing the issue of plagiarism in the *Biographia Literaria*, DeQuincey specifically characterizes Coleridge's debt as a

circumstantial plagiarism, of which it is impossible to suppose him unconscious. . . . Many of his plagiarisms were probably unintentional, and arose from that confusion between things floating in memory and things self-derived which happens at times to most of us. . . . [however] no excess of candour the most indulgent will allow us to suppose that a most profound speculation on the original relations *inter se* of the subjective and the objective, literally translated from the German, and stretching over some pages, could, after any interval of years, come to be mistaken by the translator for his own. (*TM* 226)

Because Coleridge's borrowings—already unacknowledged, unfamiliar, and unimproved—are also conscious, the appropriations are culpable, or, in DeQuincey's phrase, "barefaced" plagiarisms (*TM* 146). Although De-Quincey remains willing to entertain the possibility of "confusion" in other instances, in respect to Schelling's work the error is simply too substantial to have been accomplished without knowledge. This is a critical factor: for DeQuincey, consciousness implies a *knowing* or *witting* performance. As it turns out, Coleridge defines the unconscious rather differently.

The central disagreement between Coleridge and DeQuincey does not pertain to the categories of Romantic-period plagiarism but, rather, to the nuances brought to discussions of the unconscious and its operations in the aesthetic sphere. Georgian culture generally understood plagiarism in terms similar to those that DeQuincey outlines in his *Tait's Magazine* essays, and it was understood that unconscious plagiarism represented a legitimate avenue of defense. Indeed, both the distinction between appropriation and plagiarism and the category of unconscious plagiarism had been part of the contemporary public discourse on intellectual property for at least a decade preceding DeQuincey's essays. In fact, DeQuincey himself borrowed the argument from an 1823 essay "Recent Poetical Plagiarisms and Imitations," written by Wordsworth's friend and advocate Henry Taylor.[5] However, as early as the 1796 "Advertisement" to *The Monk*, Matthew Lewis had acknowledged the possibility of "plagiarisms . . . of which I am at present totally unconscious," and, in 1800, Anna Seward would speak of her "involuntary" and "unconscious plagiarism[s]" from Chatteron.[6] Thus, when Coleridge evokes his unconscious plagiarisms—his poems involuntarily poured forth or composed "in a profound sleep" (*STC* 102), his "genial coincidences" with Schelling (*STC* 235)—he is evoking a relationship to intellectual property that was recently familiar to his contemporaries. However, while the general parameters for understanding Romantic plagiarism were in place as early as the beginning of the nineteenth century, debates as to which particular examples constituted plagiarism persisted, largely on account of the frequently subjective criteria used to understand appropriation. Many of the terms were hotly contested: what, after all, was the threshold of "improvement"? Which works formed part of the common literary tradition? What texts could a well-versed reader be expected to recognize? Perhaps most importantly for understanding Coleridge and his borrowings in the *Biographia*, what were the limits of unconsciousness? This last category, only emergent within British culture during the early eighteenth century and a distinctive part of the Romantic-period attitude toward literary property, was particularly open to interpretation and disagreement.

Coleridge, Plagiarism, and the Psychology of the Romantic Habit

When we consider what Coleridge meant by the term *unconscious*, there is no indication that he understood the matter exclusively in terms of actions "unknowingly" performed. Indeed, in a keen but instructive irony, one definition of the term provided in the *Oxford English Dictionary*, given as "Not realized or known as existing in oneself" (A.3) and attributed to Coleridge in 1800 as its first recorded instance, seems to be precisely out of step with the nuances he brought to the term. Instead, Coleridge associated both the unconscious and his plagiarisms with the operations of habit. Even De-Quincey, in the *Tait's Magazine* essays, observes that Coleridge's plagiarisms had a habitual nature, comparable to his opium habit or to the habit of kleptomania, and he notes that, in respect to plagiarism, he had known other people who, like Coleridge, were "otherwise not wanting in principle, who had habits, or at least hankerings, of the same kind" (*TM* 147). What, then, is the Romantic psychology of the habit? The question preoccupied Coleridge, and it should perhaps preoccupy his critics, if we are keen to understand how he might have imagined his unconscious plagiarisms.

Although one answer to the question of how Coleridge understood habit and the unconscious elements of his art lies in his reading of German philosophy and in those texts he found so compelling as to borrow from wholesale, especially Kant and Schelling, his letters and journal notebooks offer extensive and often self-reflective commentary on the subject. Among his observations, the most striking is an early notebook entry, dated to 1803, in which Coleridge explicitly argues for habit as an unconscious phenomenon. He writes:

Is not *Habit* the Desire of a Desire?—As Desire to Fruition, may not the faint, to the consciousness *erased*, Pencil-mark-*memorials* of or relicts of Desire be to Desire itself in its full prominence? . . . May not the Desirelet [*sic*], a, so correspond to the Desire, A, that the latter being excited may revert wholly or in great part to its exciting cause, *a*, instead of sallying out of itself toward an external Object, B? . . . Whether the marvelous velocity of Thought & Image in certain full Trances may not be explained from the same cause?[7]

Characterizing habit as the "desire of a desire" and emphasizing its "erasure" from consciousness, Coleridge formulates a three-term analogy in which *habit: desire:: desire: fruition.* Erased from consciousness, habit is not unknown or inaccessible to consciousness but is instead a ruin, a memorial, a trace, a *mark* of erasure, still visible but serving only to point back to the thing which it no longer is. Like the Romantic ruin and its sublime landscape, habit becomes the means of return, a return to desire. Reflecting further, Coleridge proposes that habit, as the memorial of a desire once felt, is focused not on the object of desire but on the desire for desire itself. In philosophical terms, the exciting cause of the desire, i.e., habit (a) so corresponds with the desire itself (A) that the thing desired becomes not an object (B) but the exciting cause or the habit itself (a). Out of this complexity, an important fact emerges: for Coleridge, habit is not about the desire for an object, and it is not a desire for possession; instead, habit emerges as a desire to enjoy and to occupy (or perhaps figuratively to *inhabit*) the place of origin. Applied to Coleridge's habitual plagiarism, we discover a claim for an erasure from consciousness conjoined to a claim for an enjoyment of the trace, and what emerges is a partial model of the unconscious. While the desire persists in mind, the action is occluded. From this perspective, plagiarism is the desire for the thing that created the desire (a text, an idea), not in the sense of a desire to own or to possess the object but in order to continue the experience and production of the desiring itself. In short, if Coleridge plagiarized from habit, he did so both *knowingly* and *unconsciously* and because it brought a form of pleasure.

In 1814, Coleridge further elaborated on the nature of habit, and the notion of a persistence of desire and an occlusion of the act continues to inform his understanding of the unconscious nature of the habitual. Writing of his laudanum addiction, Coleridge explains that:

By the long Habit of the accursed Poison i.e. opium my Volition (by which I mean the faculty *instrumental* to the Will, and by which alone the Will can realize itself—its Hands, Legs, & Feet, as it were) was completely deranged, at times frenzied, dissevered itself from the Will, & became an independent faculty.[8]

Here, Coleridge explains how habit comes to be "erased" from consciousness in the separation of volition from the will: as actions become independent and operate irrespective of the will, it becomes possible for the subject to act "unwillingly" rather than "unknowingly." In the derangement of the faculties, the subject acts instrumentally through volition in ways that may or may not correspond with what he or she desires or wills. If consciousness is predicated on *willingness*, rather than on *knowingness*, it becomes possible for plagiarism (or any other habitual act) to be at once deliberate and unconscious. Moreover, if we understand Coleridge to mean by unconscious the operations of habit and inhabitation, produced in disassociation from the will, several of the other ways in which he speaks about his plagiarisms come into focus. Throughout his works, Coleridge describes his plagiarisms according to three predominant metaphors: the phenomenon of ocular spectra, the concept of the "genial coincidence," and—most memorably—the notion of the "divine Ventriloquist."

Coleridge's evocation of divine ventriloquism as a defense against plagiarism is, of course, well known. In respect to the plagiarisms from Schelling, he had claimed in the *Biographia Literaria*, "I regard the truth as a divine Ventriloquist: I care not from whose mouth the sounds are supposed to proceed, if only the words are audible and intelligible" (*STC* 237). One particularly important aspect of the ventriloquism image is its association with inhabitation and the unconscious. The subject of Coleridge's ventriloquism and its relationship to literary possession has been admirably discussed by Susan Eilenberg in *Strange Power of Speech: Wordsworth, Coleridge, and Literary Possession*, and Eilenberg argues for understanding ventriloquism as a model of possession that functions both legally and demonically for Coleridge. While Eilenberg's reading is productive in many respects, when Coleridge casts plagiarism as a matter of throwing one's voice into the body or (harkening back to the sixteenth-century metaphor equating body and text) the corpus of another, he is making a quite different point and one that rejects metaphors of possession or ownership in favor of metaphors of inhabitation or use. The distinction has very different implications for understanding how Coleridge imagined his relationship to intellectual property.

Coleridge's clearest statement on ventriloquism and its associations with the unconscious operations of habit is found in a letter dated 17 December 1800 to John Thelwall. In this letter, he requests that his friend

> Write to me all particulars of yourself, I mean, your present Self—& whether in the higher excitements of mind, ratiocinating or imaginative, you have been able to conjure up *religious* Faith in your Heart, and whether if only as a Ventriloquist unconscious of his own agency you have in any mood or moment thrown the voice of your human wishes into the space without you, & listened to it as to a Reality[.] (*CLSTC* 1: 656)

Here, Coleridge not only specifies that the ventriloquist is unconscious but he illuminates what is at stake in the question of the unconscious itself by emphasizing the degree to which the categories of the unconscious and the unknowing are separate. After all, even as an unconscious ventriloquist, Coleridge assumes that Thelwall *knows* of his vocalization. However, Coleridge imagines that Thelwall may not know *how it has happened*. The ventriloquist, like the plagiarist, is unconscious only of "his own agency" in creating likeness, is unconscious of his volition.

Ventriloquism and Plagiarism in *Christabel*

While ventriloquism offers a rich model for understanding the philosophical nature of Coleridge's anxieties surrounding unconscious plagiarism and the identity of voice, it has implications for reading his verse as well. Although several of his poems dramatize the unconscious operations of composition and vision, Coleridge's most direct engagement with themes of plagiarism, ventriloquism, and volition occurs in *Christabel* (1798–1800), a poem that centers, both critically and aesthetically, on the appropriation of voice and its potency.

In his 1816 preface to *Christabel*, Coleridge drew an explicit connection between the poem and questions of plagiarism. Although the first two sections of *Christabel* had been completed by 1800, the work was not published until 1816, and the long delay occasioned concerns within Coleridge's circle that his critics would misunderstand the direction of literary influence. *Christabel* had been widely circulated in manuscript among the Romantic literary coterie, and, as Coleridge knew, the poem had influenced the compositions of some of his more celebrated contemporaries, including Lord Byron and Walter Scott. He now feared that his own work would appear derivative of precisely those poems and poetic identities that it had helped to shape. Thus, the preface to the poem directly addressed his concern for "precluding charges of plagiarism or servile imitation from myself" (*STC* 66). However, while the dates of composition might have supported any claims to exclusive ownership and originality that Coleridge cared to assert, his preface further reveals the degree to which he understood literary correspondences and the inhabitation of poetic voice as part and parcel of the creative experience. He writes:

[T]here is amongst us a set of critics, who seem to hold, that every possible thought and image is traditional; who have no notion that there are such things as fountains in the world, small as well as great; and who would therefore charitably derive every rill they behold flowing, from a perforation made in some other man's tank. I am confident, however, that as far as the present poem is concerned, the celebrated poets whose writings I may be suspected of having imitated, either in particular passages, or in the tone and spirit of the whole, would be among the first to vindicate me from the charge, and who, on any striking coincidence, would permit me to address them in this doggerel version of two monkish Latin hexameters:

'Tis mine and it is likewise yours;
But an if this will not do;
Let it be mine, good friend! For I
Am the poorer of the two. (*STC* 66)

In this wry explication, Coleridge maintains that literary property has its origins in communal and natural resources and that it cannot be considered exclusive except in the most conventional or "traditional" manner. He rightly ascribes these rigid attitudes toward literary origins and originality to his contemporary periodical reviewers, for whom the plagiarism debate represented a mode of critical practice. In *Reading, Writing, and Romanticism: The Anxiety of Reception*, Lucy Newlyn offers a reading of the preface to *Christabel* and of this doggerel that emphasizes precisely this "competitive-collaborative relationship between creativity and criticism" (xii); however, Newlyn also reads the preface as internally conflicted, asking whether "there [is] not a contradiction . . . between the collaborative idea of social diffusion embodied in the practice of 'reading aloud' and the proprietorial model of authorship implied in his resentment that 'Christabel' had been plagiarized?" (64). I call attention to Newlyn's reading because it engages the traditional view of Coleridge and his relationship to literary prop-

erty—a view that does not persuasively reflect the complexity of his position or his motivations. By characterizing the tone of the preface as
resentful and the doggerel as a "disingenuous . . . device of false modesty"
(64), Newlyn reads literally a passage that is marked by ironic gestures and
that engages precisely the contradiction that she identifies. Coleridge demonstrates in his doggerel verse the degree to which ventriloquism and the
inhabitation of poetic voice undermines conventional categories of authorship. Indeed, Coleridge privileges oral culture and collaboration over proprietorial models in a rather pointed response to the position taken by the
periodical reviews, magazines whose contributors were disproportionately
trained in the legal professions. The irony is heightened in the preface by
the layers of allusion, as well; Coleridge is mimicking the poetic voice of
Walter Scott, whose popular *Lay of the Last Minstrel* (1805) was deeply indebted to the unpublished *Christabel* for its characteristic and celebrated
metrical devices—while simultaneously appropriating and translating the
actual verses of an unnamed "barbarous Latin poet."[9] Represented as a
form of ironic ventriloquism, the doggerel thus performs a complex self-
imitation, in which Coleridge introduces the poem by projecting the site of
its articulation elsewhere. The result is a poetic voice authentically original
but identifiably other, and Coleridge's point is that an author cannot have
it both ways: if the material content of poetry is communal then the poetic
identity produced by it must be as well.

In "Meter, Identity, Voice: Untranslating *Christabel*," Margaret Russett extends the discussion of plagiarism in the poem and its preface to illuminate these metrical issues that were clearly at stake in imitations of
Christabel, and in doing so she outlines a way of understanding the Romantic category of "originality" that makes a great deal of sense.[10] Coleridge
was distinctly aware that Wordsworth, Byron, and Scott had each reemployed the "peculiar meter" (*CLSTC* 4:603) of *Christabel*, and there are numerous examples in the Romantic period of meter, style, or what Coleridge
here calls "tone and spirit" being treated as elements of literary property
capable of being plagiarized.[11] Russett, however, extends this historical observation to link Coleridge's writings on the metrical innovation in *Christabel* with both the formulation of voiced poetic identity and the theory of
literary "untranslatableness" that he proposes in the *Biographia*, in order to
argue that originality was not achieved through "novelty" or invention but
rather through the process of "imbu[ing] an iterable pattern with unaccountable variation" (*Biographia*, qtd. in Russett 775–76). Understood in
terms of meter, this means transforming familiar patterns of accentuation

and stress through "countless modifications" of the inherited tradition rather than through "the introduction of new metres" (775). Or, as Russett puts it, "Originality does not consist in the repression of sonic matter, but in its mastery" (775). This succinctly articulates one of the central problems posed by plagiarism in the period and for Coleridge particularly: How are we to make sense of Romanticism's rhetorical investment in "original" expression when unacknowledged borrowing was the norm, unless early nineteenth-century originality did not depend on ex nihilo creation or on all those models of solitary genius with which Romanticism has been conventionally associated? In his early study *The Romantic Ventriloquists*, Edward Bostetter made a similar argument about Coleridge's use of the ventriloquism metaphor and its relationship to formal questions of style, voice, and poetic craft, proposing that Romantic writers adapted and assimilated the language of the "new cosmic syntax" (3) laid down by their eighteenth-century predecessors, a syntax that paradoxically defined the imagination as a form of ventriloquism.[12] Bostetter reads Romanticism (and Modernism after it) as a failed and fragmentary aesthetic precisely because these authors were unable to imagine a new poetic language; other scholars have read Romanticism's engagement with the discursive structures of their historical moment as a sign of their mastery. In either case, and as Russett's argument so ably demonstrates, there is a tension between models of autogenous originality and the simple fact that language functions through a series of repetitions.

This tension, however, is primarily a belated critical invention. Assimilation and originality were not mutually exclusive categories in Georgian Britain, and, in making aesthetic judgments—including the judgment of plagiarism—the Romantics were centrally concerned with narrative mastery, domination, and control over borrowed materials. Perhaps most importantly, the anxieties that *Christabel*'s introduction into print culture occasioned for Coleridge were focused on the questions of consciousness, inhabitation, and volition that were central to his metaphor of ventriloquism. Part of his concern was for the disjunction between the success of his poem as an oral artifact and the proprietorial and critical demands of print culture. Coleridge articulates this dilemma in his reflections on the poem's reception in the *Biographia*:

Year after year, and in societies of the most different kinds, I had been entreated to recite it [*Christabel*]. . . . This before the publication. And since then, with very few exceptions, I have heard nothing but abuse. . . . This may serve as a warning to authors, that in their calculations on the probable reception of a poem, they must subtract. . . . for the excitement and temporary sympathy of feeling, which the recitation of the poem by an admirer, especially if he be at once a warm admirer and a man of acknowledged celebrity, calls forth in the audience. For this is really a species of animal magnetism, in which the enkindling reciter, by perpetual comment of looks and tones, lends his own will and apprehensive faculty to his auditors. They live for the time within the dilated sphere of his intellectual being. (*STC* 476)

Here, Coleridge credits the sympathetic recitations of his poem with producing its initial popularity, and elsewhere in this section of the *Biographia* he acknowledges that *Christabel*'s transition into print circulation had resulted in a hostile critical reception that had surprised him. However, what interests me particularly is the way in which his account of these recitations recalls his earlier discussions of the dislocation of the will as a psychological faculty and its relationship to collective authorship. In Coleridge's model of habitual plagiarism and divine ventriloquism, the volition of the author is severed uncharacteristically from the will and internally reproduces texts irrespective of what the will intends. In contrast, the "enkindling reciter" whom Coleridge describes in this passage imposes his will onto his listeners in an inverted form of ventriloquism, in which an embodied voiced consciousness draws the external inward in a process more akin to circumscription than projection. The result of imposing or temporarily inhabiting the will of another is the alteration of sensory and aesthetic perception. However, it also functions, at least metaphorically, as the instantiation of collective authorship; Dorothy Wordsworth's claim that the poetic community she shared with William Wordsworth and Coleridge comprised "Three bodies, but one soul!" mirrors Coleridge's reflections in the *Biographia*, and the interrupted sympathy that he had shared with the Wordsworths cannot have been far from his mind when considering either the origins of *Christabel* or its final fragmentation.[13] In this passage, Coleridge likewise invokes the figure of the "enkindling reciter" as a means of suggesting that *Christabel*—or at least the version of it that was popularized and embraced within the literary coterie—was not the text he authored but was a performance brought into being by the relationship between speaker and listeners. While the effect is the opposite of plagiarism, the dilation of the speaking intellect beyond the proper boundaries of the self that Coleridge describes here is a useful figure for understanding how he understood the imposition and superimposition of voices, desires, and poetic identities, and it is clearly not a model that privileges proprietorial authorship.

In contrast to this philosophical reflection on *Christabel*'s transmission in the *Biographia*, Coleridge had also connected the problem of the poem's plagiarism with questions of consciousness as early as 1810, when responding to a correspondent's suggestion that Scott had plagiarized from his poem, and here Coleridge demonstrates how familiar the category of unconscious plagiarism was to Romantic-period readers. While acknowledging similarities between *Christabel* and the *Lay of the Last Minstrel*, Coleridge acquits Scott of charges of culpable plagiarism by observing, "An intentional plagiarist would have *translated*, not transcribed . . . [plagiarizing with] purpose implies consciousness" (*CLSTC* 3:357). Coleridge sees the transparency of Scott's obligation (and, perhaps, the presumed "familiarity" of his own poem within the literary coterie—for he writes in the *Biographia* that "[d]uring the many years which intervened between the composition and the publication of the CHRISTABEL, it became almost as well known among literary men as if it had been on common sale" [*STC* 475–76]) as evidence that the borrowing could not have been performed with "consciousness" (3:357). However, by excusing Scott from any charges of culpable plagiarism, Coleridge leaves open the possibility that Scott may have borrowed unconsciously—an obligation with potentially negative aesthetic implications for Scott. Dorothy Wordsworth, at any rate, wrote in a letter from this period that she considered the unconscious nature of the obligation to be apparent, and this likely reflected the broader view of the Wordsworth-Coleridge circle (*LWDW* 1:633).

While *Christabel*'s public presentation engages questions of ownership, identity, and voice in the literary marketplace, the poem itself, written over fifteen years earlier, engages many of the same questions raised by the preface; themes of ventriloquism, entrancement, and volition shape the narrative of *Christabel* with implications for understanding Coleridge's attitudes toward both plagiarism and authorship. Most dramatically, *Christabel* offers a model of unconscious imitation remarkably similar to (and roughly contemporaneous with) Coleridge's 1800 and 1803 notebook reflections on the habit, the trance, and ventriloquism. In those reflections Coleridge had argued that the individual was "unconscious of his own agency" or "will" and, thus, not unknowing but unable simply to render accounts. In *Christabel*, Coleridge explores these unconscious operations in a dramatic framework, focusing on the enchantment of Christabel and the possession of her voice by Lady Geraldine. Offering a figuration of passive and unconscious imitation and invoking metaphors of both ventriloquism and the trances with which Coleridge associated inhabitation of this sort, the poem enacts the drama of plagiarism that Coleridge later feared would be applied to it.

Christabel incorporates several layers of narrative disruption, including instances of ventriloquism and enchantment. The central event of the poem is, of course, the corruption of Christabel's person, both sexually and psychologically, through some unspoken and implicitly sexual liaison with the apparently supernatural Lady Geraldine, and it is significant that Christabel engages in these relations unconsciously but not unknowingly. The nature of Christabel's enchantment is peculiar in this regard. If read in the context of Coleridge's notebook entry on habit and enchantment, Christabel's trance emerges as an encounter in which her own desires are acting freely, rather than as an experience in which, as Eilenberg suggests, she is possessed and controlled by an external influence. For, as Coleridge had explained in the notebooks, the trance represents an event that is unconscious only in the sense that desire (volition) operates independently of agency (will). In short, the trance always originates internally.[14] Thus, in the consummate scene of the poem, Geraldine undresses in front of Christabel, famously revealing her breast, and the enchanted Christabel lies down to spend the night in the other woman's arms. In the aftermath, Christabel knows what has come to pass; what she cannot account for is her own agency—and in this respect alone is she unconscious. Knowledge, without the ability to communicate it, is the explicit condition of Geraldine's enchantment, such that she proclaims:

In the touch of this bosom there worketh a spell,
Which is the lord of thy utterance, Christabel!
Thou knowest tonight, and wilt know to-morrow,
This mark of my shame, this seal of my sorrow;
But vainly thou warrest,
For this is alone in
Thy power to declare,
That in the dim forest
Thou heard'st a low moaning,
And found'st a bright lady, surpassingly fair[.] (ll. 265–76)

Christabel is explicitly characterized as having knowledge of the event, both in the moment of its performance and in the aftermath.[15] She is just as explicitly characterized as being "powerless" to declare how this experience came to pass—an inability predicated, in terms of the spell itself, by Christabel's apparent volition in touching Geraldine's breast. Most tellingly, the consequences of Christabel's enchantment and of her enacted desires for Geraldine are the confusion of voice and identity, particularly through metaphors of ventriloquism.

If Christabel's enchantment by Geraldine represents a dramatic portrayal of the Coleridgean unconscious in action, the effects of this liaison show the ways in which the "deranged" or "frenzied" volition can produce ventriloquism, "passive imitation," and ultimately plagiarism. As the passage above suggests, the result of Christabel's unconscious enactment of her desires is the erasure of agency. She is an "unwilling" participant only in the most precise sense of the term: the instrumentality of the will has been suspended. Unable to render accounts and unconscious in the Coleridgean sense of that category, Christabel also experiences the vocal effects of habit and inhabitation: passive imitation and ventriloquism. Unconscious of how her own desires operate in relation to agency, Christabel's body becomes the site of an imitative identity as she begins to mimic Geraldine's speech. To the enchanted Christabel and to the visionary poetic bard within the poem, Geraldine takes on the qualities of a snake (e.g., ll. 583–85), and Christabel ultimately comes to imitate both her appearance and her vocalizations. When Christabel tries to speak, she does so in the reptilian intonation she perceives in Geraldine: in once instance she "drew in her breath with a hissing sound" (l. 459) and at another "Christabel in dizzy trance / Stumbling on the unsteady ground / Shuddered aloud, with a hissing sound!" (ll. 587–89). The product of enchantment, like the product of habit, is the complete identification with desire and with the occasions that produce it. Moreover, these imitations are explicitly characterized as unconscious: Coleridge writes that Christabel "passively did imitate. . . . With forced unconscious sympathy" (ll. 605–9). Perhaps more clearly than anywhere else in his corpus, here is a description of how Coleridge imagined the inhabitation of the voice of another to operate. Christabel imitates Geraldine—both in voice and in identity—passively, unconsciously, even unwillingly. Yet this mimicry is likewise forced upon her, not through the agency of another but through the powers of her own sympathetic desires. If read as a figure for plagiarism, Christabel reveals the degree to which such imitations involve the passive, unconscious, and interdicted processes of desire and identification, escaping the willed intent of the author.

As the throwing of the voice and of the desires into a space beyond the proper boundaries of the self, ventriloquism represented for Coleridge one of the fundamental experiences of the unconscious and one of the principle justifications for plagiarism, and tracing this theme throughout *Christabel* reveals the problem of authorship engaged by the poem itself. For, if Christabel comes to sound unwittingly like Geraldine, it is also the case that she becomes the place into which Geraldine unconsciously throws the voice of her own desires. Implicitly, at least, Christabel's body and its articulation is the site of ventriloquism, inhabited and "frenzied" by Geraldine's voice and passions. However, Geraldine also begins to sound like Christabel as the poem progresses, and it may be that the process of identification and projection is not unilateral. In other words, Geraldine and all that she represents may be equally a product of Christabel's psychological ability to create a persona for the "deranged" and autonomous volition.[16] The riddle of the poem remains the question of agency. With each woman casting onto the other the voice of her desires and integrating those desires back into the self through passive imitation, it becomes uncertain who is the author—or, indeed, if a single author of either the poem's texts or its deeds may be said to exist at all. The operations of the unconscious construct for the self and its desires a myriad of voices, and it constructs myriad places for those voices to inhabit, some of which are coterminous with the bodies and voices of others. Much like the complex self-mimicry performed in the poetic doggerel with which Coleridge prefaces this poem and which may be read as a model for reading the poem's engagement with themes of voice and appropriation, *Christabel* explores the ways that the voice of the other and the voice of the self may coincide and counterinhabit each other.

Association and the Ocular Spectra

The trance and its role in explaining unconscious processes that include plagiarism are also related to the second metaphor that Coleridge employed as justification for his intellectual obligations, the phenomenon of "ocular spectra." Coleridge's understanding of association, perception, and memory was informed by contemporary scientific and psychological models, and, as Alan Richardson has demonstrated in *British Romanticism and the Science of the Mind*, he was particularly sympathetic to early "cognitivist accounts of a modular and material brain-mind."[17] His knowledge of the "ocular spectra" was drawn primarily from the work on visual perception proposed in Joseph Priestley's *History and Present State of Discoveries Relating to Vision, Light, and Colour* (1772), which Coleridge had read in the 1790s, and he specifically associated these "spectra" with the operations of the unconscious mind and with the processes of poetic composition. In this phenomenon, which John Livingston Lowes first explicated in his early work on Coleridge and plagiarism, *The Road to Xanadu: A Study in the Ways of the Imagination*, Coleridge claimed to have experienced the return of certain images that had been impressed as "traces" on his optic nerve. Speaking of these visual experiences as word-images or "Thoughts & Images," he asserts that they appeared to him in "certain Trances" that he also associated with habit. These ocular impressions, reshaped and unified, presented themselves to his unconscious mind's eye as fully formed poetic expression, experienced as moments of intoxication, trance, reverie, or inspiration much like the process of composition described in the preface to "Kubla Khan" (1798).

Coleridge maintained that these spectra, which he attributed both to psychological and physiological factors, were part of his experiences with memory and with poetic composition, and they consequently intersect with his attitudes toward textual appropriation, external influence, and plagiarism. In an 1801 entry in the notebooks, Coleridge linked the experience of these spectra both to the unconscious and to his own production of poetic images. In vivid language, he writes:

Wednesday—Afternoon. Abed—nervous—had noticed prismatic colours transmitted from the Tumbler—Wordsworth came—I talked with him—he left me alone—I shut my eyes—beauteous spectra of two colours, orange and violet—then of green, which immediately changed to Peagreen, & then actually *grew* to my eye into a beautiful moss, the same as the one on the mantle-piece at Grasmere,—abstract Ideas—& unconscious Links!! (*NSTC* 925 21.124)

In Coleridge's account, the prismatic colors refracted through the glass of the tumbler impressed themselves upon his optical nerve so that, when he closed his eyes, they appeared first as spectra and then, through unconscious association, as an image of moss. However, with its precise and poetic attention to detail and language, the notebook entry further suggests the degree to which Coleridge understood the spectra as an experience of composition. For, while the spectra give rise to "abstract Ideas" and associations, they also are productive of specific poetic language—the word-images in which the mental perception unconsciously takes shape. Above all, the spectra are a phenomenon of memory made present, and in this instance the associative nexus centers on the experience of seeing and re-seeing the mantle-piece in Wordsworth's house. However, the source for such imagery might as well be textual in its origins: words and the images they produce can be replicated in the mind's eye. Through the imaginative processes of association and synthesis, the mind could produce or reproduce word-images (including texts authored by another writer) that had been impressed upon it previously. In this event the mode of textual transmission is not mimetic but organic and unconscious, even where the results are identical, and, in such a scenario, plagiarism, like the act of poetic composition itself, becomes a product of the imagination's visual operations within the unconscious mind. In fact, the ocular spectra are simply another manifestation of the trance, an experience that we have already seen had strong associations for Coleridge with both plagiarism and the unconscious. It is also rooted in the psychology of the Coleridgean habit. We might understand spectra rather like desire: as the *marks* of erasure and the means through which the mind returns, unconsciously and creatively, to its exciting cause.

Coleridge's evocation of ocular spectra has been generally dismissed by the critical tradition, in large part, I suspect, because the scientific investigations upon which Coleridge's theories were based did not pass into the cultural mainstream. Even Lowes, who must rank as one of Coleridge's staunchest defenders on this point, characterizes the phenomenon negatively, as a psychological trick of the mind and as a productive failure of memory that Coleridge employed to explain his obligations. Fruman and the poet's later critics dismiss the notion as absurd, self-serving, and evidence of his self-rationalizing compulsions. In both instances, the critical impulse is to cast Coleridge's borrowings in terms of a psychological disruption. Yet, the problem of the ocular spectra raises an interesting historical dilemma. As a matter of historical coherence, it becomes difficult to justify dismissing the scientific basis that Coleridge had for using the ocular spectra as a justification for plagiarism without jettisoning the theory of aesthetics that he constructed on that same foundation. Coleridge's descriptions of the phenomenon are consistent not only with his reflections on habit and its unconscious operations but also with the ideas of association and imaginative psychology he subsequently developed throughout the *Biographia Literaria*.[18] His discussion of the "inward eye" of poetic perception explicitly links the ocular spectra and its internal processes to theories of association, leading to this observation in the *Biographia*: "It is a well-known fact, that bright colours in motion both make and leave the strongest impression on the eye. Nothing is more likely too, than that a vivid image or visual spectrum, thus originated, may become the link of association in recalling the feelings and images that had accompanied the original impression" (*STC* 398). Indeed, throughout the *Biographia*, Coleridge is concerned with the ways in which visual perception produces internal correspondences and abstract categories, and he bases his theory of poetry on the creative mind's associative and "symbolic" capacities. In short, the notion of the ocular spectra is part and parcel of Coleridge's theory of poetic composition.

Genial Coincidence and Transcendental Idealism in the *Biographia Literaria*

As implausible as the experience of ocular spectra may seem to modern readers, Coleridge's justification of his plagiarisms from Schelling on account of a "genial coincidence" has elicited the most consistent critical denunciation. Indeed, the question of his debts to Schelling and to other contemporary German philosophers remains a particularly sensitive issue; as Michael John Kooy remarked in *Coleridge, Schiller, and Aesthetic Education*, the nature of the influence has been largely understudied on account of a "nervous fixation on sources" that has left us "unaccustomed, even unwilling, to think of Coleridge's relationship with other thinkers except in terms of either slavish dependence or absolute ignorance."[19] However, although the "genial coincidence" has been seen as one of the most improbable and disingenuous aspects of Coleridge's self-justification, his employment of the term also has more complex philosophical resonances and implications than often have been acknowledged. Coleridge's understanding of the term *coincidence*, in particular, warrants further consideration in respect to both the question of unconsciousness and the question of plagiarism.

In its current modern usage, "coincidence" implies a notion of the accidental and the unaccountable, but Coleridge understood the term in a distinct philosophical sense that was informed by and indebted to the very work and correspondences that he was seeking to address: Schelling's *System des transcendentalen Idealismus* (System of Transcendental Idealism). Responding in the *Biographia Literaria* to charges of plagiarism, Coleridge famously observes that

In Schelling's 'NATUR-PHILOSOPHIE,' and the 'SYSTEM DES TRANSCENDEN-TALEN IDEALISMUS,' I first found a genial coincidence with much that I have toiled out for myself. . . . It would be but a mere act of justice to myself, were I to warn my future readers, that an identity of thought, or even similarity of phrase will not be at all times a certain proof that a passage has been borrowed from Schelling, or that the conceptions were originally learned from here. In this instance, as in the dramatic lectures of Schlegel to which I have before alluded, from the same motive of self-defence against the change of plagiarism, many of the most striking resemblances, indeed all the main and fundamental ideas, were born and matured

in my mind before I have ever seen a single page of the German Philosopher[.]
(*STC* 235)

Coleridge proposes that, despite the apparent lack of originality or, more precisely, of linguistic uniqueness, the ideas and expression in the *Biographia* were the products of his creative and mental activities. The similarities, he implies, are a matter of "coincidence." This passage has been almost universally discredited because the idea of such an extended and fortuitous coincidence has seemed far too genial to grant much credence. Elsewhere, however, Coleridge is clear that he expects his readers to understand his evocation of "coincidence" in this passage precisely. By coincidence, Coleridge means something closer to the original sense of the term: that the two texts *inhabit* the same space and that they literally coincide. Put another way, Coleridge understands the matter philosophically—indeed, in terms borrowed from his reading of Schelling, who in the opening passage of the *System des transcendentalen Idealismus* had written, "All knowledge is founded upon the coincidence of an objective with a subjective.—For we *know* only what is true; but truth is generally taken to consist in the coincidence of presentations with their objects" (§1.1).[20] In the *Biographia*, Coleridge incorporated this same passage into his discussion of the authorship and the imagination (chapter 12), and the engagement with Schelling at this particular juncture in his argument suggests the degree to which he associated the processes of logical argumentation and coincidence with precise philosophical argumentation.

There are two ways of unraveling the particulars of how Coleridge imagined "coincidence" to have operated in the process of poetic and aesthetic composition. The more complex but potentially treacherous route is to attempt to recover how Coleridge read or misread Schelling's original text. Schelling, at least, is reasonably clear on the point, proposing that knowledge and truth are always experiences of coincidence between nature and self, objective and subjective, conscious and unconscious, and he writes elsewhere in the *System des transcendentalen Idealismus* that coincidence may be understood as a matter of "reciprocal concurrence" (§1.2). The second way lies in Coleridge's reflections on the subject in the notebooks. Commenting on Walter Scott's purported plagiarisms, Coleridge uses the same term, but he explains his meaning rather more clearly, writing, "Coincidence here is used as a negative—not as implying that Likeness between two Works is merely accidental, the effect of chance, but as asserting that it is not the effect of imitation" (*CLSTC* 3: 358). Here, Coleridge acknowledges that coincidences between the thoughts and expressions of writers are not what are commonly understood by coincidence at all. The contrast he develops is not between intention and chance but between original and imitation, and Coleridge asserts that, in the absence of studied or what he often calls "servile" imitation, correspondences of this nature between texts and expressions cannot be said to constitute plagiarism. Coleridge's formulation leaves open, of course, the additional possibility that these similarities arose unconsciously—which he continues to define in terms of the unwilling rather than the unknowing. Indeed, Coleridge understood Schelling to be proposing that, where the argument is philosophically true, repetition is inevitable; the works of two authors are the same simply because their individual subjective expressions (i.e., identities) have both coincided with the same objective phenomena (i.e., nature, logic). Or, put more simply, Coleridge understood it thus: that the similarities were not the result of willful imitation, but neither were they unknown to him. They were the result of the unconscious, inevitable, logical coincidence of two intelligences inhabiting the same subjective experience.

This relationship between genial coincidences and the revelation of philosophical truths is an important element of how Coleridge understood his own innocence from plagiarism, and it is obviously related to the notion of the "divine ventriloquist" discussed earlier in this chapter. Following Schelling's argument, unconscious concurrences are logically valid because the objective truth is out there to be found, and, when Coleridge proposes that his borrowings are the result of unconscious ventriloquism, he likewise emphasizes the truth-value of the shared linguistic claims. Addressing the problem of plagiarism in the *Biographia,* Coleridge insists upon both the unintentional rather than imitative nature of the coincidence and the value that he places on the truth of the perceptions. "Let it," he writes,

be not charged on me as ungenerous concealment or intentional plagiarism. I have not indeed . . . been hitherto able to procure more than two of his books, viz. The 1st volume of his collected Tracts, and his System of Transcendental Idealism. . . . I regard the truth as a divine ventriloquist: I care not from whose mouth the sounds are supposed to proceed, if only the words are audible and intelligible. (*STC* 237)

Coleridge directly associates truth and ventriloquism in this passage, and his employment of the voice metaphor further extends the range of coincidence beyond the logical content of abstract thought to include modes of expression and identity. At the same time, by associating his plagiarisms with unintentional actions, Coleridge effectively inoculates himself here and throughout the *Biographia* against the most serious form of Romantic failed appropriation, culpable plagiarism. His dilemma, however, is that he cannot acquit himself of aesthetic plagiarism. How does a writer convincingly persuade his or her readers that the work is good? As poets have always known, self-confidence does not guarantee critical applause or commercial success. The judgment of aesthetic plagiarism—based on an assessment of the degree to which an author has asserted narrative or lyric control over his or her borrowed materials and unified the voiced identity of the text— rested in the perceptions of readers and reviewers. While culpable plagiarism was concerned with where textual borrowings had come from and with the intention with which they were reemployed, aesthetic plagiarism hinged on the question of improvement and concerned only what a writer had done with his or her materials. Reading Coleridge's insistence on voice rhetorically, the metaphor of ventriloquism also operates as an attempt to argue for the internal mastery (and eternal overmastery) of his writing.

Style, Mastery, and Patchwork Plagiarisms

In its attitude toward literary property and appropriation, literary Romanticism valued texts that, however disparate their sources, maintained a unified and distinct authorial style. Simply put, an author had sufficiently changed or had "improved" upon the work of another writer if he or she had assimilated the text into his or her own literary persona, especially through control of poetic or narrative voice. Questions of the production of voice were at the center of Byron's troubles with charges of plagiarism and are discussed at length in Chapter 4. However, Coleridge also addresses this subject in the course of his reflections on imitation. Most notably, in the *Biographia* Coleridge recognizes voice as an element of literary property, and he proposes that highly personal poets such as Wordsworth have little reason for anxiety. Imitation—conscious imitation—is itself bound to fail if the original poetry is sufficiently distinct in respect to subjectivity. Perhaps responding to Wordsworth's repeated assertions that Byron had plagiarized stylistic aspects of his writing such as tone and voice, Coleridge argues that Wordsworth's poetry is characterized by a particularly identifiable and unique textual persona. He writes that "it would be difficult and almost superfluous to select instances of diction peculiarly his own, of a style which cannot be imitated without it being at once recognized, as originating in Mr. Wordsworth" (*STC* 374). The assertion is that Wordsworth's voice remains so tied to the person of the author (and the "matter-of-factness" of his existence) that it remains his own even in the context of other texts. Where Wordsworth believed that his tone and style were subject to appropriation by his literary competitors, Coleridge maintains that the efforts to mobilize his lyric voice through imitation cannot ultimately succeed because the resulting text will always be marred by the presence of two competing voices, and the imitator will fail to improve upon or to assimilate fully his or her borrowed text. The consequence of such a muddled text—irrespective of the nature or extent of the correspondences—was plagiarism. Hybrid texts of this sort, much like dramatic narratives, ran the risk of internal incoherence; in Coleridge's words, "Either the thoughts and diction are different from that of the poet, and then there arises an incongruity of style; or they are the same and indistinguishable, and then it presents a species of ventriloquism" (*STC* 397). Here, with remarkably clarity, is the contrast Coleridge imagined: plagiarism represented an "incongruity of style" and an inability to infuse the text of another with the authorial voice. Its opposite is ventriloquism: when, through mastery and projection, one voice speaks through two bodies and two texts.

Coleridge's attitude toward univocal narrative or lyric control is important for understanding the charges of plagiarism that he leveled against other Romantic-period writers. To appreciate that Coleridge's literary obligations, however extensive and silently rendered, operated in a context of intellectual-property standards that was historically distinct from our own is one matter. To appreciate why someone who availed himself so fully of this license would censure others for borrowings that often appear far less significant is another. The question of Coleridge's apparent hypocrisy remains a troubling concern for even his most sympathetic and historically imaginative readers. Coleridge was unquestionably a writer who operated, even by contemporary standards, at the margins of legitimate appropriation and in the rhetorical complexities of literary-property discourse; yet he repeatedly accused other writers—with debts apparently less extensive than his own—of plagiarism. Ungenerous at best, the matter reeks of bad faith. However, without discounting the possibility that Coleridge harbored some competitive motives and could be cranky in a plain old-fashioned way, his hypocrisy has been overstated. The charges that he brought against his literary contemporaries emphasize the critical and evaluative rather than personal or moral nature of his censure, and his commentaries on the plagiarisms of other writers clearly indicate that his investment was in assessing the narrative coherence of these texts. In other words, Coleridge was concerned with aesthetic plagiarism and not culpable plagiarism, and his concern was with the quality of their literature. In making these charges, Coleridge believed that he was responding to a deficiency in the work itself, particularly a deficiency in the matter of voice, and he based his judgments on the criteria of Romantic-period plagiarism that were broadly familiar to his contemporaries.

When Coleridge charges other writers with plagiarism, he is charging them not with deception but with a lack of genius and with the failure to unify or to individualize textual voice. The degree to which Coleridge and his Romantic-period contemporaries associated plagiarism with issues of voice cannot be underestimated. Coleridge spoke of the plagiarisms of both James Mackintosh and Matthew Lewis in terms of their having created discontinuous or "patchwork" texts, by which he meant that they had failed to assimilate their borrowed materials or to unify their work. In an 1801 letter to Thomas Poole, Coleridge wrote of Mackintosh: "I attended 5 of his Lectures—such a wretched patch work of plagiarisms from Condilliac [*sic*]—of contradictions, and blunders in matter of fact" (*CLSTC* 2: 675). In 1798, he had described Matthew Lewis's plagiarisms in *Castle Spectre* (1797) in nearly the same language: "I suspect, Mr. Lewis has stolen all his sentimentality, moral and humorous. . . . The whole plot, machinery, & incident are borrowed—the play is a mere patchwork of plagiarisms" (*CLSTC* 1: 379). In these charges, "patchwork" is as important a term as "plagiarism." For Coleridge the problem with the respective borrowings of Mackintosh and Lewis is not the fact of the appropriations per se but each author's failure to unify, transform, or *improve* upon his borrowed materials. By returning to the question of improvement, which was a question of authorial control for the Romantics, Coleridge articulates his critique within what is by now, I hope, a familiar critical discourse, and it is perhaps not surprising that, in looking at the failures of others, he should have paid particular attention to the aspect of appropriation at which he excelled: the ability to make his materials his own.

This ability to make one's materials one's own was an important component of the Romantic-period discourse on plagiarism; responding to charges of plagiarism in *Don Juan*, Byron used almost precisely those words in his defense. For both Coleridge and Byron the central issue in plagiarism was a question of voice, and Coleridge in particular considered the individuation of voice, rather than linguistic uniqueness, to be the crucial feature in identifying both plagiarism and the literary failure that it represented. The very emphasis on ventriloquism suggests, as both Eilenberg and Russett have also observed, that Coleridge understood successful and literary appropriation in terms of voice—quite specifically in terms of the unifying voice of "truth" irrespective of "from whose mouth the sounds . . . proceed" (*STC* 237).[21] When responding to Wordsworth's critique of Byron, Coleridge likewise formulated questions of literary originality in terms of uniqueness of voice, reflecting in the *Marginalia* that "W. Wordsworth calls Lord Byron the Mocking Bird of our Parnassian Ornithology; but the Mocking Bird, they say, has a very sweet song of his own, in true Notes proper to himself" (qtd. in Fruman 95). While Byron may borrow, even ventriloquize, Coleridge observes that, so long as the notes are *proper* to himself, the song must be judged lovely.

This notion of qualitative propriety—rather than exclusive property—thus emerges as the definitive aspect in judging the success and, therefore, the appropriateness of borrowing in the Romantic period. Describing his own writings and efforts at literary appropriation, Coleridge articulates this matter of voice in terms of authorial subjectivity or "spirit":

> He who can catch the Spirit of an original, has it already. It will not [be] by Dates, that Posterity will judge the originality of a Poem; but by the original spirit itself. This is to be found neither in the Tale however interesting, which is but the Canvass, no nor yet in the Fancy or the Imagery—which are but Forms & Colors—it is a subtle spirit, all in each part, reconciling & unifying all—. Passion and Imagination are its *most* appropriate names; but even these say little—for it must be not merely Passion but Poetic Passion, poetic Imagination. (*CLSTC* 3:361)

Again, in an 1804 notebook entry, he observes of his borrowings from metaphysics that quoting is a skulking trick and after all "the Soul is all *Mine*" (*NSTC* 2: 2375). In both instances, Coleridge insists that spirit pervades, unifies, and instantiates the literary text and that originality creates its own origins. From the perspective of his own metaphor, Coleridge maintains that he has thrown his voice completely into the corpus of the other; plagiarism, then, becomes unsuccessful ventriloquism, and Coleridge has succeeded. Put another way, "Coleridge's plagiarism is," as Norman Fruman first noted, "transcendental idealism in action" (154). Fruman meant something quite different when he made this claim, yet, as we have seen, Coleridge's attitude toward plagiarism cannot be easily disassociated from his readings in Schelling and in metaphysical psychology. Schelling had argued that unconscious nature surpassed conscious art in one respect: it had life.

Coleridge would claim more for art and propose that the goal of the poetic genius was to throw consciousness into the world and to make nature speak; in an act of creative ventriloquism the poet, thus, would plagiarize nature and produce living art.

My objective in this discussion has not been to suggest that Coleridge is right or wrong or to evaluate the merits of his defense. Whether Coleridge was or was not a nineteenth-century plagiarist is probably an irresolvable question, precisely because, even by Romantic-period standards, he operated at the limits of legitimate appropriation, and he justified his borrowings in philosophical and psychological terms that were either contested or unfamiliar. What we can say is that the responses that he gave to the charges of plagiarism brought against him were entirely in keeping with what was, in fact, a highly motivated argument between the Romantics and their reviewers and that the charges of plagiarism that he lodged against contemporaries were consistent with a broadly understood set of expectations regarding the deployment of the term. We can likewise say with some assurance that the critical tradition has been and remains invested in Coleridge's obligations. His alleged plagiarisms continue to occasion controversy, and this is often productive. However, unless the controversy is framed by a historical context, the debate is senseless; judged by modern standards, Coleridge is obviously guilty. Yet, as I have argued, plagiarism in the Romantic period was not formulated primarily in moral terms. More importantly, interrogating the processes of aesthetic judgment that led to assertions of plagiarism in Georgian Britain enriches our understanding of the period and its literary investments.

Early nineteenth-century critical assessments of Coleridge's borrowings demonstrate how important aesthetic judgments were for evaluating charges of plagiarism. While DeQuincey's indictment represents one of the only sustained public efforts in the period to prove another writer guilty of *culpable* plagiarism, his argument proceeds from the critical assumption of literary failure. DeQuincey asserts that Coleridge's inability to improve upon the materials borrowed from Schelling is self-evident, knowing that only such a "negation of improvement" could expose an author to the judgment of plagiarism, either culpable or aesthetic. Had Coleridge successfully assimilated his textual sources in the *Biographia*, the consciousness or unconsciousness of his obligations would have been irrelevant, regardless of their extent. The appropriations from Brun were dismissed by DeQuincey on precisely these same grounds, and because those improvements are also represented as self-evident it is difficult to know what other cultural factors might have influenced the exercise of aesthetic judgment. In both instances, however, the recognition of literary success or failure determined the outcome in regard to questions of plagiarism. Plagiarism was a function and a consequence of writing badly, and Romantic-period writers and their readers understood the stakes to be primarily aesthetic.

The critical tradition that has described Coleridge's plagiarisms, on the other hand, has focused intently on the questions of consciousness and morality. Coleridge was to a large extent responsible for initiating this trajectory. He cast his borrowings in psychological terms and availed himself fully of the avenue of defense that "unconscious plagiarism" offered to British writers in the late eighteenth and early nineteenth centuries. However, the articulation both of plagiarism and of consciousness evolved over the course of the nineteenth and twentieth centuries, and the historical and aesthetic contexts from which Coleridge's "unconscious" appropriations emerged eventually were replaced by a later sensibility that was much more deeply invested in the moral and legal aspects of authorship. It is difficult to say precisely when the definition of the unconscious as Coleridge understood that term ceased to operate as a plausible argument. DeQuincey was one of the first commentators to obscure the historical complexities surrounding consciousness when he elides in the *Tait's Magazine* essays any discussion of the contemporary philosophical arguments about psychology that his other writings make clear he knew. DeQuincey makes one argument about the limits of unconsciousness, and Coleridge makes another, but both were positioned in relation to shared Romantic-period attitudes toward literary property and its appropriation. When Sara Coleridge defended her father from plagiarism in the late 1840s, unconscious plagiarism apparently no longer operated so freely as a legitimate form of appropriation, and she unwittingly adopted DeQuincey's definition of the unconscious rather than her father's.[22] When J. F. Ferrier and C. M. Ingelby documented Coleridge's plagiarisms at the end of the nineteenth century, they did so without examining what the term might have meant for an earlier generation and at a time when notions of intellectual property and ownership were still in transition.[23] By the time John Livingston Lowes and Adrien Bonjour came to psychoanalyze Coleridge in the early twentieth century, his neuroses had already been defined and his plagiarisms became, for both his defenders and his critics, a matter of uniquely personal desires and needs.[24] His borrowings continued to be documented in the 1950s by scholars as prominent as Joseph Warren Beach and René Wellek without historical interrogation into what might have constituted plagiarism in another century, and even the monumental works of Thomas McFarland, Jerome Christensen, and Norman Fruman have cast the debate in terms of both twentieth-century attitudes toward intellectual property and post-Freudian categories of the unconscious.[25] Defending Coleridge, McFarland ironically argues precisely the thing that would have most horrified the poet: that his plagiarisms in the *Biographia Literaria* reveal a pattern of implicitly unassimilated "mosaic organization" (27). Condemning the poet through assiduous research, Fruman judges Coleridge according to standards that his contemporaries never would have thought to apply to his borrowings. In the end, the critical tradition surrounding Coleridge tells us more about the ways in which the category of literary property has evolved and about our own relations to it than it tells us about the poet or the stakes being contested when charges of plagiarism were made in early nineteenth-century Britain.

Yet, while the historical contexts of Romantic plagiarism have been elided from the critical tradition surrounding the poet, it may be that Coleridge has, in some respect, albeit indirectly, shaped the current postmodern critical discourse on literature and literary property. The perspective most resonant with Coleridge and with Romantic-period categories of literary property remains psychoanalysis, and Coleridge's unconscious plagiarism represents a prototype of the form of expression that Roland Barthes or Jacques Lacan call *jouissance*—and, surprisingly, to use the term is not anachronistic. The word was current in Britain during the eighteenth century and had long-standing use in continental property law as a notion associated with the use, enjoyment, or occupation of an estate or property, rather than outright possession, ownership, or right of disposal.[26] There is much here in common with Coleridge's characterization of plagiarism as inhabitation of various kinds. In current psychoanalytic terms, *jouissance* has come to signify textual excess or, in the early analysis laid out by Barthes in *The Pleasure of the Text*,

criticism always deals with the texts of pleasure [plasir], *never the texts of bliss* [jouissance]. . . . With the writer of bliss (and his reader) begins the untenable text, the impossible text. . . . you cannot speak "on" such a text, you can only speak "in" it, *in its fashion*, enter into a desperate plagiarism, hysterically affirm the void of bliss (and no longer obsessively repeat the letter of pleasure)[.][27]

Criticism, indeed, has not dealt with Coleridge's "texts of bliss," although works such as the *Biographia Literaria* might be read precisely as such a joyfully desperate plagiarism and as an effort to speak in the text and corpus of the other. In the final analysis, it may be that the very elements that have made Coleridge's texts impossible and, perhaps, untenable have been mis-recognized, along with the poet's relation to the tradition that he inhabited and to the literary texts that surrounded him.

Chapter 3
Property and the Margins of Literary Print Culture

The idea of literary property in the Romantic period, as in the present moment, depends upon a legal and rhetorical principle that is essentially a contradiction. At the heart of both plagiarism and copyright is the belief that a text is simultaneously public and private or, more precisely, is simultaneously offered to the public on the condition of continued private ownership. This concurrency was resolved as a matter of copyright law early in the eighteenth century and was, for obvious reasons, welcomed by authors and booksellers as a means of circulating their productions while retaining title to them. However, this chapter considers the situation in the late eighteenth and early nineteenth centuries for texts located at the extremes of either category—texts that were avowedly private, such as journals, patently public, such as folktales, legends, or ballads, or simultaneously public *and* private, such as commonplace books and certain manuscripts circulated in a coterie fashion. What were the standards for appropriating from these materials, and how were the categories of "private property" and "literary property" complicated by cultural productions of this sort? What was the attitude toward texts that were not obviously "literary" at all? In many instances, the answers to these questions are closely linked to another set of complications posed by issues of gender and by the status of particular genres and particular modes of transmission in the period. Women participated with far fewer cultural restrictions in the production and dissemination of works located at the limits of literary print culture, and, as I will demonstrate, these texts often appear to have enjoyed fewer protections as property than works identified as literature. At the same time, there is the curious fact that, during the Romantic period, it was extremely rare for a male author to be persuasively charged with plagiarism from a female author, even in instances where the texts participated in "high-culture" genres. Yet, the role that gender played in evaluating the legitimacy or illegitimacy of particular textual obligations is vexed because it is often very difficult to disentangle issues of authorial identity from contemporary cultural attitudes toward particular types of texts that circulated at the margins of literary culture. This chapter begins with an overview of how gender related historically to issues of copyright law and the ownership of intellectual property, and I discuss textual appropriations by Coleridge and, later, William Wordsworth from Friederike Brun, Mary Robinson, and Dorothy Wordsworth. Despite often extensive and unacknowledged verbal parallels, none of these borrowings were considered plagiarism as that charge operated rhetorically during the Romantic period, for reasons that might have had as much to do with attitudes toward genre—and particularly toward magazine culture and the domestic circulation of private journals and commonplace books—as with authorial identity. In the second part of the chapter, I consider examples of appropriation in texts that were closely associated with oral traditions, including the Gothic "plagiarisms" of Percy Bysshe and Elizabeth Shelley and of Matthew Lewis.

Gender and the Circulation of Private Property

The relationship among plagiarism, private property, and gender is a particularly relevant concern for scholars of the Romantic period, but the subject is unusually difficult to address. The historical record suggests that, in practice, plagiarism was primarily a charge leveled by one gentleman against another, and, although there were occasionally instances when women accused each other of this form of appropriation, it was remarkably rare for the term *plagiarism* to be used to describe instances in which a male author borrowed from a women author.[1] Even on those occasions when the term was invoked for borrowings from women's writing, the context is complicated by other factors. I return in the course of this chapter, for example, to DeQuincey's contention that Coleridge did not plagiarize from the poetry of Friederike Brun because he improved upon her work. The claim of improvement was sufficient to justify an obligation almost regardless of any other element, but it is impossible to know to what extent aesthetic judgments of this sort were based on cultural expectations regarding gender. In Chapter 4, I discuss Byron's borrowings from the travel narrative of Miss Tully, yet the gendered aspects of the obligation are muddied by the fact that her journal (a private genre) was published by her brother as *A Narrative of Ten Years' Residence at Tripoli in Africa; from the Original Cor-*

respondence in the Possession of the Late Richard Tully, Esq., the British Consul (1816), a title that implied male ownership if not male authorship. Moreover, there was a contemporary perception among many writers and readers that travel narratives, as documentary rather than literary texts, were implicitly authorless materials, available for appropriation elsewhere. Most often, however, the term *plagiarism* was not used to describe borrowings of this sort, and, quite simply, men were not charged with plagiarism from women's texts with any frequency during the early nineteenth century, although they borrowed from women writers on many occasions.

Understanding the historical silences regarding plagiarism from women's texts in the Romantic period is largely a matter of balancing what we know or can discover about cultural attitudes toward women's claims to intellectual property with what we know or can discover about the status of particular modes of textual circulation and the different protections afforded to particular genres. It is my own sense that, in the final analysis, issues of genre were more significant factors than issues of gender in the period, but it is also the case, of course, that gender and genre often were intimately connected. What we can say with assurance about the conditions of female authorship in the late eighteenth and early nineteenth centuries is that women had, as a matter of law, limited rights to the private ownership of property and personhood. At the same time, their intellectual and rational capacities were underestimated as a matter of cultural convention. In these circumstances, women's relationships to both intellectual property and expressivist aesthetics were necessarily complicated. The circumscribed rights of women to property were detailed by Sir William Blackstone in his *Commentaries on the Laws of England* (1765–69) in the 1760s, and the conditions that he outlines make clear how precarious a woman writer's—and especially a married woman writer's—relationship to her own text could be. In the late eighteenth century and into the Romantic period, the only women who could be said to own either their person or property independently were those claiming the legal status of *feme sole*, a category limited to unmarried women over the age of twenty-one and to widows. Children and especially women under the age of majority were, according to Blackstone, under the "empire" of the father, and the violation of the parent's authority (or of the person of a woman under such authority) was considered a form of "trespass" against his property and his rights.[2] While the law was particularly concerned to prevent the loss of this female property through unauthorized marriage, women in their minority were not entitled to manage their own property or to negotiate contracts except by parental permission. As a matter of strict interpretation, then, a woman under the age of twenty-one could only by way of parental concession control the productions of her own intellect or retain the copyright monies that she might earn.

Eighteenth-century law restricted the property rights of a married woman even more profoundly. For, while an unmarried woman in her minority retained, in most instances, the right to have her personal inheritance preserved, a married woman or *feme covert* had no legal existence and, therefore, no independent legal rights and no protections of private property, apart from those vested in pin money and paraphernalia. As Blackstone described her condition: "the very being or legal existence of the woman is suspended during the marriage, or at least incorporated and consolidated into that of the husband. . . . If the wife be injured in her person or her property, she can bring no action for redress without her husband's concurrence" (*Commentaries* 1: 15). Not only was a married woman at the end of the eighteenth century denied the ability to take legal action on her own behalf, but any property that she might receive or create belonged, as a point of law, to her husband. Again, Blackstone argued that her "chattels personal, whether it be in possession, or in action [i.e., in bond or contract] . . . these a husband may have if he pleases" (*Commentaries* 2: 29). Having no independent legal personhood, a married woman under *coverture* was likewise debarred from drawing valid contracts or from drafting wills, except with the consent of her spouse. The implications for women's rights to intellectual property during the period are unambiguous: a married woman could not be said to own the texts that she wrote. She was not entitled to control the circumstances in which her text was or was not published, and, if she sold her copyright, the earnings were not hers to manage.

In concrete terms, the laws of the British Romantic period meant that Mary Shelley, who had married in 1816, had no legal identity apart from Percy Bysshe Shelley and did not own the intellectual property of a work such as *Frankenstein* (1818) except through his goodwill. Nor is the example simply rhetorical, for, while many husbands encouraged the literary efforts of their wives and granted them the autonomy to manage these intellectual properties, this was a matter of courtesy alone. As late as the 1850s, the writer Caroline Norton, a member of the well-placed literary family that included Richard Brinsley Sheridan and the novelist Caroline Sheridan, confronted the legal realities of a woman's entitlement to her own literary property, which she described in a pamphlet entitled *English Laws for Women in the Nineteenth Century* (1854). Norton's case, although coming at midcentury, had its roots in the Romantic era. During the 1820s, she emerged as a popular late-Romantic woman author with the publication of works such as *The Sorrows of Rosalie* (1829), and her legal entanglements began in the 1830s, when she fled her abusive husband and was left in precarious financial circumstances.[3] Norton turned to writing as a means of support but found her husband prepared to avail himself of his legal rights to her intellectual productions. As she wrote in her pamphlet, "I turned my literary ability to account, by selling the copyright of my first poem. . . . [and] [i]t is not without a certain degree of romantic pride that I look back and know that the first expenses of my son's life were defrayed from the price of that first creation of my brain" (25).[4] However, she soon discovered that English law "gives a woman's earnings even by literary copyright, to her husband" (22). In law, her literary efforts and their fruits belonged to her spouse, and they continued to do so until the passage of the Divorce and Matrimonial Causes Act in 1857.

If Blackstone's *Commentaries* represents the legal and cultural attitude toward women's writing by the second half of the eighteenth century, then Norton's testimony and her legal difficulties show the degree to which gender continued to shape a woman's relationship to her intellectual property well into the Victorian era. However, women writers working in the Romantic period were at a particular disadvantage when it came to questions of plagiarism. While the ownership and infringement of copyright was a charge with concrete legal and financial implications in the early nineteenth century, it remained distinct from allegations of plagiarism, which were focused during the Romantic period on the category of improvement and its related elements of mastery, voice, and subjectivity. The legal restrictions placed on the feme covert and her incorporation into the person of her spouse had cultural implications for women generally, regardless of their legal status at a particular moment, for it was expected that a woman would and, in fact, should spend the majority of her life under the protection and authority of a male relative or a husband. As a result, the personhood of a woman was both legally and rhetorically subject to assimilation by men. In an expressivist aesthetic culture, in which the identity, voice, and persona of the author was sufficient to constitute literary property and essential to the judgment of poetic achievement, it is not difficult to anticipate the potential textual consequences of a woman's conditional right to independent personhood. If men could assimilate her person, then why could they not assimilate her personal expressions as well? Perhaps more importantly, how would a Romantic-period woman writer, especially a married woman writer, succeed at all, under the conditions outlined for her? Early nine-teenth-century aesthetics demanded that a writer craft a masterful textual persona, at a time when many women spent significant parts of their lives with their legal personhood suspended.

An argument that reads the absence of contemporary charges of pla-giarism from women's texts as essentially a matter of gender bias would proceed, I think, along the grounds laid out above, and, as I have suggested, there are some reasons to anticipate that female authors might have faced particular challenges in an aesthetic climate so firmly rooted in the mastery of identity and in the person of the author. However, at the same time, there clearly were successful women writers during the Romantic period who did, despite the legal rhetoric, find their own voices and live with a clear sense of self. Indeed, male contemporaries often praised women writ-ers for their literary accomplishments, suggesting that the idea of women's genius was not a cultural impossibility. However, these male contemporar-ies also borrowed, often extensively, from the works of women writers, and they were not charged with plagiarism for these appropriations. At a histor-ical moment when accusations of plagiarism were flung fast and furious in the literary gazettes and were brought against authors as original as Byron or as attentive as Wordsworth, this omission hints at some form of larger exclusion from Romantic literary culture, its competitions, and its stakes.

However, if gender and a woman's legal relationship to intellectual property during the period is one way of understanding the scarcity of pla-giarism charges that followed from the appropriation of women's texts, cul-tural attitudes toward particular genres and particular patterns of cultural production is another, and, of course, the two elements often cannot be viewed in complete isolation. Yet, it is also possible to understand the ab-sence of plagiarism charges in relationship to the texts of individual women writers in the context of a broader set of assumptions both about what con-stituted plagiarism and about how that charge applied differently to works depending on their mode of transmission or relationship to a consciously literary culture. Plagiarism during the Romantic period was a primarily aesthetic criticism and was an allegation of the misappropriation of conven-tionally literary property. The authors of texts that were predominantly rec-ognized as subliterary genres—journals, ballads, folktales, newspapers, and criticism or reviews consistently, travel narratives and histories fre-quently—were typically not charged with plagiarism, and the authors of lit-erary texts who appropriated from these materials often distinguished between these sources and sources with literary origins. In *Cultural Capital:*

The Problems of Literary Canon Formation, John Guillory argues this point clearly in regard to commonplace books, "vernacular works," and "popular" Romantic genres. Guillory's contention is that the production of "literature" as a form of cultural capital during the eighteenth century depended upon its discursive isolation from other oral or textual traditions, and he locates the Romantic period particularly as a moment of aesthetic crisis when, "[f]or the first time poetic genres and prose genres are comparable as *literary* genres."[5] It is for this reason, Guillory proposes, that

Wordsworth can conjure an apocalyptic scenario in which the works of Milton or Shakespeare are swallowed up in the sea of popular writing only because the distinction between serious and popular genres produces no corresponding linguistic differentiation. . . . [The result is a] division of literary production into "literature" and the genres which are by definition subliterary or nonliterary[.] (132–33)

Guillory suggests here that Romantic writers were *particularly* concerned with articulating a distinction between literary and subliterary genres, for reasons that were both aesthetic and essentially bourgeois. This argument is confirmed, I think, by the different ways in which the rhetoric of plagiarism seems to have applied to texts identified with particular genres or modes of production. As part of the critical language of literary Romanticism, the exclusion of certain texts (and perhaps certain authors) from discussions of plagiarism would have functioned as a means of affirming the distinction between literary and subliterary genres—a distinction in which many of the period's most familiar writers were deeply invested.

Gender and Improvement in the "Hymn before Sun-rise"

Among Coleridge's literary obligations, his appropriations from a poem by the German poet Sophie Christiane Friederike Brun (1765–1835) have been particularly celebrated, and Coleridge's borrowings in this instance are a clear example of the ways in which issues of gender and subliterary modes of transmission such as newspaper circulation become difficult to separate conclusively. The correspondences between Brun and Coleridge were first noted publicly by DeQuincey in the *Tait's Magazine* essays, where DeQuincey claimed that Coleridge's "Hymn before Sun-rise, in the Vale of Chamouny" (1802), published as part of his writing for the *Morning Post* newspaper, was a little more than a translation of Brun's "Chamonix, beim Sonnenaufgange" (Chamounix, with the Sun Rising), which had been published in 1795.[6] Adrien Bonjour documented the full extent of the debt to Brun's work, demonstrating in parallel text comparisons the extensive correspondences between the "Hymn before Sun-rise" and both Brun's poem and her notes. Norman Fruman later revealed that Coleridge misled even his closest intimates about the nature of the poem's composition, claiming to have "involuntarily poured forth" the hymn.[7] However, despite the obvious nature of the parallels, the modern academic controversy exemplifies an ahistorical understanding of Romantic-period plagiarism generally and highlights Coleridge's attitude toward transitory genres in particular.

Considered in terms of the Romantic-period definition of plagiarism, Coleridge's reemployment of Brun's verse was legitimate because it met the standard of improvement. Even DeQuincey argues that it was, stating that charges of plagiarism could not be brought against Coleridge in this instance because his poem had improved upon Brun's original. Improvement represented one of three instances (along with unconsciousness and familiarity) in which borrowing, however extensive, was permitted, and it is true, of course, that Coleridge turns a twenty-line original into a eighty-five-line hymn. While as modern critics we are keen to understand the role of gender in late eighteenth- and early nineteenth-century attitudes toward literary appropriation, the case of Coleridge's debt to Brun offers little insight because, by contemporary standards, no plagiarism had occurred. This is not to say, of course, that the influence of gender still might not have been central to this assessment: it is possible—I suspect, even likely—that the judgment of improvement in respect to a woman's text was a foregone conclusion in some instances. DeQuincey treats the improvement as obvious and dismisses the charges in a brief paragraph; the obligation was never the subject of an extended Romantic-period critical discussion elsewhere, making it impossible to know for certain the degree to which gender might have influenced DeQuincey's evaluation. However, in regard to Coleridge and the question of his culpability, at least, the question of gender is secondary. Whatever the prejudices upon which DeQuincey and his contemporaries based their judgments, Coleridge's amplification of Brun's original verse would have been considered a species of improvement. This would have been true even had Coleridge not extended the length of the poem, for improvement did not require any change or addition to the *language*; it only required that the new author unify the *voice* of the poem. And, certainly, the guiding subjectivity of the poem is a voice that, with the hindsight of history at least, we have come to recognize as distinctively Coleridgean.

Quoting and Poetic Dialogue in the *Morning Post*

However, while the degree to which the contemporary assessment of Coleridge's debts to Brun was shaped by the element of gender can only be a matter of speculation, Coleridge's relationships with other women writers provide a fuller picture of his attitude toward his female contemporaries and toward texts associated—as Brun's poem was—with transitory genres and periodical publication. For it is also possible that the mode of circulation affected the judgment of improvement in regard to the debt to Brun. Part of the dilemma is that Coleridge, like many of his contemporaries, does not seem to have considered as entirely literary those works published in ephemeral or periodical sources such as the newspaper, regardless of genre. His exchanges with the Della Cruscan poet Mary Darby Robinson in the *Morning Post* from 1797 to 1800, in particular, offer considerable information on the ways that Coleridge perceived aspects of literary property, competition, and exchange, but in ways that make it difficult to disentangle how the influence of gender operated as distinct from attitudes toward certain paths of cultural transmission. The exchanges between Coleridge and Robinson have never been a question of plagiarism; however, their poetic dialogue is replete with instances of influence, assimilation, and verbal echoes that suggest that, at least as a matter of rhetorical posturing, Coleridge was willing to engage with Robinson as a colleague in the context of the newsprint media.

The poetic conversation between Coleridge and Robinson includes a series of poems that each author composed primarily for publication in the *Morning Post*. Out of financial necessity, Coleridge began writing for the paper in early December of 1797 and, after a year's unofficial hiatus while touring Germany, resumed work for the publication in late November of 1799. Robinson had begun supplying pieces for the *Morning Post* as early as 1794 and, by 1799, in no less dire financial circumstances, had become a poetry editor for the newspaper. This professional proximity led to a series of poetic responses to each other's work between 1797 and 1800.

The dialogue between Coleridge and Robinson can be characterized as falling into three distinct sets of exchanges, the first beginning in late 1797 when Coleridge arranged to have his poem "The Visions of the Maid of Orleans" appear directly before Robinson's "Ode to the Snow-Drop" in the 26 December edition. While Coleridge's intent behind this initial juxtaposition was at least partly political, his publication in the issue of 3 January 1798 of a direct (although pseudonymous) response to Robinson suggests that his interest in her poem went beyond editorial convenience.[8] In this response, entitled "The Apotheosis, or the Snow-Drop," Coleridge sympathetically responds to Robinson's self-identification with the passing and forgotten snowdrop, bested by its springtime rival "The *gaudy* Crocus" (l. 21). While Coleridge's poem demonstrates the conventional elements of sensibility, it also represents a genuinely collegial gesture by introducing into the dialogue the explicit attention to Robinson as a poet. In the course of the "Apotheosis," Coleridge argues that, through "imitative sympathy" (l. 15), Laura (a figure for Robinson and one of her pen names) has magically transported the snowdrop beyond time to the Muses' eternal Pieria. As a gesture toward another poet, Coleridge's characterization of Robinson in the "Apotheosis" suggests that he was not reluctant either to acknowledge her as a fellow professional or to place—pseudonymously at least—his work in relation to hers.

These pseudonymous exchanges between Coleridge and Robinson were suspended during the period in 1798 and 1799 when Coleridge was in Germany and out of contact with the paper, but the dialogue resumed, this time more openly, in 1800 when Coleridge had renewed his involvement with the *Morning Post* and its poetry section. The more direct nature of the second exchange was undoubtedly a result of the personal friendship that had developed between Coleridge and Robinson in January and February of 1800, and William Godwin's diary records several instances where the two poets met socially.[9] Robinson initiated the exchange this time, publishing her "Ode Inscribed to the Infant Son of S. T. Coleridge, Esq." in the 17 October 1800 edition of the *Morning Post*. In this poem Robinson at once accepts and returns the collegial gesture that Coleridge had made in "The Apotheosis" by publicly celebrating Coleridge as a poet (e.g., "the magic of his loftier muse" [l. 82]) and by casting her poem as an exchange between two writers. Coleridge responded by publishing on 24 November a brief poem entitled "Alcaeus to Sappho," which E. H. Coleridge identified as having been addressed to Robinson, and by also sending privately to Robinson his poem "A Stranger Minstrel."[10] The public-private bifurcation of Coleridge's response to Robinson is critical for understanding the ways in which self-representation was essential to this public dialogue.

Both of Coleridge's poetic responses to Robinson enact the rhetorical gesture characteristic of the public dialogue between them from the beginning: each poem offers the acknowledgment of the interlocutor as a professional colleague and fellow poet. In "Alcaeus to Sappho," the literary nature of the address is obvious, but it was also meant particularly, since "Sappho" was a pseudonym with which Robinson had been associated openly in the *Morning Post*. In "A Stranger Minstrel," however, the collegial gesture is far more extensive. In this poem, which Coleridge even after Robinson's death made an effort not to have published, he applauds Robinson in superlative terms as a poet of "divinest melody" (l. 51). More importantly, the poem engages for the first time in a direct textual assimilation from Robinson's work. In creating this panegyric, Coleridge quotes at intervals from lines of Robinson's verse, drawing from her recent poems "The Haunted Beach" (1800) and "Jasper" (1800). The public-private distinction that Coleridge made between these two poems and his reluctance to publish "A Stranger Minstrel" suggest his ongoing concern with issues of voice, ventriloquism, and the mastery of style.

In both "Alcaeus to Sappho" and "A Stranger Minstrel," Coleridge's relationship to the text of another poet was becoming increasingly intimate but in markedly different ways and to markedly different ends. Coleridge appears not to have been troubled by the publication of "Alcaeus to Sappho," an identifiable but textually distinct tribute to a colleague, while the more dialogic text of "A Stranger Minstrel" gave him pause. In the context of his broader relationship to Robinson, this hesitation is understandable. With the publication of *The Lyrical Ballads* (1798), Coleridge's professional star was rising. He had long viewed his writings for the *Morning Post* as hackwork and, mirroring a broader cultural distinction between literary and subliterary genres, had prevented his serious poetic efforts from appearing in its pages, even when short of copy. As he explained to Josiah Wedgwood in January of 1798: "The few weeks I have written for the Morning Post, I have felt thus—Something must be written and written immediately—if any important Truth, any striking beauty occur to my mind, I feel a repugnance at sending it garbled to a newspaper."[11] His reluctance did not stem from any high estimation of "A Stranger Minstrel," a poem he dismissed in 1802 as "silly" and regrettable (*CLSTC* 2: 903–6). Rather, Coleridge's concern was lest his poetry—especially his serious poetry—be linked too closely in the public arena either with Robinson's verse or with a periodical mode of production. Not only did "A Stranger Minstrel" develop through quotation and allusion a lyric voice in internal dialogue with Robinson's works; it celebrated poems that were particularly close to Coleridge's imaginative territory. The allusions in the poem to Robinson's "Haunted Beach" were particularly treacherous for the manner in which they drew attention to the intimate relationship her verse had with his own. In November of 1800 Robinson had published a collection of poems under the title *Lyrical Tales*, and her choice of title was undoubtedly intended as a nod toward Wordsworth and Coleridge's recent volume. The Wordsworth family, at any rate, was irritated by the proximity, since they feared confusion between Robinson's volume and the planned second edition of *The Lyrical Ballads*, in progress at just that moment. As Dorothy Wordsworth complained to a correspondent in September of 1800: "Mrs. Robinson has claimed the title and is about publishing a volume of *Lyrical Tales*. This is a great objection . . . as they are both printed at the same press and Longman is the publisher of both" (*LWDW* 1: 293). Even more particularly, the *Lyrical Tales* had included Robinson's "Haunted Beach," which, in its portrayal of a "shipwrecked mariner" and a "band of Spectres," clearly appropriated themes and incidents from Coleridge's *Rime of the Ancient Mariner*. Meanwhile, as Coleridge may have known by December of 1800, Robinson was also at work on an additional poem, addressed "To the Poet Coleridge," in which she adopted the themes, imagery, and language of "Kubla Khan." In these poems Robinson continued to make the collegial gestures that had been the foundation of their professional friendship and public exchanges, but she appears not have appreciated the distinction that Coleridge made circa 1800 between his writing for the *Morning Post* and his serious literary efforts. His willingness to publish one poem and not the other was a function of Coleridge's investment in crafting for himself in his serious publications a voice uncontaminated by popular contexts or by other subjectivities. While "Alcaeus to Sappho" might acknowledge the talents of a contemporary and bear his name, it was a poem consigned to the ephemera of newsprint. As part of the printed exchange with Robinson, the piece served to identify Coleridge as a poet publicly, without jeopardizing the reputation of his loftier efforts. On the other hand, by mixing Robinson's texts with his own, "A Stranger Minstrel" blurred lines that Coleridge preferred to keep publicly distinct and called attention to the intimate dialogue and gracious ventriloquism their poems enacted. As a private piece of correspondence, the poem testifies to the genuine esteem and affection in which he held Robinson; but publicly, Coleridge had the professional sense to appreciate the dangers of associating himself too closely—either textually or personally—with a woman whose social and professional reputation was not and could not be entirely respectable or with a genre as indiscriminate as newsprint. The exchange suggests that Coleridge was more than willing to complicate the categories of gender and authorship—willing to acknowledge a female contemporary in public and willing to foster a friendship with her privately. However, in the end, what Coleridge was not prepared to do was publicly place his poems in the same sort of dialogue or collaboration that he had embraced with Wordsworth, and it is difficult to know to what extent this was a matter of gender rather than genre.

Coleridge's willingness to publish "Alcaeus to Sappho" in the *Morning Post* has a final twist. While the exchanges between Coleridge and Robinson involved familiar themes of quoting (a form of ventriloquism, after all), assimilation, allusion, and voice, the textual history of "Alcaeus to Sappho" brings Coleridge's readers squarely back to the issue of plagiarism. As Norman Fruman discovered, Wordsworth actually had written the poem and sent a copy of the verses to Coleridge in a letter of 27 February 1799 (45–46). Coleridge had suggested some revisions to the poem, but Wordsworth had quickly abandoned the piece, written in the context of the Lucy poems, as one for which he did not "care a farthing" (*LWDW* 1: 256). When it came to a matter of farthings, however, Coleridge apparently could take the trouble to care for it. Coleridge was consistently pressed to fulfill his copy requirements for the *Morning Post*, and the poem was sent, apparently with Coleridge's revisions, to the paper's general editor, Daniel Stuart, on 7 October 1800. There are several ways to understand this additional instance of unacknowledged borrowing: its composition followed a period of intimate exchange between Wordsworth and Coleridge, and Wordsworth may have given Coleridge leave to use the poem as a token of friendship; indeed, the revision Coleridge made to the poem (changing its subject from Lucy to Sappho, for example) was perhaps sufficient, to his mind, to voice and to "improve" the poem. Perhaps the borrowings were even unconscious in the sense that Coleridge brought to that term. However, I suspect that the truth of the matter is that neither Wordsworth nor Coleridge considered the poem sufficiently well crafted to merit treatment as literary and consequently consigned it, as piecework, to the ephemera of paid professional writing. Whatever the case, the normally territorial Wordsworth did not express dismay about the reemployment of this abandoned poem. In fact, the context of the appropriation is finally more interesting than the particulars of the occasion: it is curious that so many of Coleridge's "plagiarisms" should be concentrated in the paid work that he performed in order to make a living or in professionalized genres, ranging from the poems in the *Morning Post*—which included the publication of the "Hymn before Sunrise" on 11 September 1802—to his late public lectures and the extended critical review that is the *Biographia Literaria*. While Coleridge often protested the financial disadvantage that serious literary authors faced and participated in shaping the emerging rhetoric of the poet as professional writer, his investment in ownership and intellectual property had little to do with those poems, essays, and lectures by which he often made a living. In drawing this final contrast between Grub Street and the literary, Coleridge was reflecting an element central to Romantic-period appropriation: the clear distinction between literary property and commercial print culture. Yet, as a number of scholars have shown, genre was often gendered, and late eighteenth- and early nineteenth-century writers frequently cast literary genres as masculine and denigrated subliterary commercial genres as feminine. As Peter Manning argues in *Reading Romantics: Texts and Contexts*, Byron specifically discriminated between literary and popular texts, and in his mind commercial success and "professionalization [was] equated with the feminine."[12] Coleridge's relationship to commercial print culture and to the texts of other writers may have reflected a similarly complex intersection of genre and genre.

Domestic Circulation and the Journals of Dorothy Wordsworth

If Coleridge's borrowings from Friederike Brun and Mary Robinson reflect the subliterary status of texts that circulated in the context of commercial print culture, the borrowings from the unpublished journals of Dorothy Wordsworth by various members of the Wordsworth-Coleridge circle reveal the contemporary attitude toward texts that remained ostensibly private. As an unmarried woman, Dorothy Wordsworth was entitled to the fullest measure of property rights available to a woman at the end of the eighteenth century. Yet, her language and imagery were routinely reemployed in the poetry of both William Wordsworth and Coleridge, and these borrowings were not characterized as instances of plagiarism during her lifetime, although the obligations are apparently considerable.[13] The most familiar of these appropriations is William Wordsworth's recourse to the language of Dorothy Wordsworth's Alfoxden journal in "I wandered lonely as a cloud" (1804). William Wordsworth's familiar poem announces:

I wandered lonely as a cloud
That floats on high o'er vales and hills,
When all at once I saw a crowd,
A host, of golden daffodils;
Beside the lake, beneath the trees,
Fluttering and dancing in the breeze.

Continuous as the stars that shine
And twinkle on the milky way,
They stretched in never-ending line
Along the margin of a bay:
Ten thousand saw I at a glance,
Tossing their heads in sprightly dance.

The waves beside them danced; but they
Out-did the sparkling waves in glee:
A poet could not but be gay,
In such a jocund company:
I gazed—and gazed—but little thought
What wealth the show to me had brought:

For oft, when on my couch I lie
In vacant or in pensive mood,
They flash upon that inward eye
Which is the bliss of solitude;
And then my heart with pleasure fills,
And dances with the daffodils.[14]

The textual correspondences between his poem and Dorothy Wordsworth's journal are apparent. In her journal, she had described how:

When we were in the woods beyond Gowbarrow park we saw a few daffodils close to the water side. We fancied that the lake had floated the seeds ashore and that the little colony had so sprung up. But as we went along there were more and yet more and at last under the boughs of the trees, we saw that there was a long belt of them along the shore, about the breadth of a country turnpike road. I never saw daffodils so beautiful they grew among the mossy stones about and about them, some rested their heads upon these stones as on a pillow for weariness and the rest tossed and reeled and danced and seemed as if they verily laughed with the wind that blew upon them over the lake, they looked so gay ever glancing ever changing. This wind blew directly over the lake to them. There was here and there a little knot and a few stragglers a few yards higher up but they were so few as not to disturb the simplicity and unity and life of that one busy highway. (109)[15]

William Wordsworth clearly finds the source for his poem's imagery in his sister's journal, and he uses several of her particular expressions in its articulation. However, while the extent of the borrowing is significant, charges of plagiarism during the Romantic period did not depend on the degree of correspondence but, rather, on judgments concerning consciousness, familiarity, and improvement, and, as I will argue, evaluations of improvement, in particular, often intersected with broader cultural attitudes toward genre, literary status, and perhaps gender. In addition to these obligations to Dorothy Wordsworth's journals in "I wandered lonely as a cloud," William Wordsworth also relied upon his sister's text in early poems that included "A Night-piece" (1798), "A whirlblast from behind the hill" (1798), "Repentance" (1802), "Alice Fell" (1802), "Beggars" (1802), "To a butterfly" (1802), "To a small celandine" (1802), and "The redbreast chasing the butterfly" (1802). While it is impossible to know without specific historical commentary how contemporary readers might have applied the aesthetic judgment of improvement in particular instances, contemporary evidence suggests that authors were often given considerable license to borrow from works such as private journals that circulated beyond the margins of literary print culture. Works of this sort were often cast as implicitly authorless texts, making the mastery of voice and, therefore, the judgment of improvement remarkably uncomplicated. In fact, in her writings, Dorothy Wordsworth struggled with her own ambivalence about identifying herself as a poet and frequently disavowed the literary nature of the texts that she produced. In doing so, she was participating, of course, in a conventional set of assumptions about the impropriety of female authorship. However, the marginal modes of transmission that she adopted—the coterie circulation of her poems, the public-private nature of her private journal, and the collaborative nature of her commonplace book—also marked her texts as available for appropriation in ways that contemporary literary texts often were not. Quite simply, private unpublished journals, regardless of the author's gender, did not typically enjoy the protections granted to public literary texts.

I have suggested that the manner or medium in which a text was presented to the public had an effect on the extent to which it was considered private intellectual property. At the same time, I want to be clear that, as in the case of genre, the mode of transmission was principally important insofar as it was a signal of the literary or subliterary nature of the production, at a moment in history when the individuation of style was essential to the positive aesthetic judgment that a text's identification as literary represented. As a result, subliterary texts tended to be treated as voiceless and, therefore, implicitly authorless texts that could be assimilated successfully into other works (i.e., could be infused with a new subjectivity) with relatively little effort. The coterie circulation of Coleridge's literary poem *Christabel* (1798) in light of his silent debts in the work to Dorothy Wordsworth's journals highlights the extent to which aesthetic judgments and explicitly literary competitions were involved not only in charges about plagiarism but also in the anxiety produced by particular borrowings. The publication history of Coleridge's text and his desire to cast the work as a literary production, despite its early private mode of transmission, even while he appropriates from other unpublished writings that he treats as subliterary, offers a particularly rich example of the permeable discursive boundaries between literary and nonliterary genres, of the ways in which those boundaries might have been influenced by gender, and of the importance of a controlling authorial subjectivity or style in contemporary aesthetic judgments.

I discussed in Chapter 2 the concerns that surrounded the publication of this poem for Coleridge and the various stratagems that he employed in the public presentation of the work to forestall charges of plagiarism. The preface directly engages the question of plagiarism and goes so far as to acknowledge other writers whose works were indebted to *his* literary innovations. In light of this abundance of caution, it is striking that Coleridge does not mention borrowings from private materials, even in general terms. Yet, his poem appropriated from Dorothy Wordsworth's journals. On 7 March 1798, for example, she had written in her journal, "One only leaf upon the top of the tree—the sole remaining leaf—danced round and round like a rag blown by wind" (*Journals* 9), and this image and vocabulary reappeared in *Christabel* when Coleridge wrote: "The one red leaf, the last of its clan, / Which dances as often as dance it can, / . . . . / On the topmost twig that looks up at the sky" (ll. 49–52). In addition to this correspondence, Mary Moorman has identified another half-dozen parallels between Dorothy Wordsworth's journals and *Christabel*, suggesting a pattern of unacknowledged assimilation. However, these borrowings do not appear to have produced particular concern or resentment, in large part because unpublished private journals such as Dorothy Wordsworth's texts generally were not considered to have inherently literary properties. Within the Italian Shelley-Byron circle, the private journals of Edward Ellerker Williams were treated in much the same manner as Dorothy Wordsworth's journals, and Williams's notebooks were likewise used an unacknowledged source of material for the consciously literary poems and novels of Edward Trelawny and Thomas Medwin in ways that never elicited controversy or contemporary charges of plagiarism.[16] Borrowing successfully from private materials of this sort and "improving" upon them simply did not represent a significant aesthetic challenge. Transforming a subliterary private expression into a component of a literary work likely represented an obvious degree of improvement and one sufficient to forestall charges of poetical plagiarism.

While Romantic period attitudes in general cast subliterary materials such as private, unpublished journals as implicitly authorless texts, Dorothy Wordsworth frequently disavowed any investment in asserting the literary nature of her texts or her authorial rights to them. In her private correspondence, she frequently claimed to "detest the idea of setting myself up as an Author" (*LWDW* 2: 453), and she represented herself as writing simply for the private pleasure of her family. In an 1806 letter to Lady Beaumont, she wrote to refute the suggestion that she was "capable of writing poems that might give pleasure to others besides my own particular friends" and even insisted that she could never be "bold enough the hope to compose verses for the pleasure of grown persons" but only for children (*LWDW* 2: 24). Regarding the Grasmere journal, in particular, she claimed to have written only to "give Wm pleasure by it" (*Journals* 15–16), and it is likely that the extended Wordsworth household took her at her word and understood these materials as communal resources intended for private entertainment. In making these statements, Dorothy was drawing upon a set of familiar eighteenth-century cultural conventions regarding the impropriety of female authorship. As Robert Halsband and Irvin Ehrenprein argued some time ago, there were essentially two kinds of women writers in the period: "respectable women who wrote primarily for their own or their friends' amusement, and the faintly or frankly disreputable women who published for profit."[17] In her correspondence, especially with Lady Beaumont, Dorothy Wordsworth is careful to place herself firmly in the former category. There were significant social pressures placed on genteel women writers (or women aspiring to gentility), regardless of their marital status, to imagine their literary works in relation to a limited coterie and to the genres suitable to domestic circulation, especially subliterary genres such as commonplace books, travel journals, manuscript or vanity-press poems, and private theatricals. This localization of women's writing within a domestic sphere likely had additional implications for the ways in which the private nature of their property was understood. If for male "authors" private intellectual property typically was synonymous with individual ownership and attribution in the public arena of literary print culture, the same was not always true for women "scribblers" of a certain class whose private texts were often treated as shared domestic or social resources. In many instances, women's writing was regarded as communal, even when the work made its way into print, and to charge another writer, and especially a male writer, with plagiarism from such a text—a charge that implied the unsuccessful interpenetration of authorial subjectivities—would have been regarded as both unwelcome and inappropriate.[18] Dorothy Wordsworth's journals, as private domestic texts kept separate from the public contests of print culture, may not have represented a species of literary property and may not, therefore, have been subject to the critical and aesthetic evaluation that charges of plagiarism implied at all.

However, Dorothy Wordsworth's explicit disavowal of authorship and her gestures toward the private household nature of her texts stand in contrast to other reflections in which she recorded feeling "more than half a poet" (*Journals* 104), and there is some evidence that she was sensitive to the appropriations from her writing. Her journals and, later, her circulating commonplace book incorporate several self-consciously literary efforts, and at least one of these poems, "Thoughts on my sick-bed" (1833), engages with the issues of appropriation and textual interpenetration that shaped her experience as a writer in the Wordsworth-Coleridge circle. In the poem, Dorothy asks:

And has the remnant of my life
Been pilfered of this sunny Spring?
And have its own preclusive sounds
Touched in my heart no echoing string?

Ah! Say not so—the hidden life
Couchant within this feeble frame
Hath been enriched by kindred gifts,
That, undesired, unsought-for, came

With joyful heart in youthful days
When fresh each season in its Round
I welcomed the earliest Celandine
Glittering upon the mossy ground;

With busy eyes I pierced the lane
In quest of known and *un*known things,
—The primrose a lamp on its fortress rock,
The silent butterfly spreading its wings,

The violet betrayed by its noiseless breath,
The daffodil dancing in the breeze,
The carolling thrush, on his naked perch,
Towering above the budding trees.

Our cottage-hearth no longer our home,
Companions of Nature were we,

The Stirring, the Still, the Loquacious, the Mute—
To all we gave our sympathy.

Yet never in those careless days
When spring-time in rock, field, or bower
Was but a fountain of earthly hope
A promise of fruits & the *splendid* flower.

No! then I never felt a bliss
That might with *that* compare
Which, piercing to my couch of rest.
Came on a vernal air.

When loving Friends an offering brought.
The first flowers of the year,
Culled from the precincts of our home.
From nooks to Memory dear.

With some sad thoughts the work was done,
Unprompted and unbidden.
But joy it brought to my *hidden* life,
To consciousness no longer hidden.

I felt a Power unfelt before,
Controlling weakness, languor, pain;
It bore me to the Terrace walk
I trod the hills again;—

No prisoner in this lonely room,
I *saw* the green Banks of the Wye,
Recalling thy prophetic words,
Bard, Brother, Friend from infancy!

No need of motion, or of strength,
Or even the breathing air:
—I thought of Nature's loveliest scenes;
And with Memory I was there.[19]

The poem was included at the end of Dorothy Wordsworth's journal for 1833 and was also copied into the commonplace book that she kept at this time and circulated among her social circle. The inclusion of the poem in the commonplace book suggests that it was something she was reasonably proud to have written. Susan M. Levin was one of the first critics to call attention to the metaphors of authorship and appropriation that Dorothy

Wordsworth develops in the poem.[20] In her reading of "Thoughts on my sick-bed," Levin draws particular attention to the word "pilfered" (l. 2), which suggests, she argues, a comparison with the manner in which "[h]er observations were taken little by little (pilfered) by other writers" (136) and to the flowers described in the poem. The flowers, Levin observes, "are those of William's poetry: 'the celandine,' 'the primrose,' 'the violet,' 'the daffodil'" (135). While Levin's claim is that "the poem is in ambiguous dialogue with William's great decade" (135), I extend this reading and propose that Dorothy Wordsworth's poem rhetorically discovers her "hidden" role in the collaborative authorship from which William Wordsworth's public works emerged. William Wordsworth was particularly indebted to Dorothy Wordsworth's journals in the early years of his career for information on the details of the local landscape, and her invocation of the daffodil and the celandine recall the close textual relationship between her descriptions and his poems "I wandered lonely as a cloud" and "To a small celandine." However, the final lines of "Thoughts on my sick-bed" represent not only the conflation with the Lucy poems that Levin recognizes (135) but also part of a larger pattern of ventriloquism—or, more accurately, self-ventriloquism in the poem. The last stanza of "Thoughts on my sick-bed," with its emphasis on "I thought of Nature's loveliest scenes; / And with Memory I was there," recalls not only "Tintern Abbey" and its prophecy of future memory but also the last stanza of "I wandered lonely as a cloud," in which William Wordsworth had described how "oft, when on my couch I lie / . . . . / They [the daffodils] flash upon that inward eye / . . . . / And then my heart with pleasure fills, / And dances with the daffodils." Returning to the language of William Wordsworth's poem and, therefore, circuitously to the public context of the language of her journal, Dorothy Wordsworth claims for her own "couch of rest" (l. 31) the agency of her brother's. She echoes William Wordsworth's appropriations from her journals in order to locate the origins of both literary works in a domestic context. The recuperation performed by the allusive textual relationships represents, while not perhaps a claim to authorship, a form of complex self-imitation and a projection of the voice of the self elsewhere that confirms Dorothy Wordsworth's mature perception of herself as something "more than half a poet" and suggests that she remained personally invested in those texts that she saw silently reemployed in the public literary sphere.

While the borrowings from Dorothy Wordsworth's journals cannot be said to represent instances of Romantic plagiarism, both the manner of the appropriations and her literary reflections upon them gesture toward some of the ways that the conventions of gender and class complicated the ideas of authorship and intellectual property in the context of a cultural moment that distinguished between the individual possession of literary texts and the more communal property of subliterary texts. In practice, Romantic-period plagiarism was a mode of criticism, centered in the periodical reviews and concerned fundamentally with issues of public representation and the aesthetic development of persona. Texts that remained either rhetorically (as in the case of genteel women's writing) or literally (as in the case of unpublished journals such as Dorothy Wordsworth's) private were beyond its scope of inquiry.

Gothic Plagiarisms in *Original Poetry by Victor and Cazire*

Far more troubling for nineteenth-century reviewers than these appropriations from private texts were those from subliterary productions that were manifestly public and yet did not have their origins in commercial print culture—elements drawn from legend, folktale, popular song, and oral history. These stories occupied a position within print culture but were simultaneously beyond it, and charges of plagiarism from these sources are among the most illuminating examples in the period. The controversy surrounding another collaborative partnership highlights the difference. In 1810, Percy Bysshe Shelley and his sister Elizabeth published a coauthored volume of poetry, under the pseudonyms of Victor and Cazire, in which they appropriated from the Gothic writings of Matthew Lewis—a writer whose own plagiarism from folktale and legend had been the subject of sustained critical controversy.

Many of the details surrounding the composition and publication of this volume, entitled *Original Poetry by Victor and Cazire* (1810), are uncertain, in large part because most of the print run was destroyed following the discovery of extensive borrowings and because its existence remained apparently unknown even to Percy Bysshe Shelley's most intimate friends and to his early biographers. Published in the autumn of 1810 by Joseph Stockdale, the work contained recent poetry written by both Percy Bysshe and Elizabeth Shelley. Percy Bysshe Shelley's first love, Harriet Grove, recorded in her journal having "Received the Poetry of Victor & Cazire" (*SHC* 2: 590) on 17 September, and the book was advertised in the *Morning Chronicle* on 18 September.[21] Several brief and dismissive reviews of the volume were eventually published, including reviews in the 1810–11 volume of

The Poetical Repository and the April 1811 edition of *The British Critic*; apart from these few notices, the poems disappeared from public attention until their rediscovery and republication at the end of the nineteenth century.[22] While both Percy Bysshe and Elizabeth Shelley contributed poems to the volume, their productions are not identified within the work, and the authorship of individual verses is difficult to confirm positively. *Original Poetry by Victor and Cazire* comprises seventeen poems, some of which directly imply female authorship (e.g. "To Miss ——, from Miss ——"), while others have clear connections to later publications by Percy Bysshe Shelley. Various pieces of correspondence hint at the individual authorship of particular items but not always reliably. Neil Fraistat and Donald H. Reiman, the most recent editors of Shelley's juvenilia, conclude that Elizabeth Shelley probably wrote five poems in the volume and that Percy Bysshe Shelley probably wrote another eleven.[23] The remaining poem was, as the Shelleys' publisher first noticed, not written by either of the volume's authors: it was a poem by Matthew Lewis.

John Stockdale had observed this literary appropriation in the *Victor and Cazire* volume only after the work had been published and advertised. Upon informing Shelley of this discovery, it was agreed that the book should be removed from circulation and all remaining copies destroyed. In 1827, Stockdale published an account of these events, writing:

Some short time after the announcement of the poems I happened to be perusing them, with more leisure than I had till then had leisure to bestow upon them, when I recognized one which I knew to have been written by Mr. M. G. Lewis, the author of "The Monk," and I fully anticipated the probable vexation of the juvenile author when I communicated the discovery to Mr. P. B. Shelley. With all the ardour natural to his character he expressed the warmest resentment at the imposition practiced upon him by his coadjutor, and entreated me to destroy all the copies, of which about one hundred had been put into circulation.[24]

The poem that Stockdale recognized was Lewis's "The Black Canon of Elmham, or, Saint Edmond's Eve; An Old English Ballad," which had been included in his collected *Tales of Terror* (1801), a book that was a particular favorite of the young Percy Bysshe Shelley. The *Victor and Cazire* edition had included a poem, entitled "St. Edmond's Eve," that was, in fact, nothing more than a reprinting of Lewis's poem.

While Percy Bysshe Shelley's efforts to cast the blame for this deception onto his anonymous "coadjutor" are understandable, it is difficult to believe that he was unaware either of Lewis's poem or of the placement of it in the volume.²⁵ In fact, the question of personal responsibility is the least compelling aspect of the entire affair. Far more interesting is the fact that the obligations in the *Victor and Cazire* volume have been taken as an incontrovertible example of plagiarism. The borrowings are word-for-word, the original author is not cited, and the similarities are, ipso facto, plagiarism—or so the critical argument has run. This term has been used in each of the major editions of the Shelley juvenilia to describe the borrowings in *Victor and Cazire*, beginning with the first Garnett edition of 1898 and continuing through the Cameron edition of the 1960s and the Fraistat and Reiman edition of 2000. Yet, the appropriations in the *Victor and Cazire* volume were not labeled plagiarism in the Romantic period, either by Stockdale or by the periodical reviewers, who had not failed to notice that "[t]here is no 'original *poetry*' in this volume" (*Poetical Repository* 617). This absence of contemporary charges of plagiarism surrounding the *Victor and Cazire* volume could simply be a matter of chance, of course. However, it is more likely that the omission signals an important distinction. The liberties taken with "St. Edmond's Eve" in *Victor and Cazire* may not have represented a matter of plagiarism so much as a matter of imposture and copyright violation. It is difficult to imagine that contemporary readers would not have recognized the inclusion in the volume of a poem drawn from Lewis' popular horror collection and published under the same title as the original. The borrowing was hardly recondite, and, as we have already seen, where a work was broadly familiar and where readers could be expected to credit the actual author, culpable plagiarism, in the Romantic-period sense, would not have occurred.

By reprinting Lewis's poem rather than assimilating it, however, Percy Bysshe and Elizabeth Shelley had opened Stockdale to charges of copyright violation and themselves to charges of imposture or fraud. Shelley's editors have suggested that the inclusion of Lewis's poem in the volume was probably deliberate and intended as an elaborate prank, on the order of the Rowley hoax. In his *Life of Percy Bysshe Shelley* (1858), Thomas Jefferson Hogg recorded that the youthful Shelley "had a certain sly relish for a practical joke, so that it were ingenious and abstruse, and of a literary nature; he would often exult in the successful forgeries of Chatterton and Ireland," and the publication of an unoriginal poem in a volume entitled *Original Poetry* might well qualify as adolescent humor of precisely this sort.²⁶ However, the consequences of forgery and imposture were, in fact, rather more severe than the consequences of plagiarism. After all, Thomas Chatterton was reputed to have killed himself as a result of his literary impostures and the subsequent disgrace they brought upon him, and the very fact of this cultural representation, regardless of its accuracy, reveals how grave the social consequences of such deception could be. William Henry Ireland's Shakespearean frauds were the subject of considerable legal inquiry, and the infamous eighteenth-century cleric William Dodd was sentenced to hang for forging financial instruments and impersonating Lord Chesterfield in writing.[27] Percy Bysshe and Elizabeth Shelley were not, of course, in danger of consequences this dire, but the fraudulent representation created in the *Victor and Cazire* volume exposed them to more serious criticism than either might have imagined. For, as Jack Lynch has argued, the eighteenth-century attitude toward literary duplicity made little distinction between it and other forms of imposture; Samuel Johnson considered it a form of "treason" and characterized "[t]he nature of fraud, as distinct from other violations of right or property [as] consist[ing] in this, that the injured man is induced to concur in the act by which the injury is done."[28] Nicola Trott has shown that, as late as 1825, textual impersonation (including the use of pseudonyms) was satirically associated with fears of "being hanged for forgery."[29] While plagiarism was a primarily aesthetic transgression during the Romantic period, having no direct consequence in law, both copyright piracy and fraud were violations of property with concrete legal and financial implications. The fact that Stockdale was moved to suppress the *Victor and Cazire* edition and to destroy an entire print run of nearly 1,500 volumes suggests that he understood the more serious nature of the jeopardy in which this prank might have placed them all. After all, nineteenth-century publishers had little incentive to worry about charges of plagiarism, the consequences of which affected the reputation of the author almost exclusively. John Murray never proposed to destroy editions of Byron's poetry simply because Wordsworth or the periodical reviewers were alleging plagiarisms, and none of the numerous contemporary commentaries that I examine in this book suggest that plagiarism was a publisher's concern. However, booksellers and publishers did have good reasons for protecting themselves from the scandal and from the potential legal consequences of printing a work that might be viewed as a fraud, imposture, or copyright violation, and Stockdale's reproduction of "St. Edmond's Eve" in its entirety and under the original (albeit truncated) title was arguably precisely such a violation.

While the inclusion of Lewis's "The Black Canon of Elmham, or, Saint Edmond's Eve" in the *Victor and Cazire* volume, then, may have represented an instance of fraud or infringement rather than plagiarism, there are other appropriations throughout the volume that we might expect to have occasioned more conventional charges of illegitimate borrowing. There are several poems in *Victor and Cazire* that silently borrow from the works of contemporary writers and in ways that are more directly associated with the complex conditions of early nineteenth-century plagiarism. The presence of one of these appropriations was first noted by Thomas Medwin, who wrote in his *Life of Shelley* (1847):

Chatterton was one of his [Shelley's] great favourites; he enjoyed very much the literary forgery and successful mystifications of Horace Walpole and his contemporaries. . . . One of his earliest effusions was a fragment beginning—it was indeed almost taken from the pseudo Rowley:

Hark! the owlet flaps his wings
In the pathless dell beneath;
Hark! 'tis the night-raven sings
Tidings of approaching death.[30]

Although Medwin apparently was not aware of the *Victor and Cazire* volume, he is quoting (with minor inaccuracies) in this passage from the first stanza of a poem that Percy Bysshe and Elizabeth Shelley had published under the title "Ghasta; or, the Avenging Demon!!!" Percy Bysshe Shelley probably was the author of this poem, and there can be little doubt that in composing the work he borrowed directly from Chatterton's verse. Richard Garnett characterized this debt in 1898 as "an audacious plagiarism" (xxiii), and, indeed, the stanza is lifted, with a few changes, from the "Mynstrelles Songe" in *Aella: A Tragycal Enterlude . . . wrotten by Thomas Rowlie* (1777), in which Chatterton had written:

Harke! the ravenne flappes hys wynge,
In the briered delle belowe;
Harke! the dethe-owle loude doth synge,
To the nyghte-mares as heie goe; (ll. 982–85)[31]

While Percy Bysshe Shelley has altered the archaic language and has reversed the order of his ornithology, the image and style are substantially the same. Had *Victor and Cazire* been subject to serious literary criticism in the contemporary reviews, this borrowing might well have occasioned charges of poetical (but perhaps not culpable) plagiarism. Both the critical notices of the volume, at any rate, agreed that the poetry in the volume had little to recommend it, and it seems unlikely that the Shelleys' borrowings would have been considered improvements.

However, the appropriations in the *Victor and Cazire* volume also need to be understood in relation to the broader anxieties about origins that Gothic literature elicited among contemporary readers. Gothic texts were remarkably allusive and assimilative in their narrative and verse conventions and were prone to highly contested charges of plagiarism. As E. J. Clery has argued in *The Rise of Supernatural Fiction, 1762–1800*, there was throughout the period a "perceived tension between originality and imitation in commericalised Gothic fiction" that stemmed from the systematic textual interpenetration practiced by authors writing in the genre.[32] In noting Percy Bysshe Shelley's obligation to Chatterton, Medwin had taken some pains to place the discussion in the context of Gothic literature and questions of its originality. Immediately following the quotation from "Ghasta," Medwin explained:

I had had lent me the translation of Bùrgher's "Leonora". . . . It produced on Shelley a powerful effect; and I have in my possession a copy of the whole poem, which he made in his own hand. The story is by no means original, if not taken from an English ballad. For the *refrain*,

> How quick ride the dead,

Which occurs in so many stanzas, Burgher is indebted to an old *Volkslied*[.] (*Life of Shelley* 1: 62–63)

Medwin calls attention here to a common feature of eighteenth- and early nineteenth-century Gothic literature: it often drew specifically from folklore, including ballads, ghost stories, and local legends, for its materials. Lewis had emphasized the folk "origins" of "The Black Canon of Elmham" by appending the identification "An Old English Ballad," and one of the central questions in assessing plagiarism in Gothic genres, and in the *Victor and Cazire* volume more specifically, concerns the degree to which "common" oral narrative or verse traditions qualified as private literary property during the Romantic period.

This question of the relationship between plagiarism and the folk tradition in Gothic genres emerges more directly at another point in Shelley's "Ghasta," when he appropriates additional materials for the poem from Lewis's novel, *The Monk* (1795). The central narrative of "Ghasta" can be traced to Lewis's novel and, particularly, to the scenes in the fourth chapter describing the apparition of the Bleeding Nun. In addition to similarities of incident and characterization, there are several direct verbal parallels, including Shelley's reemployment of the nun's ghastly incantation. In *The Monk*, the scene focuses on Raymond mistaking the nun for his paramour, Agnes, whom he assumes has arrived in disguise. He clasps her to his bosom and professes his devotion to her, only to discover the next morning from the peasants that no woman had been seen. The next evening, she returns, and he recognizes her as the Bleeding Nun of local legend when she exclaims:

Raymond! Raymond! Thou art mine!
Raymond! Raymond! I am thine!
In thy veins while blood shall roll,
I am thine!
Thou art mine!—
Mine thy body, mine thy soul! (166)

The climactic scene of Shelley's "Ghasta" borrows from this passage. In Shelley's poem, the central character is confronted with a female ghost who claims him as her lover with the pronouncement

Thou art mine and I am thine,
Till the sinking of the world,
I am thine and thou art mine,
Till in ruin death is hurled—(ll. 73–76)

Modern readers may quarrel with the idea that this borrowing represents a substantial plagiarism, but there is little doubt that some Romantic-period readers would have charged Shelley with plagiarism for his appropriation in this instance. For, while Lewis was Shelley's immediate source, Lewis had borrowed as well in writing this passage and had been charged with plagiarism for the same obligation. Lewis's sources had been equally familiar, and, if anything, Lewis could claim an avenue of defense not available to Shelley: his materials had included not only other literary works but also narratives drawn directly from the arena of folklore and oral tradition.

Gothic Literature and the Possession of Folklore

As Louis F. Peck has observed, "Lewis' reputation as a shameless plagiarist became quickly established [after the publication of *The Monk*] and has survived to this day."[33] The periodical reviews that followed the publication of his Gothic romance were nearly unanimous in decrying the tale's lack of originality and its obligations to, by Peck's calculation, "more than fifty works and authors" (21). In fact, Lewis drew from a wide range of source materials, primarily German and French. Syndy Conger, for example, has demonstrated extensive and often direct borrowings from the lyric poetry of "Storm and Stress" Romanticism, including works such as Bürger's "Lenore" (1773), Herder's "Der Wasserman" (The Waterbearer) (1779), and Schubart's "Der ewige Jude" (The Wandering Jew) (1784).[34] Other important characterizations and narrative events in the novel Conger identifies as drawn from texts including Musäus's "Die Entführung" (The Elopement) (1782–86), Schiller's "Der Geisterseher" (The Ghostseer) (1787–89), Flammenberg's *Der Geisterbanner* (1792) and its English translation *The Necromancer; or, a Tale of the Black Forest* (1794), and Weber's "Die Teufelsbeschwörung" (The Exorcism) (1791). However, the status of these works as literary property was not a straightforward matter in the Romantic period, because many of the stories Lewis appropriated were based on narratives drawn from ghost stories, local legend, ballads, and oral tradition. Claims that Lewis had plagiarized from these sources suggest that the definition of familiarity as a standard in evaluating early nineteenth-century plagiarism was complicated by borrowings from outside the self-consciously literary tradition and particularly by narratives that represented a communal, oral inheritance.

Many readers assumed that Musäus's "Die Entführung" was Lewis's textual source of the Bleeding Nun legend, and the controversy surrounding these obligations is intensified by Lewis's claims, probably truthful, not to have encountered the story in this print version until the publication of Musäus's *Volksmärchen der Deutschen* (German Folktales) in 1805, a decade after the first edition of *The Monk*. Yet, as Conger demonstrates, Musäus's tale includes all the central details and some of the precise language present in the Bleeding Nun scenes. To make matters worse, Lewis had already been charged with plagiarizing these same passages from a different source: Stephanie de Genlis's *Les Chevaliers du Cygne; ou la Cour de Charlemagne* (1795). In the fourth (expurgated) edition of *The Monk* in 1798, Lewis had responded to these allegations in a preface that explained the source of his materials:

I can only account for it [the resemblance between his Bleeding Nun episode and that in "Les Chevaliers du Cygne"] by supposing that Madame de Genlis had heard, while in Germany, the same tradition which I have made use of. . . . The story which was related to me, was merely, that the castle of Lauenstein was haunted by a spectre habited as a nun (but not as a bleeding one); that a young officer by mistake ran away with her, instead of the heiress of Lauenstein. . . . and that the words which she used to repeated to him were in the original, "Frizchen! Frizchen! Du bist mein! / Frizchen! Frizchen! Ich bein dein! / Ich dein! Du mein! / Mit leib' und seel." (Conger 95)

Lewis explains here that his source was not, in fact, Genlis—nor would it later be Musäus—but was instead a version of this familiar folktale that had been orally communicated to him. Indeed, in *The Monk*, the Bleeding Nun tale is explicitly identified as an oral tradition that has escaped textual history. Agnes asks Raymond "can you possibly have lived in Lindenberg for three whole months without hearing of [her]?" (Lewis 151) and proceeds to explain, "All my knowledge of her history comes from an old tradition . . . handed down from father to son. . . . It is surprising that in all the chronicles of past times this remarkable personage is never once mentioned" (Lewis 152). Lewis's veracity in recounting his own exposure to the story is possibly suspect, but the point in respect to matters of literary property and plagiarism remains the same: Lewis evokes the traditional oral transmission of the tale as a justification for his reemployment of it, and the suggestion is that folktales, like ancient ballads, were understood as authorless texts and as part of a shared national history.

However, although Lewis claimed not to have borrowed the legend of the Bleeding Nun from a printed source, he was careful to acknowledge the obligation to the oral tradition in his prefatory advertisement published in the first edition of *The Monk*. In that advertisement, he had identified three textual sources from which he had borrowed, and he noted, once again, that the story of the Bleeding Nun had its origins in folk tradition:

The first idea of this Romance was suggested by the story of Santon Barsisa, related in The Guardian [31 August 1713].—The Bleeding Nun is a tradition still credited in many parts of Germany; and I have been told that the ruins of the castle of *Lauenstein*, which she is supposed to haunt, may yet be seen upon the borders of *Thuringia*.—The *Water-King*, from the first to the twelfth stanza, is a fragment of an original Danish ballad—And *Belerma and Durandarte* is translated from some stanzas to be found in a collection of old Spanish poetry. . . . I have now made a full avowal of all the plagiarisms of which I am aware myself, but I doubt not that many more may be found of which I am at present totally unconscious. (Lewis 32)

In light of this "full avowal," the charges of plagiarism brought against him are extraordinary, and it is particularly curious that his appropriation of the

Bleeding Nun story generated some of the most intense criticism. While his other explicitly textual attributions were accepted and while the suggestion of additional "unconscious" plagiarisms prompted a more thorough investigation of his reading than he might have desired, there appears to have been a critical reluctance to accept the folkloric source of the Bleeding Nun. Lewis's reviewers, in other words, persisted in their efforts to locate the print origins of his tale, despite his identification of it as part of an oral cultural tradition. Instead, Lewis's periodical reviewers attempted to discover in Musäus or in Genlis—texts that had drawn from the same folk traditions from which Lewis was appropriating—the real source of his borrowings. These repeated allegations of plagiarism in the periodical reviews suggest that folkloric materials, or what would have called until the second half of the nineteenth century "Popular Antiquities, or Popular Literature," disrupted and complicated the conventional attitudes toward private property and authorship.[35]

It is not surprising that oral or folk materials should have been a topic of some uneasiness when it came to matters of literary property, particularly because Romanticism as an aesthetic and a national movement was tied to the emerging interest in popular traditions during the eighteenth and early nineteenth centuries in both Britain and Germany. In Britain, the revival of interest in the oral tradition was closely associated with the development of imperial identity at the end of the eighteenth and beginning of the nineteenth centuries, as Katie Trumpener argues in *Bardic Nationalism: The Romantic Novel and the British Empire*. Charting the relationship between the revival of Scottish nationalism and the "restoration" of a lost oral tradition in the *Poems of Ossian*, Trumpener demonstrates that folk traditions operated as powerful embodiments of a shared national and racial past.[36] If these imperial effects offered an invitation to Romantic-period subjects to identify with and to assimilate an imagined cultural heritage held in common, at the same time popular antiquities were being transformed legally into a category of private property at the beginning of the nineteenth century, as those who had previously been seen as collectors gathering together a shared cultural heritage became the owners of private manuscripts and materials. As Penny Fielding has argued in *Writing and Orality: Nationality, Culture, and Nineteenth-Century Scottish Fiction*, the rise of connoisseurship in the early nineteenth century generated a contemporary debate regarding the ownership of cultural artifacts, including the ballad tradition.[37] Rhetorically positioned as both culturally common and privately collected, popular antiquities occupied territory beyond the conventional arenas of either print culture or proprietorial authorship, and as a result there was a resistance to seeing works in the oral tradition as "literary" material.

At the same time, the ownership of oral culture in the Romantic period is additionally complicated by extent to which it highlights the disjunction between commercial and aesthetic categories of authorship. Like other texts located at the margins of literary print culture, oral materials were understood as implicitly authorless and, therefore, available for appropriation in a relatively straightforward manner. The problem, of course, is in defining what constituted the "absence" of authorship in a text at this period. Vernacular works typically lack authors in the most literal sense because they cannot be associated with individual-specific origins and because they are part of a larger national or communal process of composition and transmission that escapes private ownership. However, vernacular works may also have been understood in the Romantic period to lack authors in a more narrow aesthetic sense: the *literary* ownership of a work depended primarily on the production of a controlling "spirit" or "style" (in other words, on the production of an "author") that improved and appropriated any borrowed materials. Style, however, is a rhetorical effect that to some extent depends upon a textual articulation to fix its individual identity. Oral traditions, ironically, were among those materials in the late eighteenth and early nineteenth centuries that were most likely to be understood as voiceless and as most readily available for assimilation. The internal and aesthetic production of literary identity, however, was not the same thing as the external production of legal ownership, just as plagiarism is not the same thing as copyright infringement, and the appropriation of vernacular materials was often controversial because it revealed a fissure in the structure of authorship, namely, the extent to which authorship as a term operated simultaneously in two discourses that could not always be reconciled.

This bifurcation and the ways in which its was revealed and complicated by the possession of vernacular materials are explored at some length in the works of James Hogg, where the production of voice dominates both his aesthetic concerns and his mediated relationship to both print and oral culture. Peter T. Murphy, in *Poetry as an Occupation and an Art*, devotes a chapter to Hogg's complicated textual relationship with John Lockhart, who inserts the voice and persona of Hogg into the *Noctes Ambrosianae* (1822–35) and, in doing so, parodies Hogg's novel *The Three Perils of Man: War, Women, and Witchcraft* (1822)—a work that itself explores the problem of an author claiming to own oral productions.[38] Murphy makes two important points about this exchange: first, that the ownership of voice in a literary context is complicated by the simultaneous impossibility of owning vernacular traditions and the necessity of mastering them in print; and second, that Lockhart's strategy of appropriation—his "brain-sucking" (124)—is based on models of domination and absorption over the voice of the borrowed text. As Murphy writes, "the subject [Hogg] becomes enslaved to his absorbing Master. . . . Contest over voice, as I have argued again and again, is not superficial, not purely 'formal'" (124). From the legal perspective on authorship, Lockhart's caricatures of Hogg and his textual style are perfectly permissible. From the aesthetic perspective, Lockhart has appropriated (or misappropriated) one of the central elements of Hogg's literary property and in ways that threaten the coherence of his authorial persona.

While Murphy reads this literary competition as it played out in contemporary print culture, Penny Fielding offers a more particular analysis of Hogg's novel that highlights the ways in which the literary ownership of oral materials depends on textual mediation, perhaps particularly in instances where the origins are a common vernacular tradition. Reading the scene in the novel in which the character Colley Carrol humorously claims to be the author of a popular traditional song, while asking the audience to remind him of some of the verses, Fielding considers the problems with the ownership of oral materials generally in Romantic-period culture and proposes that the "authority [of ownership] depends on the text's becoming fixed, with a stable existence before any particular telling; that is, the text's being written down" (*Writing and Orality* 13). Read in this context, the investment of Matthew Lewis's reviewers in locating the print sources of his oral materials can be understood as a reaction to the ways in which the vernacular disrupted the aesthetic and commercial judgments that constituted the production of authorship. At the same time, the textual imperatives of Romantic-period authorship, which required that oral traditions be "fixed" before their assimilation into print culture, may have helped to produce the fashion for collecting ballads and songs in the late eighteenth and early nineteenth centuries.

This same tension between the public and private nature of the oral tradition is apparent even in the prefaces to *The Lyrical Ballads* (1798). In the 1798 "Preface," Wordsworth and Coleridge famously set out to justify and to describe a form of poetry that was both spontaneous and written in the language of the common man, and in striking these particular notes they were reflecting an earlier eighteenth-century fashion, first popularized by Joseph Addison and Richard Steele, for regarding traditional ballads as national poetry.[39] William Wordsworth later reiterates this point about the importance of the ancient folk-ballad tradition for the development of British Romanticism in the "Essay Supplementary to the Preface" (1815) when he defends the "compilation[s]" of Thomas Percy.[40] In praising Percy's *Reliques of Ancient English Poetry* (1765), Wordsworth addressed the problems of authorship, assimilation, and influence raised by works in the oral and historical tradition, describing the *Reliques* as

collected, new-modelled, and in many instances (if such a contradiction in terms may be used) composed by the Editor, Dr. Percy. This work did not steal silently into the world, as is evident from the number of legendary tales, that appeared not long after its publication; and had been modelled, as the authors persuaded themselves, after the old Ballad. The Compilation was, however, ill suited to the then existing taste of city society. . . . The critic triumphed, the legendary imitators were deservedly disregarded, and, as undeservedly, their ill-imitated models sank, in this country, into temporary neglect; while Bürger, and other able writers of Germany, were translating or imitating these Reliques, and composing, with the aid of inspiration thence derived, poems which are the delight of the German nation. . . . The Editor of the *Reliques* had indirectly preferred a claim to the praise of invention, by not concealing that his supplementary labours were considerable! . . . I have already stated how much Germany is indebted to [the *Reliques*]; and for our own country, its poetry has been absolutely redeemed by it. I do not think that there is an able writer in verse of the present day who would not be proud to acknowledge his obligations to the *Reliques*[.] (*PWWW* 3: 76–77)

Wordsworth negotiates in this passage some of the central "contradiction[s]" raised by Percy's reemployment of folk tradition: Percy is at once poet and editor; his works are at once composed and collected. "Fixing" the textual identity of the vernacular tradition, in an environment where authorship was to some extent a judgment of voiced mastery and personal labor, represented an act of creative and commercial invention. However, while Wordsworth argues for the poetic accomplishment achieved by Percy in his "supplementary labours," many of Percy's contemporary critics had dismissed the literary merits of the *Reliques* out of hand and had argued for the merely historical and editorial nature of his volume. While Percy's right to draw from the "old Ballad" tradition and the print ephemera or private manuscripts in which it had been recorded went largely uncontested, the aesthetic consequences of these borrowings were more problematic. What was not clear was the degree to which Percy had created a literary work and, by doing so, appropriated as private property his common sources.

Lewis faced a similar dilemma. At stake in the plagiarism controversy surrounding *The Monk* was not so much Lewis's reemployment of German ballads and folk tales—stories that, as Wordsworth observes, were themselves the result of a far more complicated process of cultural transmission and often had their historical origins in the English oral tradition—as the question of his literary accomplishment. Borrowing from works designated as literary was a relatively straightforward matter in the Romantic period, although the critical evaluation of these obligations was subject to a particular set of interpretive judgments. However, if Lewis's appropriations were to other authored print sources, then the operative categories of evaluation became questions of consciousness, improvement, and familiarity. Having acknowledged the possibility of "unconscious" plagiarisms in the "Advertisement" to *The Monk*, Lewis had effectively forestalled charges of culpable plagiarism, and the critical stakes remaining would be exclusively aesthetic: questions of the degree to which Lewis had improved upon or assimilated his borrowed materials, which was another way of asking whether Lewis had succeeded or failed as an author. With materials drawn from an anonymous and oral tradition, however, there was no clear process for coming to critical judgment. Certainly, an author could not have been charged persuasively with culpable plagiarism, an allegation that functioned in the Romantic period to prevent harm being done to the reputation of the individual author. Likewise, in cases of an obligation to a folkloric national tradition, the category of familiarity and the distinctions used to evaluate it collapsed under the weight of the obvious, making it irrelevant whether the debt was unconscious or demonstrated improvement. However, in matters of aesthetic plagiarism—the part of the charge that mattered most to the Romantic writers and to their reviewers anyhow—the obstacle was serious. In evaluating aesthetic plagiarism, the absence or presence of improvement was the judgment that finally mattered, and, as we have seen, improvement in the late eighteenth and early nineteenth centuries depended upon the consciously literary elements of voice, subjectivity, and style rather than on changes in word-for-word linguistic correspondences. If these oral materials were not literary but were historical, if they were not the productions of a unified author expressing his or her subjectivity and infusing the work with his or her style but were documentary, common, or traditional records, then how to decide if improvement had occurred? And if one could not come to judgment about improvement, then how to come to judgment about aesthetic merit when the two were inextricably linked? The cultural rhetoric followed from the legal conditions of the period: in the eighteenth century, it was literary property that copyright protected as privately owned, and it was borrowings from literary property that charges of plagiarism were equipped to negotiate. This is not to suggest that published histories were not subject to copyright protections or to charges of plagiarism. Rather, the point is that the definitions of history and its relationship to private authorship were also in transition during the Romantic period, and certain genres of "popular antiquities," including oriental tales, travel narratives, and the Gothic, were considered as less privileged forms of private property on account of their close associations with the alternative narrative conventions and ontological claims of what we would now designate as science, history, archaeology, and geography.[41] In light of this complexity, one can perhaps forgive Lewis's reviewers for their desire to locate his borrowings and to formulate their judgments in the context of literary print culture.

Lewis's tendency in *The Monk* to borrow from sources in or related to the oral folk tradition is characteristic of Gothic literature—or of what Nick Groom has called the "national Gothic"—more generally.[42] As a genre, Gothic literature challenged the contemporary expectations regarding private authorship, and this often made these works particular targets for charges of plagiarism. As a result, they also became the subject of important critical discussions about literary judgment and its limits. The Gothic genre's particularly intimate relationship to legend, like the ballad form's relationship to oral song, represented a version of the problems of multiple-use property that occupied eighteenth- and early nineteenth-century British culture at large. After all, these traditional and often rural tales and stories were part of a common literary inheritance that predated the legal and rhetorical isolation of private authorship and intellectual property. Yet, as the controversy surrounding *The Monk* demonstrates, the reemployment of these materials in print forms could often only be evaluated by a different set of conventions, emerging from the discourse of literary property and plagiarism.

In this respect, the charges of plagiarism surrounding Gothic literature are a function of the same cultural conventions that produced the silent appropriations from the private domestic texts of women writers or from works published in transitory and commercial media. As the examples from both the Wordsworth and Shelley households demonstrate, plagiarism in early nineteenth-century Britain was inextricably connected to judgments of literary status and merit, and texts located at the boundaries of literary print culture were frequently viewed as implicitly authorless at a historical moment when aesthetic achievement was a function of uniquely identifi-able textual subjectivity. As Andrew Bennett has argued, "A key element in the modern conception of 'literature' . . . is the commodification of author-ship," and, as we have seen, participation in early nineteenth-century print culture to a large extent determined the literary status of a text and the pro-tections of ownership and identity afforded to its author.[43]

Chapter 4

"The Slip-Shod Muse": Byron, Originality, and Aesthetic Plagiarism

Although the critical tradition has focused primarily on the plagiarisms of Samuel Taylor Coleridge, Lord Byron was the Romantic figure whose intellectual debts were most familiar to his contemporaries. Over the course of his career, Byron was publicly or semi-publicly charged with plagiarism on numerous occasions, and, as with Coleridge, his friends and intimates uncovered for the popular press additional obligations in the decades after his death. The scandal surrounding Byron's plagiarisms was perpetuated vigorously by the periodical press as part of a sustained literary attack on his reputation as a poet, and this history reveals the extent to which accusations of plagiarism represented a mode of criticism in the Romantic period. Most often, the attacks were intended to contradict Byron's emerging reputation as one of the era's most original poets, and the critical emphasis on originality reflects the cultural shift that occurred during the second decade of the nineteenth century in attitudes toward imitation, literary property, and plagiarism. Byron's rising celebrity as an author coincided with the debates surrounding the Copyright Act of 1814 and with the revision in attitudes toward genius and originality that Wordsworth articulated in the "Essay Supplementary to the Preface" (1815). As a result, the highly visible and popular young poet became an object of particular scrutiny, and the criticism surrounding Byron and his alleged plagiarisms became a crucible in which Romantic standards of appropriation were refined.

Byron was charged with plagiarism from a variety of sources, ranging from travel narratives and German literature to the works of his literary contemporaries. While periodical correspondents from across the political spectrum made accusations against the poet, the critical debate was, in many respects, a conflict between Byron and Wordsworth and, by extension, between what has conventionally been designated first- and second-generation Romanticism. At stake in the controversy was the poet's relationship to his literary production. Writers such as Wordsworth were increasingly concerned with copyright and sought to define poetry in essentially Lockean terms: as a property closely centered in the physical person of the author, whose intellectual labor had appropriated it for private ownership.[1] The aristocratic Byron, who gave his copyrights as gifts and who declined to negotiate with publishers over finances, was far less invested in metaphors of personal labor, preferring to see poetry as the production of multiple imagined subjectivities and dramatic personae.[2] As Romantic-period authors, both writers agreed that voice and identity were elements of literary property, but for Wordsworth this subjectivity coincided with the "matter of factness" of his existence in a way that it did not for Byron. In this conflict, of course, the two writers were playing out the terms of the eighteenth-century debate over copyright—a debate that had been reinvigorated with the confirmation of *Donaldson v. Beckett* in the 1814 Copyright Act.

While both the charges of plagiarism levied against Byron and his aesthetic conflict with Wordsworth stemmed from a larger set of competing cultural attitudes toward literary property and originality, it would not be fair, of course, to blame Wordsworth for the ensuing scandal. Although Wordsworth was hostile toward the younger poet and was responsible for bringing Byron's appropriations to public scrutiny in the 1820s, Byron was charged with plagiarisms on several other occasions and quite independently. However, in these instances the critical objective was the same: the question of Byron's originality was at stake—and, therefore, also the question of how to define the aesthetic objectives of literary Romanticism.

Originality in the Oriental Tales

Byron was first publicly charged with plagiarism in periodical reviews during 1818, although semi-public accusations had been circulating in literary circles since at least 1816, partly as a result of Byron's early scruples about acknowledging his debts. The public censure in 1818, carried on in *The Gentleman's Magazine*, focused on Byron's appropriations in the oriental tales, with particular attention to *Lara* (1814) and *The Siege of Corinth* (1816). Although the intellectual obligations in question barely rose to the Romantic-period standard of plagiarism and certainly would not rise to modern standards, the nature of the critical exchange reveals how closely connected plagiarism was with aesthetic judgments. As I have argued, the

Romantic-period attitude toward plagiarism was not only culturally distinct from twenty-first-century perceptions of intellectual property, but it also distinguished between two kinds of plagiarism: culpable and aesthetic. While modern readers often view allegations of plagiarism in exclusively moral or legal terms, early nineteenth-century readers and writers understood the charge along a wider spectrum. In the Romantic period, moral or "culpable" plagiarism was the term applied only to debts that were *simultaneously* unacknowledged, unfamiliar, unimproved, and conscious. In the absence of any one of these conditions, an author could not be held culpable for a moral breach of conduct, and, as I have suggested, the charge was almost impossible to lodge conclusively during the period. However, an author might very well be guilty of aesthetic plagiarism—in other words, of writing bad poetry. Insofar as plagiarism represented an inability to control the narrative or lyric voice within a text or to assimilate fully one's borrowed materials, the charge was an accusation of literary failure.

The charges brought against Byron in *The Gentleman's Magazine* reflect the literary and aesthetic subtext of Romantic-period plagiarism. The controversy, which took place in the pages of the review magazine from February to May of 1818, focused on Byron's debts in the oriental tales to primarily contemporary authors and was inaugurated by A. Dyce in a letter to the readers on 6 February. Reflecting the contemporary language of plagiarism, Dyce writes, "Reviewers of different parties, so often biassed, in other cases, by political opinion, have all conspired to eulogize him [Byron] as the first of the living Poets. In his works, however, (generally the productions of haste) several plagiarisms may be found, of which, no doubt, the author was unconscious."[3] Dyce proceeds to delineate Byron's appropriations in *Lara* (1814) from Thomas Parnell's "Night-piece on Death" (1722), Alexander Pope's various letters to Richard Steele, Ann Radcliffe's *The Mysteries of Udolpho* (1794), and Voltaire's *Henriade* (1728). Considered in the context of Romantic-period attitudes toward plagiarism, this review demonstrates how familiar the category of the unconscious was to early nineteenth-century readers. Yet, by suggesting that Byron's obligations may have been unwitting, Dyce also absolves the poet of any moral censure. The stakes in bringing the charge are, as this review hints, primarily aesthetic: Dyce is concerned to counteract the popular perception that Byron was "the first of the living Poets," presumably by eroding faith in his originality. This, at least, seems to have been how a subsequent contributor to the debate understood Dyce's critical objectives. In the May edition of the journal, a letter by "Vertumnus" was published, in which the pseudonymous reviewer observes that "Lord Byron, notwithstanding all his 'original daring', has often condescended to imitate his brother bards. . . . In addition to those plagiarisms or imitations [in the late number], I beg leave to present you with a few resemblances as follows."[4] This is followed by a brief account of correspondences between Richard Polwhele's "Fair Isabel" (1815) and Byron's *The Siege of Corinth* (1816). Here, "Vertumnus" specifically intends to refute Byron's status as an original poet, and this was the underlying objective of both critiques. The obligations might have been morally justified on any number of grounds, ranging from familiarity or improvement to unconsciousness, and the reviewers do not hesitate to absolve Byron of culpable theft. However, in offering unconsciousness as the mitigating factor, the reviewers also chose the justification most likely to suggest that Byron was not in complete control of either his (hasty) compositional process or his verse. By publicly observing avowedly unintentional debts, Byron's critics were suggesting not that he was a thief but, rather, that the aesthetic merits of his poetry and his status as an original writer were inflated.

Many of these same points were made in the public defense of Byron that also appeared in *The Gentleman's Magazine* in the March 1818 edition. Here the anonymous correspondent ("C. C.") develops an extended argument that both recognizes the literary stakes in the critical combat and proposes appropriation as a condition of authorship, articulating a position similar to the one Byron repeatedly described in his letters and conversations. In a long passage the reviewer writes:

Dr. Johnson observes, "that when the excellence of a composition can no longer be contested, and malice is compelled to give way to the unanimity of applause, there is yet one expedient (the charge of plagiarism) by which the Author may be degraded." Does your correspondent, A. Dyce . . . mean the Lord Byron should stand a convicted Plagiary? If so, why do away the accusation by immediately adjourning "of which, no doubt, the author was unconscious?" Does he wish us to understand this as an ironical sarcasm, or does he forget the meaning of the word Plagiarism? For, surely, if a Plagiary be . . . one who endeavours the clandestine appropriation of a borrowed thought; if allowed to be unconscious of its pre-existence, he cannot with much propriety be accused of stealing it. Having, thus, therefore, acquitted his Lordship of the charge, why then bring forward those instances?. . . . "[T]he flowers of fiction are so widely scattered, and so easily cropped, that it is scarcely just to tax the use of them as an act by which any particular writer is despoiled of his garland; any more than it is to consider every instance of similitude as proof of imitation[.]"[5]

Here, Byron's reviewer clearly demonstrates that to be unconscious of an obligation was to be absolved of the charge of plagiarism, at least at any

culpable or legal level. The legal metaphors, in fact, are predominant, with
"C.C." observing that Byron is simultaneously represented as a "convicted
Plagiary" and "acquitted" of the charge. With the legal rhetoric obviated,
why persist with detailing the obligations, the correspondent queries, unless
the stakes are merely literary: a backhanded means of degrading an author
and his composition out of "malice"? This question recognizes the unspoken context. Charges of plagiarism were part of a sustained aesthetic critique of Byron conducted in the pages of the periodical reviews throughout
the course of his career, sometimes with merit and sometimes without, and
at stake was the question of authorial originality—a term that I have argued
did not exclusively imply autogenous invention in the period.

Unsurprisingly, the charges of plagiarism brought against Byron in
The Gentleman's Magazine were also highly selective in nature and focused
on borrowings from works that were considered consciously literary. While
the public allegations of plagiarism in the oriental tales were part of a motivated assault on Byron's reputation as a poet, there were real correspondences between his works and those of his contemporaries, but the
controversy surrounding these parallels was often influenced by categories
of genre and cultural status. In writing the oriental tales, Byron, like his
contemporaries, drew from Eastern histories and travel accounts, and, in
respect to situation, the oriental tale, like the Gothic tale, remained a genre
that drew from "common" cultural materials. Yet, these early allegations
focus exclusively on Byron's debts to works written in identifiably literary
genres, further reflecting the degree to which aesthetic questions were being
negotiated. As Byron's personal correspondence reveals, the oriental tales
were indebted, often extensively, to a far broader commercial print-culture
context, and appropriations from these materials were often subject to different standards of evaluation. In 1813, for example, an acquaintance, the
travel writer John Galt, observed a "remarkable coincidence" between Byron's *The Bride of Abydos* (1813) and a project of his own, prompting Byron
to write to Galt on 10 December 1813:

My dear Galt—The coincidence I assure you is a most unintentional & unconscious
one nor have I even a guess where or when or in what manner it exists . . . I certainly
had read no works of his [Mr. Semple] or yours when this story was written that at
all contained the likeness. . . . but what is *still* more extraordinary a living poet
writes to me—that I have actually *anticipated* a tale he had ready for the press.[6]

Byron evokes once again the familiar language of Romantic literary property, assuring Galt that any similarities were mere coincidence and express-

ing surprise only at having "anticipated" a poem that the "living poet" Thomas Moore had recently completed. The poem in question was the oriental tale *Lalla Rookh* (1817), in which Moore had intended to develop the same cultural themes that Byron's poem narrated. Clearly, however, neither Moore nor Byron had invented (or personally witnessed) all the details of oriental history, geography, or society replete in both poems, and the two works, like other Romantic-period oriental tales, drew from a wide range of contemporary sources that included Eastern poetry, travel narratives, histories, and other oriental tales. I am not suggesting that these obligations should be viewed as instances of plagiarism, for they clearly were not considered in that light in this instance. Rather, it is the frequent exclusion of certain genres from charges of plagiarism and the selective nature of the critical controversies surrounding literary property that the omission curiously reveals. Borrowing from works that were historical, traditional, or foreign—and were, therefore, implicitly authorless in some respect within British print culture—was often (but not uniformly) permissible, and, as with the investigations into Matthew Lewis's reemployment of the Bleeding Nun legend that I discuss in the previous chapter, where suspicions of plagiarism arose the critical effort was to locate the source for the material in contemporary literary contexts.

The sometimes shifting distinction that Romantic-period writers and reviewers drew between appropriation from popular genres and from works that were recognized as literary is highlighted by Byron's concerns over the relationship between *The Siege of Corinth* (1815) and Coleridge's *Christabel*. Like Byron's other oriental tales, *The Siege of Corinth* drew from a range of popular and especially foreign sources; however, in the months before the publication of the poem, Byron anticipated that the correspondences between his work and Coleridge's text would be the parallels most likely to occasion charges of plagiarism. Walter Scott had been circulating Coleridge's poem in literary circles, and Byron had heard the poem recited during the summer of 1814. In October of 1815, he received a manuscript copy of the poem from Coleridge and, upon reading the text, recognized similarities between two passages in the poems.[7] On 27 October 1817, Byron wrote to Coleridge:

I am partly in the same scrape myself as you will see by the enclosed extract from an unpublished poem which I assure you was written before (not seeing your "Christabelle" for that you know I never did till this day) but before I heard Mr. S[cott] repeat it—which he did in June last—and this thing was begun in January &

more than half written before the Summer—the coincidence is only in this particular passage and if you will allow me—in publishing it . . . I will give the extract from
you—and state that the original thought & expression have been many years in the
Christabelle. (*BLJ* 4: 321)

The dating of Byron's manuscript for *The Siege of Corinth* suggests that this
timing is an accurate reflection of his composition process, but the fact remains that Byron was in the midst of composing the poem precisely at the
juncture when he was introduced to Coleridge's tale. While Byron represents the similarities as a matter of unconscious "coincidence," he is nevertheless attentive to the aesthetic question of originality and proposes to
credit Coleridge with the authorship of a passage that will not strike many
modern readers as plagiarism at all. In fact, the correspondences between
the two poems are not extensive and are largely confined to those "immate-
rial" elements of tone, voice, and diction. Stanza 14 of *The Siege of Corinth*
offers a series of questions and answers:

Was it the wind, through some hollow stone,
Sent that soft and tender moan?
He lifted his head, and he looked on the sea,
But it was rippled as glass may be;
He looked on the long grass—it waved not a blade;
How was that gentle sound conveyed?
He looked to the banners—each flag lay still,
So did the leaves on Cithaeron's hill,
And he felt not a breath come over his cheek;
What did that sudden sound bespeak?
He turned to the left—is he sure of sight?
There sate a lady, youthful and bright! (ll. 476–87)

This passage, as Byron recognized, resonated with Coleridge's lines from
Christabel:

Is it the Wind that moaneth bleak?
Is there not Wind enough in the Air
To move away the ringlet Curl
From the lovely Lady's Cheek—
There is not Wind enough to twirl
The One red Leaf, the last of its Clan,

. . . .
There She sees a Damsel bright (ll. 44–58)[8]

The similarities in particular expression between these two texts are not extensive, but Byron suspected the parallels might occasion charges of plagiarism from his contemporaries, presumably on account of broader correspondences in imagery and voice. As we have seen repeatedly, style and tone functioned as elements of literary property in the Romantic period, and borrowings sometimes too subtle to trouble twenty-first-century critics preoccupied nineteenth-century ones. Byron at any rate was so certain that the parallels would be noted and subject to censure that the poem was published with a note acknowledging the debt, even as Byron maintained that it was the result of coincidence. In the subsequent note added to stanza 14, Byron wrote:

I must here acknowledge a close, though unintentional, resemblance in these twelve lines to an unpublished poem of Mr. Coleridge, called "Christabel". It was not until after these lines were written that I heard that wild and singularly original and beautiful poem recited; and the MS. of that production I never saw till very recently, by the kindness of Mr. Coleridge himself, who, I hope, is convinced that I have not been a willful plagiarist. The original idea undoubtedly pertains to Mr. Coleridge, whose poem has been composed above fourteen years. (*LBCPW* 3: 486)

Byron's emphasis on originality throughout the passage indicates that this was a crucial matter for him in respect to poetry and to charges of plagiarism, and it mirrors the implied critiques of his work in the periodical reviews. However, Byron also suggests that it is the superlative aesthetic merit of Coleridge's work and the difficulty of improving upon a "singularly original and beautiful poem" that has occasioned such a public acknowledgment of the obligation, even when the appropriation had been unconsciously performed. Byron's anxiety in this instance reflects his sensitivity to the larger literary combats at stake in charges of plagiarism, and, in the case of *The Siege of Corinth*, he effectively forestalls the controversy by granting Coleridge ownership of a passage that does not match the word-for-word particulars. Perhaps most surprisingly, Byron inoculates himself against charges of plagiarism by evoking questions of coincidence, will, and consciousness—a characterization of literary property not unlike the justifications for which Coleridge has been historically derided. Whatever the nature of his obligations, Coleridge was not merely casting about for self-serving rationales, as the critical tradition has sometimes maintained. Both Coleridge and Byron, in their exchanges with each other and with their literary contemporaries, were responding to a shared context regarding intellectual property and its limitations.

Henry Taylor and the Principles of Aesthetic Plagiarism

While the critical attacks on Byron in *The Gentleman's Magazine* and his early anxieties about appropriation in the oriental tales shaped his investment in originality, Byron's most extended engagement with questions of plagiarism occurs in *Childe Harold's Pilgrimage*, canto 3. The third canto of the poem was published in November of 1816, and by 1817 semi-public allegations of plagiarism were being circulated by Wordsworth. These charges were later made publicly in an 1823 essay, written by Wordsworth's friend Henry Taylor for *The London Magazine*, and, unfortunately for Byron, they followed on the heels of the periodical attacks in 1821 occasioned by his obligations in the early volumes of *Don Juan*, to which I will return. Although Wordsworth was not responsible for the charges of plagiarism made against Byron in respect to the oriental tales, he was closely involved in the controversy surrounding the third canto of *Childe Harold*.

Wordsworth began voicing his complaints about Byron's plagiarisms from him to his literary correspondents as early as 1817. He wrote, for example, to Henry Crabb Robinson on 24 June 1817: "I have not seen Lord B's . . . last canto of *Childe Harold*, where I am told he has been poaching on my manor."[9] Thomas Moore recalled that Wordsworth likewise had complained to him in October of 1820 regarding "Byron's plagiarisms from him [alleging that] the whole third canto [was] founded on his style and sentiments. The feeling of natural objects . . . caught . . . from him . . . and spoiled in the transmission—*Tintern Abbey* the source of it all."[10] As late as 26 December 1823, Wordsworth was repeating the charge to Henry Taylor, although he ultimately acknowledges that there have been substantial "plagiarisms from Mr. Coleridge" as well. In this long letter, a response to Taylor's request for evidence of Byron's appropriations, Wordsworth writes:

I have not, nor ever had, a single poem of Lord Byron's by me, except the Lara . . . and therefore could not quote anything illustrative of his poetical obligations to me. As far as I am acquainted with his works, they are most apparent in the 3rd canto of Childe Harold; not so much in the particular expressions, though there is no want of these, as in the tone (*assumed* rather than natural) of enthusiastic admiration of Nature. . . . Of my writings you need not read more than the blank verse poem on the Wye to be convinced of this. Mrs. W. tells me that . . . she was much disgusted with the plagiarisms from Mr Coleridge [in *The Siege of Corinth*]. If I am not mistaken there was some acknowledgment to Mr C. which takes very much from the reprehensibility of literary trespasses of this kind. Nothing lowered my opinion of Byron's poetical integrity so much as to see "pride of place" carefully noted as a quotation from Macbeth, in a work where contemporaries, from whom he had drawn by wholesale, were not adverted to. It is mainly on this account that he deserves the severe chastisement which you, or some one else, will undoubtedly one day give him, and may have done already, as I see by advertisement that subject has been treated in the "London Mag." (*LWDW* 4: 236–37)

This is an extraordinary passage both for its passion and its hesitations. Not only does Wordsworth claim not to have copies of Byron's verse in his library, but he suggests that his familiarity with the poetry is slight. Yet, Wordsworth details Byron's literary crimes with personal disdain and animosity uncharacteristic of the elder poet. In fact, the literary conflict between the two poets was surprisingly intense, especially on Wordsworth's part, and the language of his complaints reveals the imagined—and imaginative—stakes in the argument. While these passages provide considerable information on the precise nature of Romantic-period attitudes toward plagiarism, notably the continued emphasis on style rather than "particular expressions," Wordsworth's avowed disgust and his desire to see Byron chastised suggest that the charges had a personal element. Indeed, plagiarism and literary property were to become increasingly important to Wordsworth in the nineteenth century and in ways that were often deeply personal.

By 1815 Wordsworth had become invested in defining the nature of the literary and, particularly, the nature of poetry, both in terms of aesthetic merit and in terms of property. After several years of relative inactivity, he had also become deeply concerned about his own legacy as a poet. For Wordsworth, both represented issues of labor and, as I discuss in the final chapter of this study, to a larger extent of class. In his correspondence of the period, Wordsworth repeatedly begins to define the poet as a laborer, and, from his perspective, plagiarism was a productive failure with feudal overtones: it was poaching on the manor of diligent poets. Wordsworth makes this connection among poetry, "literary" merit, labor, and plagiarism explicit in a letter of 15 April 1816 to R. P. Gillies, in which he writes:

Gray failed as a Poet . . . filching a phrase now from one author, and now from another. I do not profess to be a person of very various reading; nevertheless if I were to pluck out of Grays tail all the feathers which, I know, belong to other Birds he would be left very bare indeed. . . . There are Poems now existing which all the World ran after at their first appearance . . . that do not deserve to be thought of as *literary* Works. . . . But I need not press upon you the necessity of Labour. (*LWDW* 3: 301–2)

Chief among those contemporary writers whose works had been celebrated by society, of course, was Byron, whose sales far outstripped Wordsworth's own and whose work the elder poet would characterize in April of 1816 as "wretched" and "fiend-like . . . productions" (*LWDW* 3: 304–5). Like Byron's anonymous critic in *The Gentleman's Magazine,* Wordsworth's complaint was that works composed in "haste" lacked the labor required both for the "literary" production of poetry and for its appropriation to the author as private property. From Wordsworth's perspective, while he toiled with nature, working the imaginative landscape of the mind and creating new sensibilities, Byron declined similar intellectual labors. Thus, Wordsworth's animosity in his indictment of Byron reflects deeply personal concerns and genuine outrage, but it is an outrage that has as much to do with the aesthetic implications of plagiarism and authorship as with the circumstances of appropriation.

In his letter to Henry Taylor, Wordsworth expressed the wish that Byron would be—perhaps already had been—publicly chastised for his obligations, and in the December 1823 issue of *The London Magazine* the wish had been granted. Taylor offered an extended consideration of Byron's appropriations from Wordsworth and Coleridge, and his essay articulates the nuances that Romantic writers brought to their understanding of plagiarism. Published under the title "Recent Poetical Plagiarisms and Imitations," Taylor's piece provided his readers with a detailed definition of plagiarism, and it offers another extended clarification of early nineteenth-century attitudes toward plagiarism and its relationship to aesthetic judgments.[11]

Many of the elements of Taylor's argument are already familiar from other contemporary sources. Like the essays on plagiarism that Thomas De-Quincey later wrote for *Tait's Magazine,* Taylor's essay outlines three instances in which the appropriation from the text of another writer may not be considered plagiarism: where there is familiarity, improvement, or unconsciousness. Like Byron's earlier periodical reviewers, Taylor also distinguishes clearly between the moral and aesthetic components of the charge, arguing for two separate types of plagiarism, culpable and poetical. Finally, like numerous eighteenth- and early nineteenth-century contemporaries, Taylor makes clear the degree to which intangible elements of a text such as tone, style, and voice are considered literary property. Within this context, Taylor contends that Byron was unquestionably guilty of aesthetic plagiarism in the third canto of *Childe Harold's Pilgrimage.*

Taylor's essay begins by making apparent how immediately recognizable Byron's borrowings from Wordsworth and Coleridge were to the Romantic-period reading audience, and this transparency becomes a critical factor in excusing Byron from charges of what Taylor calls "culpable" or moral plagiarism. He writes, "Lord Byron has borrowed the most beautiful passages Mr. Coleridge ever wrote, [but] Mr. Coleridge has not suffered by this, and the plagiarism has availed nothing to Lord Byron, because it is obvious and unqualified; and therefore, by every reader acquainted with poetry, it is appropriated to its author" (597). Taylor indicates that Byron's plagiarisms in *Childe Harold* 3 are so obvious and his sources so familiar that no learned reader could fail to recognize Coleridge as the true author of this imagery. To borrow this overtly and from a poet this well known was tantamount to an open acknowledgment of one's literary debt. This distinction is critical, because it is on the grounds of implicit "avowal" of appropriation that Taylor ultimately acquits Byron of any criminal wrongdoing. However, distinguishing between poetical plagiarism and culpable plagiarism, Taylor's discussion encompasses the possibility of both an aesthetic and a moral component to the charge, and it is an aesthetic failure for which Byron is publicly censured.

In Taylor's clarification of Romantic-period attitudes toward plagiarism, intention—rather than the fact of appropriation itself—becomes the critical factor in determining culpable wrongdoing. He writes: "New thoughts and new modes of expression are literary property; and culpable plagiarism is the conscious and unavowed appropriation, without improvement of them" (597). While Taylor read Byron's borrowings as clearly conscious, he ultimately determines that they cannot be considered "unavowed": Byron's reemployment of Coleridge's verse was so faithful to the original expression as to count as obvious and, therefore, as implicitly *acknowledged* appropriation. Taylor explains clearly that even when "occurring between rivals, it is innocent when obvious" (598), and, thus, he will not hold Byron morally accountable for any intentional deceit. However, not a willful thief and, therefore, not a culpable plagiarist, Taylor proposes instead that Byron is merely a poor poet.

According to Taylor's definition, Byron remains only a literary plagiarist, and his sole "crime" is bad poetry. For Taylor posits that the superior poet and the "man of great genius" *will* appropriate freely from his predecessors, often consciously and without acknowledgment; but such a man *will not* fail to improve upon the original and by improving transform it. Through improvement, the great poet "regenerate[s] the thoughts of his inferiors, giving them the cast of his own mind" (598). This, in Taylor's argument, is Byron's failure: he has not improved upon his appropriated material, and such a "negation of improvement" is a sign of poetic inferiority. The ultimate charge is aesthetic—of poetical plagiarism only: Byron is unable to imbue this borrowed material with his own "cast of mind," and his text remains a mere collection of quotations and an imitation of poetry.

Here, the failure to improve upon one's borrowed materials is revealed as a serious aesthetic criticism, in which an author is charged with an inability to maintain lyric control over his or her own production. Seen from this perspective, Wordsworth's complaint that "Tintern Abbey" had been "spoiled in the transmission" is pointed, since it addresses itself to one of the critical components necessary for a charge of literary plagiarism. In fact, this issue of the "negation of improvement" remains the crucial—but typically undefined—factor in Romantic-period views of literary appropriation. Transforming a predecessor's text did not necessarily mean changing the words or the imagery of the original expression in any respect. Instead, improvement rested simply upon the author's ability to give the borrowed material the "cast of his own mind." In Byron's case, this "cast of mind," or what he ultimately calls the machinery of "my own spirits," is poetically achieved through the control of authorial voice and the production of a guiding subjectivity.

The nature of this speaking self, however, is a critical issue for analyzing the problem of plagiarism and literary "failure" in *Childe Harold* 3. As I have already argued and as other scholars have also suggested, plagiarism emerges as primarily a problem of voice throughout the period.[12] Ultimately, both Taylor and Byron agree that the poem is marked by a fundamental aesthetic failure, and they even agree that the central problem is a matter of voice. But what constituted a successful authorial voice? On this question, Taylor and Byron disagreed. Each construed the limits and possibilities of this speaking subjectivity in different ways and with different implications for understanding the process of aesthetic judgment in the Romantic period.

Plagiarism and the Mastery of Voice in *Childe Harold's Pilgrimage*, Canto 3

Taylor and Byron agreed that the poet-narrator of canto 3 of *Childe Harold's Pilgrimage* was a second-rate poet and a plagiarist. Byron's traveling poet-narrator is a self-acknowledged literary failure, ultimately silenced by his inability to assimilate his textual sources. The point on which Byron and Taylor disagree, however, is finally more illuminating: for Taylor, the subjectivity of the poem, dramatic frame or no, represents the historical ("real") author and his shortcomings, while, for Byron, the "literary" is located in the possibility of an autonomous imagined self, who is no less real for being a product of "romance." Both agree that *Childe Harold* 3 fails, but from Taylor's perspective it is a matter of too little history and from Byron's a matter of too little romance. Or, put another way, at stake in the critical disagreement was how to understand the relationship between voice and the author in early nineteenth-century British poetry.

In *Childe Harold* 3, there can be little doubt that literary plagiarism occurs, as Taylor defines it. Even Byron's modern critics agree that much of what he borrowed was unacknowledged, conscious, and "spoiled in the transmission." Philip Martin, for example, has argued in *Byron: A Poet before His Public* that the appropriation of Wordsworth's imagery is disastrous; Byron attempts to "master new material," and the unfortunate result is verse that "stumbles into vagueness," "a number of uncomfortable stanza endings," and some "particularly awkward alexandrine[s]."[13] Scholars have typically seen the work both as technically flawed and as characterized by a certain adolescent grandiosity. However, the "Byronic" poet-narrator of *Childe Harold* 3 is represented as a flawed figure throughout the course of the poem, and his self-acknowledged aesthetic limitations become the central focus of the third canto. The question, finally, is whether Byron is in control of his narrator's "bad" poetry.

The poet-narrator of *Childe Harold* 3 is, of course, a struggling English poet and tourist whose materials for his own travel account are largely the versified scenic tours of his literary contemporaries, which he reinscribes compulsively and unsuccessfully. Unable to assimilate these materials into his own experience of the Swiss alpine landscape or to control the representations that have influenced him, the poet-narrator experiences a disintegration of voice within his own text that ultimately makes him both a plagiarist and a self-acknowledged literary failure. Quite simply, the poet-narrator fails to improve upon his borrowed materials. The unfortunate result is a poem that he ultimately finds inadequate for the expression of his own subjectivity. Canto 3 primarily focuses on the poet-narrator's thwarted literary efforts to "wreak / [His] thoughts upon expression" (97.906–7) and the intrusion of textual influences into this project.

As both poet and tourist, the narrator is faced with negotiating the textually constructed nature of his experience abroad, and the control these precursors exercise over him indicates the critical importance within Romantic-period verse of successfully assimilating one's materials. Repeatedly, the speaker attempts to find a natural scenery that is free from the influence of human culture, and repeatedly this effort to avoid the "things of Man" is figured as an anti-textual impulse. However, the poet-narrator is unable to maintain the distinction between these categories. Indeed, the objects of human culture are represented as texts; they are at once the "tome / Of his land's tongue" (13.115–16) and (in a delightful pun) that "mingling with the herd [which] penn'd me in their fold" (68.652). More importantly, his perceptions of nature lapse back into language borrowed from the scenic tours of the Lake School poets. Setting out to write a travel poem, he ends up tangled in the language of Wordsworth and Coleridge, his sensibilities mediated by national and poetic conventions. The canto begins, for example, with the poet-narrator turning away from "the white city's sheen" (61.582) and the ruins of empire that he observes touring the Rhine. As these images recede into a view of the Alps, the poet-narrator describes the mountains as:

> . . . palaces of Nature, whose vast walls
> Have pinnacled in clouds their snowy scalps,
> And throned Eternity in icy halls
> . . . .
> [Where] All that expands the spirit, yet appals,
> Gather around these summits, as to show
> How Earth may pierce to Heaven,
> Yet leave vain man below. (62.591–98)

The language of his own expression indicates how clearly "vain man" has not been left behind in his perception of this view: the poet-narrator's imagery here is borrowed from Coleridge's "Hymn before Sun-rise":

> On thy bald awful head, O Sovran Blanc,
> . . . .
> . . . thou, most awful Form!
> . . . .
> . . . Deep is the air and dark, substantial, black,
> An ebon mass: methinks thou piercest it,
> As with a wedge! But when I look again,
> It is thine own calm home, thy crystal shrine,
> Thy habitation from eternity! (ll. 3–12)

While the mountain's "bald awful head" becomes a "snowy scalp," and while "habitations" of eternity are exchanged for "thrones," the imagery the poet-narrator employs in his description is recognizably derivative. The result of these repeated borrowings is a rather sharp irony at the poet-narrator's expense, in which the authenticity of his own response as poet and as traveler is undermined by its primary relationship to Coleridge's text.[14]

In the subsequent stanzas of canto 3, this movement from escape to reinscription is repeated obsessively. In each case, the poet's descriptions echo Lake School poetry. Throughout, the poet-narrator stumbles over Wordsworth's and Coleridge's poetry in a series of unassimilated phrases and images drawn from works that include "The world is too much with us" (1807), "Tintern Abbey" (1798), and the Immortality Ode (1807). Byron writes, for example, "There is too much of man here, to look through / With a fit mind the might I behold" (68.648–49), evoking Wordsworth's sonnet. Even more pointedly, Byron's lines "I am become a Portion of that around me; and to me / High mountains are a feeling, [still] the hum / Of human cities torture [me]" (72.680–83) draw from imagery found in several passages in "Tintern Abbey," including "The mountain, and the deep and gloomy wood, / Their colours and their forms, were then to me / An appetite; a feeling and a love" (ll. 78–80) and Wordsworth's proclamation that "oft, in lonely rooms, and 'mid the din / Of towns and cities, I have owed to them / . . . sensations sweet, / . . . . / As have no slight or trivial influence / On that best portion of a good man's life" (ll. 25–32). And, of course, Byron's "breathless, as we grow when feeling most / And silent, as we stand in thoughts too deep:—/ . . . . . / [A] solitude, where we are *least* alone" (89–90.834–43) resonates with Wordsworth's "thoughts that do often lie too deep for tears" ("Intimations" l. 203). In short, here is a poet whose language reflects his fundamental failure to perceive or to write individually. Not only is he unable to assimilate his borrowed materials into an expression of his own subjectivity, but the poet's borrowed literary sources dominate his work. This apparently unimproved repetition of images and attitudes appropriated from the Lake School poets clearly leaves the narrator of *Childe Harold* 3 a plagiarist, at least in the literary sense. In this respect, Byron's periodical reviewers were justifiably anxious. However, the poet-narrator's inability to improve upon, transform, or appropriately assimilate his textual influences is a reflection of his own self-acknowledged aesthetic failure within the canto. Moreover, it is a failure that he ultimately represents as a problem of voice.

The relationship between the poet-narrator's struggle to find poetic voice and this inability to assimilate his literary influences is most clearly

indicated by the expression of frustration with which he concludes this series of densely allusive stanzas on the alpine landscape. He writes:

Could I embody and unbosom now
That which is most within me,—could I wreak
My thoughts upon expression, and thus throw
Soul, heart, mind, passions, feelings, strong or weak,
All that I would have sought, and all I seek,
Bear, know, feel, and yet breathe—into *one* word,
And that one word were Lightening, I would speak;
But as it is, I live and die unheard,
With a most voiceless thought, sheathing it as a sword. (97.905–13)

In these lines, the poet articulates his own problem clearly: he is unable to
give unified expression to his thoughts and unable to transform passionate
subjectivity into the appropriate language. More importantly, the narrator's
recognition of his own failure here is complete. At the conclusion of a considerable poetic effort, his text remains "voiceless." With his thoughts unspoken, he laments that he will "live and die unheard." The inability to
transform one's borrowed materials results not only in a muddled, awkward text but also in the effective silencing of the speaker's voice.

In this respect, the poet-narrator of *Childe Harold* 3 represents a literary example of the dangers of textual appropriation. Unable to move beyond the language of the Lake School poets, his aesthetic failure is
represented as a contamination by his literary influences and as an inability
to assimilate these representations into his own experience. Seen as a figure
for the British poet and his engagement with national literary influences, he
stands as well for the potential disintegration of English subjectivity in an
era of tourism and territorial expansion. In both cases, the result of the
poet's inability to assimilate fully his outside influences results in a multipli-
cation of voices in the text, which simultaneously emerges as a problem of
inarticulation, as literary failure, and in charges of plagiarism.

The "Byronic" poet-narrator's status as a plagiarist and a failed writer
is not at issue. However, the relationship between the historical author and
the poem's speaking self remains a matter of serious concern. With Taylor,
we are led to question whether, satirical or not, Byron is not ultimately responsible for the literary failure that is *Childe Harold* 3. Does the placement
of bad poetry and plagiarized texts within a dramatic structure change Byron's personal responsibility for the poem's aesthetic shortcomings? Taylor
maintains that bad poetry, like plagiarism, remains the responsibility of the
actual author. Voice in a text is not fictional for Taylor, and its disintegra-

tion therefore accrues directly to the poet. In Taylor's formulation, voice is the self-representation of the historical and factual author, whether he chooses to maintain a dramatic (i.e., fictional) stance or not. The concept of selfhood from which Taylor is working does not permit the mediation of that self by the text that structures it. Essentially, voice is documentary, and the "real" is historical. For Taylor, there is no escape from objectivity, and he adopts a position on satire that is remarkably similar to the one Wordsworth implies when alleging plagiarisms from his work in the satirical poems of Peter Bayley. For Byron, however, the relationship between self and the voice in a text is conceived differently. In Byron's formulation, the self in a literary work—and perhaps in life, as well—engages with forms of fiction. In other words, the production of subjectivity involves both instances of historical fact and strategies of fiction, and the speaking self is always located somewhere between documentary and romance.

Certainly, Byron works to develop in *Childe Harold* 3 the concept of a self fundamentally mediated by fiction. The opening stanzas of the canto propose the actual privileging of fantasy over fact. The purpose of poetry and of an imagined selfhood is, he writes:

. . . to create, and in creating live
A being more intense, that we endow
With form our fancy, gaining as we give
The life we image, even as I do now.
What am I? Nothing: but not so art thou,
Soul of my thought! (6.46–51)

A creature of fancy and romance, this fictive self is explicitly identified as more real than his historical author—the "I" is nothing compared to the "soul of my thought." This privileged reality of "imagined" subjectivity implies, for Byron, the genuine possibility of a text "voiced" by a character independent of his or her historical author.

This investment in the possible expression of a voiced subjectivity that is at once "fictional" and "real" is central to the concept of literary Romanticism that Byron's work develops, and he acknowledges his failure to strike this balance in *Childe Harold* 3. In the poem, Byron is unable to maintain an imagined self that is independent of his own circumstances, and, like the failure encountered by the poet-narrator in this canto, his romance is finally contaminated by documentary impulses and historical influence. Byron admits as much in the prefatory letter to John Cam Hobhouse with which he introduced canto 4, writing:

With regard to the conduct of the last canto [3]. . . . it was in vain that I asserted, and imagined that I had drawn, a distinction between the author and the pilgrim; and the very anxiety to preserve this difference, and disappointment at finding it unavailing, so far crushed my efforts in the composition, that I decided to abandon it altogether—and have done so. . . . the work is to depend on itself, and not on the writer. (*LBCPW* 2: 122)

The problem, ultimately, is an unproductive confusion of historical and "romantic" selves and inability to transmute fiction into poetic reality. Thus, in the end, Byron does experience literary failure in the course of composing *Childe Harold* 3, but it is manifestly not the literary failure that Taylor outlines. Taylor sees the voice of the historical author as too weak to unify the poem. From Byron's perspective, the problem is precisely the opposite: despite his best efforts, the voice of the "real" author remains more audible than the voice of the "Byronic" speaking subject that he would like to call into being. *Childe Harold* 3 becomes, like the travel writings it imitates, a text poised uncomfortably between fact and fiction, history and romance.

The question remains as to what are we to make of this poem, one of Romanticism's most successful failures. Perhaps it is that Byron's Romanticism is an aesthetic predicated upon failure: Byron's very project—to transform fiction into a poetic reality, more real than history, or to become the author of his own imaginative sources—is impossible. If so, the success of *Childe Harold's Pilgrimage* is that it works at the very limits of this poetic language and occupies, without drawing, that tense, ungainly, and powerful line between what we imagine and what we are. At any rate, the controversy surrounding Byron's plagiarisms in the poem are finally about these very questions of aesthetics, and, whatever his personal responsibility, the poet-narrator's self-conscious inability to assimilate his textual materials demonstrates that Byron understood contemporary charges of plagiarism well enough to parody those conventions. Likewise, Taylor's public chastisement of the younger poet dramatizes the emerging conflict between the first- and second-generation Romantics and their perceptions of lyric voice.

Borrowings in *Childe Harold's Pilgrimage*, Canto 4

While the third canto of *Childe Harold's Pilgrimage* directly engaged questions of voice, plagiarism, and authorship as part of its thematic focus, there were likewise contemporary suggestions that plagiarism had occurred in the poem's fourth canto. Although little was made of the allegations during the Romantic period, the charges emphasize both the historically distinct standards of early nineteenth-century plagiarism and the shifting critical attitudes toward literary appropriation that have shaped the assessment of these authors. The most substantial notice of Byron's obligations in *Childe Harold* 4 appeared in an 1818 review of the poem published in *Blackwood's Edinburgh Review,* in which the author suggests that Byron has "borrowed not a little of the spirit, and even of the expressions, of the Fourth Canto" from an elegy written by the German poet A. W. Schlegel. Although the review did not belabor the correspondences and, in fact, dismissed charges of plagiarism, Byron later returned to the public discussion in 1821, at the same time that he was coming under intense public scrutiny for his appropriations from popular print materials in *Don Juan.* Writing to Thomas Moore on 2 August 1821, Byron explained:

I know S[chlegel] well—that is to say, I have met him occasionally at Copet. . . . In a review of Childe Harold, Canto 4th, three years ago, in Blackwood's Magazine, they quote some stanzas of an elegy of S's on Rome, from which they say I *might* have taken some ideas. I give you my honour that I never saw it except in that criticism. . . . The fact is easily proved; for I don't understand German, and there was I believe no translation. (*BLJ* 8: 164)

While these correspondences with Schlegel's poem were largely thematic and judged as legitimate even by an otherwise hostile periodical reviewer, Byron's response suggests that he was not eager to represent his work as influenced by Continental literature. This raises some question as to the status of European texts in late eighteenth- and early nineteenth-century British print culture. As I have already argued in the context of Byron's oriental tales, "foreign" literature often was considered implicitly authorless and available for appropriation in ways that were similar to the standards that applied to historical genres such as travel narratives, biographies, or histories. However, the category of "foreign" literature in the period does not appear to have included *literary* works by European authors. Matthew Lewis, we recall, was charged during the Romantic period with plagiarism from contemporary German and French novelists, and Byron took pains to disguise his debts to Continental literary sources (as he did not, for example, with travel narratives), presumably out of a concern that notice of the borrowings would occasion unwelcome critical commentary.[15]

   The fourth canto of *Childe Harold's Pilgrimage* was particularly indebted to the literature associated with Italo-German Romanticism, and scholars in the second half of the nineteenth century and in the twentieth catalogued several additional instances in *Childe Harold* 4 where Byron borrows directly from sources that included Germaine de Staël's Italianate novel *Corinne* (1807) and Vincenzo da Filicaia's seventeenth-century sonnet "Italia, Italia o tu, cui feo la sorte" (Italy, Italy, O you, to whom fate has given). The lack of contemporary charges in these instances cannot be credited simply to Byron's successful evasion of his critics. They were many and vigorous, and I think there is little doubt that they recognized his borrowings in these instances. *Corinne* was among the most popular novels of the early nineteenth century, and, according to one reviewer writing in 1824, "Italia, Italia [was] repeated by every pretender to learning."[16] The relatively recent nature of the plagiarism charges is, rather, a function of the shifting historical context in which Byron's work has been evaluated. Byron's wholesale appropriations—including the insertion of Filicaia's entire sonnet (translated) into *Childe Harold* 4 [stanzas 42–43]—went unremarked by his contemporary readers, who could not have failed to recognize that well-known poem or the other resonances in the canto with de Staël's novel, because neither could be considered culpable plagiarism.[17] As both De-Quincey's and Taylor's essays demonstrate, the appropriation from texts this familiar were considered *implicitly* acknowledged. Indeed, in Taylor's explicit formulation, even when "occurring between rivals, it is innocent when obvious" (Taylor 598). Yet, by the late nineteenth century, when both the print-culture context and the evaluative standards of plagiarism had shifted, these obligations were occasioning critical comments such as Peter Culkin's 1863 observation that "Byron . . . had an ugly tendency to plagiarizing books whose obscurity offered but a remote chance of being detected" (53). Culkin's indictment suggests that familiarity continued to operate as an element in considering charges of plagiarism at midcentury, although perhaps not to the same extent as previously. However, what specific texts a reader could be expected to recognize had clearly changed. Culkin's readers may not have been intimately familiar with the novels of de Staël or the poetry of Filicaia, but Byron's were. This is an instance of Byron's intellectual debts being judged according to standards that do not account for the contemporary print-culture environment or the historical constructions of plagiarism.

While the post-Romantic critical tradition has inflated some of the charges against Byron in the poem, it has likewise by and large dismissed the allegations of plagiarism in *Childe Harold* 4 that Wordsworth made against Byron. Wordsworth's accusations, however, illuminate the peculiar role questions of improvement played in Romantic-period attitudes toward literary appropriation. In his 26 December 1823 letter to Henry Taylor, Wordsworth details Byron's obligations in the poem to a contemporary travel account of Switzerland:

I remember one impudent instance of his thefts. In Raymond's translation of Coxe's travels in Switzerland, with notes of the translator, is a note with these words, speaking of the fall of Schaffhausen: ". . . *Voilà un enfer d'eau!*" This expression is taken by Byron and beaten out unmercifully into two stanzas, which a critic in the Quarterly Review is foolish enough to praise. They are found in the 4th canto of Childe Harold. Whether the obligation is acknowledged or not I do not know. (*LWDW* 4: 237)

The textual correspondences that Wordsworth notes here are, of course, slight, amounting to a mere five words, and his point is not that such slender linguistic correspondences, in themselves, constituted plagiarism. After all, Wordsworth acknowledges that Byron expands upon the theme for two stanzas—and, of course, then not in the context of the Schaffhausen at all. Most importantly, however, Wordsworth indicates that he does not know or, indeed, care whether Byron has acknowledged the debt. For his purposes, the point is irrelevant. Wordsworth's interest here is to charge Byron not with culpable but with poetical plagiarism: having failed to improve upon his borrowed materials, having "beaten [them] out unmercifully," Byron has contaminated his poem with the unassimilated materials of another writer. The consequences are as much aesthetic as moral. For, while the casual nature of the theft makes it "impudent," the real point is that Byron's poetry fails. While acknowledgment, familiarity, or unconsciousness could palliate the charges of moral wrongdoing, in the absence of improvement, nothing could protect a poet from the judgment of literary failure that aesthetic plagiarism represented. As curious as it may seem, by the standards of the Romantic era, Wordsworth was alleging a potentially real instance of plagiarism, the consequences of which both he and Byron understood to be aesthetic.

Travel Writing, Plagiarism, and the Disintegration of Voice

When Byron was charged in 1821 with plagiarism in the second and third cantos of *Don Juan* (1819, 1821), the periodical press engaged many of these same issues regarding appropriation and its aesthetic implications. Like the allegations made against Byron in *The Gentleman's Magazine* in 1818, these notices were part of a critical attack on the poet and his merits, and Byron's responses provide some of his most direct statements on plagiarism, originality, and poetic composition. Although notices appeared in several reviews over the course of 1821, the articles "Plagiarisms of Lord Byron detected" that appeared in *The Monthly Magazine* in August and September prompted the most extended response.[18] These articles, written by an anonymous reviewer ("C. E. S."), detailed Byron's extensive obligations to Sir J. G. Dalyell's collection of seafaring narratives *Shipwrecks and Disasters at Sea* (1812), and the account provided its readers with several pages of parallel text comparisons.

While the objective of *The Monthly Magazine* reviews was to charge Byron with plagiarism, the critique is remarkably generous, and the author's introductory remarks offer additional insight into the ways in which appropriation from documentary texts such as travel writing was regarded during the Romantic period. The reviewer writes:

Possessed, as his Lordship is, of an imagination, fertile beyond most, it is impossible for a moment to suppose that he could have occasion to borrow from the writings of anyone; and doubtless his motive in thus illustrating his narrative with incidents which are well authenticated . . . was to render his descriptions more natural. But from what cause is it that there are no notes subjoined, acknowledging the sources from which he derived them? ("Plagiarisms of Lord Byron" 19)

The suggestion, of course, is that a poet might do well to borrow "authenticated" details from such narratives for the purpose of rendering the literary work more realistic. In fact, Byron was particularly concerned with accuracy and with facts in the composition of his poems. His letters are replete with references of this sort in which he praises, for example, William Beckford's *Vathek* (1786) for its correctness of costume or criticizes Wordsworth's failure to get the "facts" about Greece correct in his poetry.[19] Byron was particularly invested in the accuracy of *Don Juan*, a poem about which he famously claimed, "The truth is that *it is too true*" (*BLJ* 7: 202). While this investment in realism explains some of Byron's interest in travel sources throughout *Don Juan*, his failure to provide notes citing his sources was at the heart of a disagreement in the Romantic period about the authored status of popular and historical genres such as travel writing.

On 23 August 1821, Byron responded to these charges of plagiarism from Dalyell's shipwreck narratives in a letter to his publisher John Murray, and in this account he offers two reasons why he considered the inclusion of notes superfluous: the historical and factual nature of the details and the anonymous publication of *Don Juan*. Byron writes:

With regard to the charges about the "Shipwreck"—I think that I told both you and Mr. Hobhouse years ago—that [there] was not a *single circumstance* of it—*not* taken from *fact*—not indeed from any *single* shipwreck—but all from *actual* facts of different wrecks.—Almost all Don Juan is *real* life—either my own—or from people I knew.——By the way much of the description of the *furniture* in Canto 3d. is taken from *Tully's Tripoli*—(pray *note this*)—and the rest from my own observation.——Remember I never meant to conceal this at all—& have only not stated it because D Juan had no preface or name to it.—If you think it worth while to make this statement—do so—in your own way.—I laugh at such charges—convinced that no writer ever borrowed less—or made his materials more his own.——Much is Coincidence[.] (*BLJ* 8: 186)

In this passage, Byron engages the rhetoric of plagiarism in various ways, perhaps most notably by reminding Murray of the possibility of "coincidence" and by arguing for manifest improvement to the extent that he has made the materials his own. However, the emphasis on the historical nature of the borrowed material and on the anonymous mode of publication are particularly interesting as further clarifications of the Romantic-period attitude toward plagiarism. Byron had, of course, culled his descriptions from a broad collection of narratives, and he repeatedly emphasizes the factual nature of the accounts from which he is borrowing. The passage suggests that Byron considered the citation of documentary texts unnecessary, and this was a perspective that many eighteenth- and early nineteenth-century writers had toward the literature of travel, in particular.

Eighteenth- and early nineteenth-century travel writing was often formulaic, reflecting the rise of leisure-class tourism and the establishment of standard itineraries, and travel writers frequently reemployed the materials presented by previous voyagers. Byron himself had written in an early letter to his mother, "Of Constantinople you have of course read fifty descriptions by sundry traveler, which are in general so correct that I have nothing to add on the Subject" (*BLJ* 1: 244). Partly as a result of this repetition, travel accounts were particularly prone to plagiarism throughout the period, and they were often associated with scientific and historical rather than literary genres. Percy Adams has demonstrated that Byron's era "was an age of plagiarism and travel [writers] appropriated materials from other travelers," and Irena Gross has observed that "the list of writers whose 'travel plagiarisms' have been documented is endless."[20] In his early study *Wordsworth and the Literature of Travel*, Charles Coe showed that even

Wordsworth appropriated freely and without attribution from travel sources on numerous occasions—although, as we have also seen, Wordsworth did not hesitate to note Byron's obligations to this same genre when aesthetic judgments were at stake. Coleridge's debts to travel narratives have been discussed in Chapter 2 and were extensively documented in the early part of the twentieth century in Lowe's *The Road to Xanadu*. Some writers treated travel materials as implicitly authorless vehicles of information, while others were inclined to read these texts as creative productions subject to the protections of literary property. There was not uniform consensus on these matters during the Romantic period, and the disparity between *The Monthly Magazine* review and Byron's attitude toward "factual" materials reveals the presence of a broader cultural conflict that focused on questions of genre and popular print culture.

Byron's response to the charges made against him in *The Monthly Magazine* also points to the anonymous publication of *Don Juan* as the primary reason that any attribution had been unnecessary. In fact, under copyright laws of the early nineteenth century, anonymous publications had few of the protections afforded the authors or publishers of named productions, and *Don Juan*'s anonymous status had involved Murray in a series of legal contests in an effort to prevent pirate editions of the poem. Because charges of plagiarism during the period so closely involved elements such as authorial persona, tone, and style, anonymous publication seriously complicated the questions of identity, enslavement, kidnapping, or profit suggested by the etymological origins and historical connotations of the term. At the same time, the evidence from the periodical press suggests that Romantic-period plagiarism, reflecting the rise of a legal rhetoric surrounding intellectual property as real estate, focused on metaphors of injury and appropriation—ranging from the "plucking" of another songbird's feathers to the "poaching" of game. In instances of anonymous publication, the harm would have been more difficult to determine. After all, Byron was not claiming the text as his own or attempting to appropriate it (following the Lockean argument) for his private use. Metaphorically, at least, the private property in question had been left within the domain of the attributed author, and it was not clear how Byron himself had benefited. In his 1823 indictment of the poet, Henry Taylor had excused Byron's plagiarisms in *Childe Harold* 3 precisely on the grounds that "Mr. Coleridge has not suffered by this" (597), and in 1817 Robert Southey had been denied a petition to suppress the publication of his abandoned *Wat Tyler* (composed in 1794) because the law did not permit an author to benefit from seditious works.[21]

Harm or benefit represented one of the standards in determining culpable theft or copyright infringement, and by publishing anonymously Byron had complicated these evaluative measures. In reality, of course, Byron had benefited because his authorship of *Don Juan* was an open secret, but, according to the legal fictions of his era, he was probably correct in point of law when he suggested that the poem's anonymous publication granted him liberties with the texts of others.

Perhaps most importantly, however, Byron's response to *The Monthly Magazine* review engages the questions of authorial persona and voice that lay at the heart of Romantic-period charges of plagiarism. When Byron writes to Murray "I laugh at such charges—convinced that no writer ever borrowed less—or made his materials more his own," he is simultaneously defending not only his originality as a writer but the aesthetic merits of his work. Byron dismisses charges of plagiarism not because he has not borrowed but because he is confident that, where he has appropriated, he has done so fully. While Byron had acknowledged to Hobhouse both his inability to create a unified subjectivity in *Childe Harold* 3 and the aesthetic consequences of this confusion, in respect to *Don Juan* he was certain that he had succeeded. As he explained to Thomas Medwin, his own "spirits, good or bad" guided the machinery of the poem, and the "Byronic" narrator was, he maintained, in full possession of both the poem and its materials.[22]

While defending himself from charges of plagiarism in the letter to Murray, Byron also reveals one of the additional sources from which he appropriated in writing *Don Juan*. Byron identifies Tully's *Narrative of a Ten Years' Residence at Tripoli in Africa* (1816) as his guide for some of the "facts" in the poem's third canto, observing that the descriptions of the "furniture" were drawn from this travel narrative. However, as Peter Cochran has argued, the correspondences were in fact rather more extensive. In "A Note on Some Sources of the Feast in *Don Juan*, Canto III," Cochran demonstrates that in certain stanzas "nearly all the imagery is from Tully," and he locates word-for-word obligations to both Beckford's *Vathek* and Voltaire's *Candide* interspersed throughout these borrowings as well.[23] While these borrowings were not the subject of plagiarism charges in the contemporary reviews, Byron nevertheless anticipated, somewhat cynically, that they might be. It was not that Byron himself considered the obligations to be instances of plagiarism; his letter to Murray makes it clear that the reemployment of "facts" and "furniture" was to his mind unquestionably legitimate. Rather, he suspected that hostile reviewers might seize upon the matter and use it to critical advantage. Plagiarism, and especially plagiarism from materials that were arguably historical and documentary, involved a series of interpretive and aesthetic judgments, and Byron had little confidence in the intellectual generosity of his reviewers. To charge the poet with plagiarisms from Dalyell was to adopt a particularly conservative and polemical stance in regard to issues of ownership and literary property, and he had no reason to expect that the borrowings from Tully, if discovered, would occasion a different response. Byron understood, in short, that charges of plagiarism represented a mode of critical attack.

The appropriations from Tully are particularly interesting because they suggest an emerging pattern of appropriation from travel texts and, specifically, from travel texts written in the context of British colonialism within *Don Juan*. At the same time, there were concrete ways in which the discourse surrounding eighteenth-century and, later, Romantic-period plagiarism also drew from the colonialist language of miscegenation, mastery, slavery, and nativism for its operative metaphors. I hesitate to overemphasize this point because the similarities are necessarily only rhetorical—certainly the parallel does not encompass the complex legal and historical realities of the colonialist or subaltern experience. At the same time, it is not surprising that the articulation of one form of appropriation and assimilation should mirror the other; as I demonstrate in Chapter 6, the articulation of plagiarism was also deeply tied in the period to the language of real estate and enclosure. The metaphor of "servile imitation" was one of the earliest used to describe plagiarism, dating at least to the seventeenth century and ultimately back to the etymological origins of the term as a form of enslavement and kidnapping, and, while it is therefore not historically specific to the early nineteenth century, its cultural connotations cannot have been entirely neutral in a period as consumed with the question of abolition as the Romantic era was.[24] Indeed, as Debbie Lee has observed, imitation and metaphors of aping were central to the early nineteenth-century discourses on slavery.[25] In *The Forger's Shadow*, Nick Groom reminds us that this trope, which is central to discourses of plagiarism, has its roots in a medieval pun on *singe* (monkey) and *signe* (sign) and has been importantly theorized within accounts of racial signification (38).[26] However, while the slavery metaphor had a long history in relation to plagiarism, figures of miscegenation and nativism were far more directly tied not only to the evolving imperial context of the eighteenth century but also to the Romantic-period emphasis on voiced unification, narrative or lyric mastery, and domination of identity.

Both Dalyell and Tully wrote from perspectives informed by the imperial project of the late eighteenth and early nineteenth centuries, and *Don Juan* thematically engages issues of empire—British, Ottoman, Russian, and French—at several levels. The question is to what extent the appropriation from travel texts mirrored the ideological effects of the narratives themselves and to what extent the articulation of plagiarism mobilized other contemporary discourses as part of its contexts. The similarities between implicitly authorless travel texts and the "unclaimed" resources of orientalized nations suggests a slippage between the textual and the geographical that has been noted in other contexts by historians of both Romanticism and colonialism, and, as I have already suggested, travel texts were often viewed in Georgian Britain as materials available for reemployment.[27] At the same time, Romantic-period travel narratives, perhaps more clearly than any other nineteenth-century texts, participated in both the literal and figurative aspects of the British imperial project in the East, and as such these narratives were particularly tied to the administrative concerns of colonial expansion. These narratives could function, simultaneously, as an ethnographic and scientific instrument of territorial expansion, as an imaginative reflection of Western cultural anxieties and fantasies, and as a concrete guide and ideological training manual for imperial subjects. In these texts, colonization and nationalism frequently intersect as competing desires. One demands the assimilation of East into West, while the other resists this incorporation as cultural contamination. Hybridity, miscegenation, and unified national subjectivity were particular administrative and cultural concerns during the early nineteenth century, and it should come as little surprise that the rhetoric of plagiarism, especially plagiarism from orientalist texts, mirrored the Romantic-period discourse on colonialism in important ways. Like contemporaneous forms of colonial failure in the period, plagiarism represented the inability to establish mastery over one's materials and signaled an author's contamination by foreign sources, bodies, and voices.

One example of the ways in which discourses of plagiarism and colonialism intersected during the Romantic period is demonstrated by Edward Trelawny's Byronic travel novel *The Adventures of a Younger Son* (1831), a text that emerged directly out of the context of literary borrowing that was associated with the Shelley-Byron circle in Italy. An intimate of the coterie, Trelawny's modeled his self-representation after the corsairs of Byron's oriental tales, and his novel belatedly engaged a series of literary works, cultural representations, and travel texts closely associated with second-generation Romanticism. However, *The Adventures of a Younger Son* likewise appropriated from a set of orientalist works circulated at Pisa and written by Edward Williams and by Percy Bysshe Shelley's cousin, Thomas Medwin—works indebted to contemporary travel accounts and deeply engaged in the conventions of borrowing associated with nineteenth-century exploration literature. Read as a narrative of cultural assimilation and its textual mediation, *The Adventures of a Younger Son* dramatizes the dangers of cultural appropriation in terms that emphasize voice and that mirror the contemporary discourses on both plagiarism and colonial administration.

When Thomas Malthus summarized the cultural conditions of early nineteenth-century imperialism in India, he observed that young men "at an age little exceeding childhood" were being sent to colonize a continent.[28] At the same time, popular literature, including volume after volume of oriental tales and travel accounts, imagined the East as a gendered and violently eroticized space. The allure of this cultural fantasy can only be imagined, and young Englishmen "going native" represented an ongoing administrative struggle. Hybridity was a national anxiety in nineteenth-century imperial Britain, and, as a contamination of the West by its Eastern subjects, nativism signaled an undeniable failure of colonization, exposing the inherent risks of territorial expansion to national identity.

In contemporary texts, this cultural contamination was frequently represented as textual miscegenation. Incoherent or muddled speech is the consequence of "going native" and results from the conquest of the local language and its means of signification over the body and voice of the Englishman. In *The Adventures of a Younger Son*, Trelawny depicts the monstrous product of hybridity in the image of the Zaoo Englishman, an East India Company seaman gone native. As a figure the Englishman represents both the contamination by and possession of the West by the East. He is described as:

A very tall, thin and bony man [who] would have been strikingly handsome in figure and bearing, were it not for the extraordinary and grotesque manner in which he was tattooed. . . . The figure of a hideous serpent was wreathed around his throat, as if in the act of strangling him . . . its [forked and poisonous] tongue . . . darting into his mouth. [Later,] when our callians were lighted, he commenced his narrative; but in so strange an idiom, and with so many breaks and stops that, at first, I had great difficulty in comprehending his meaning. For the benefit of others, I take the liberty of amending his phraseology.[29]

The predominant features of this deserter are the possession of his body by an Eastern text, which is visually signaled by the peculiar tattoos that appear to constrict his ability to speak at all. Contaminated by native markings, the Englishman's body becomes an Eastern sign; he is branded with the "marks of [a] savage life," which prevent him from ever returning to life in European society. The textual conflict inscribed on his body, which is marked by the Orient, irrevocably confuses both his national identity and his voice, and the struggle between text and voice that the Zaoo Englishman's body represents is a figure for the conflict between Eastern and Western systems of signification that runs throughout the *Adventures.* The Zaoo Englishman becomes inarticulate as the East contaminates him, but his tattooed body can be read as an intelligible sign and as testimony to the grotesque results of nativism. The Western observer, meanwhile, maintains narrative mastery and is able to unify and to retell in unadulterated English the seaman's experience.

The failure to assimilate fully one's borrowed materials and to maintain narrative mastery over the signs that one has appropriated emerges in Trelawny's text as monstrous and grotesque, and my point is that similar anxieties and aesthetic judgments surrounded the discourse of plagiarism in the Romantic period. The silencing of Trelawny's Zaoo Englishman mirrors the distortion and possession of voice that is experienced by Christabel in her encounter with the "foreign" Lady Geraldine, for example. (Lady Geraldine, it is worth recollecting, is described as "most beautiful to see, / Like a lady of a far countrèe" [ll. 224–25]). Likewise, Byron was particularly concerned with the disintegration of voice and its contamination by other influences in *Don Juan*, a poem narrating Juan's encounters with empire and the allure of nativism. As we have already seen, Byron's response to the charges of plagiarism from Dalyell's travel narratives emphasized the degree to which he made his materials his own by exercising narrative mastery over the texts from which he has borrowed, and part of the difficulty that writers appropriating from travel narratives faced was the question of how to cast in one's own voice language that was implicitly historical and, therefore, rhetorically "authored" by its foreign contexts. Byron reflected upon the consequences of failure in an 1820 letter to Murray. He takes issues, he writes, with "that false trashy stilted style, which is a mixture of all the styles of the day," condemning as "neither English nor poetry" hybrid texts that proliferate voices (*BLJ* 7: 182). Byron associates stylistic unity with the accomplishments of a national poetics. In contrast, mixed works became literary failures and examples of plagiarism, the consequences of which were, simultaneously, the contamination of one's text as monstrous

and the disintegration in an expressionist aesthetics of individual poetic
voice.

Satire and Borrowings from Continental Literature

In the years after his death in 1824, Byron continued to be the object of
controversy in the periodical press, and during the 1820s and 1830s his plagiarisms were publicly discussed by two of his intimate acquaintances,
Thomas Medwin and Lady Blessington. Byron, of course, was in no position to defend himself or his work, and the posthumous memoirs often
represented Byron as a knowing and occasionally devious plagiarist, even
as they engaged the language of originality and unconsciousness that characterized Romantic-period attitudes toward literary property. Medwin's accusations of plagiarism from Italian comic literature in the first canto of
Don Juan participated in the critical attacks on the poem, but more importantly his accounts emphasize the degree to which neither satirical intent
nor the effects of translation mitigated Romantic-period charges of plagiarism. Lady Blessington's recollections testify to the abiding aesthetic judgments that Byron and his reviewers understood to be at stake in questions
of illegitimate appropriation.

Medwin publicly discussed the issue of Byron's plagiarisms on numerous occasions and with little variation. Drawing from a circumscribed set
of reminiscences and textual observations, he called attention to Byron's
literary appropriations in works that included his *Conversations of Lord
Byron* (1824), a review essay published in the periodical press in 1833, a curious volume entitled *Some Rejected Stanzas of "Don Juan" . . . after Casti's
manner, an Italian author from whom Byron is said to have plagiarized many
of his beauties* (1845), and his *Life of Shelley* (1847). In the *Conversations*
Medwin first alluded to a series of alleged obligations that had not been the
subject of controversy during the poet's lifetime, including debts to Goethe,
Southey, Beckford, and Casti, and the memoirs contain Byron's reported
responses to many of the public charges brought against him. Repeatedly,
Medwin characterizes Byron has having privately reveled in his plagiarisms,
especially those that had gone undetected. Discussing the debts to Coleridge
in *The Siege of Corinth*, Medwin claimed that Byron had boasted of additional "almost verbatim" obligations to Beckford (*Conversations* 258); in
Childe Harold's Pilgrimage Byron allegedly claimed additional appropriations from *Christabel* (*Conversations* 177). Perhaps most importantly, Med-

win hints here for the first time at Byron's intellectual obligations to the Italian satirical poet Giambattista Casti. Medwin records Byron as having one day explained to him:

"I am taxed with being a plagiarist, when I am least conscious of being one; but I am not very scrupulous, I own, when I have a good idea, how I came into possession of it. How can we tell to what extent Shakespeare is indebted to his contemporaries, whose works are now lost?. . . . The invocation of the witches was, we know, a servile plagiarism from Middleton. Authors were not so squeamish about borrowing from one another in those days. If it be a fault, I do not pretend to be immaculate. I will lend you some volume of Shipwrecks, from which my storm in 'Don Juan' came."

"Lend me also 'Casti's Novelle,'" said I.

"The Germans," he said, "and I believe Goethe himself, consider that I have taken great liberties with 'Faust' [but as] to originality, Goethe has too much sense to pretend that he is not under obligations to authors. . . . who is not?" (*Conversations* 141–42)

Medwin's account reflects, of course, the Romantic-period understanding of unconscious plagiarism as a legitimate species of appropriation, and the simultaneous emphasis on borrowings *and* on originality is further evidence that these categories were not considered mutually exclusive for Byron or his contemporaries.[30] Medwin also characterizes Byron here as invested in what was a characteristically eighteenth-century set of attitudes toward authorship, imitation, and tradition. However, the glancing remark regarding Casti in the middle of this account of Byron's plagiarisms was to become the source that most interested Medwin and that he felt compelled to detail for his reading public in subsequent publications.

Medwin's public elaboration of this elliptical remark came in an article (published serially) entitled "A Cast of Casti. By Lord Byron."[31] Appearing in *The New Anti-Jacobin* in April of 1833 (and later reprinted in *The Life of Shelley* in 1845), the article detailed extended correspondences between the first canto of *Don Juan* and Casti's poem *La Diavolessa* (The Female Devil) (1790) and characterized the obligations as obvious plagiarisms. The similarities leave little doubt that Casti was one of Byron's sources for the poem, and there are numerous instances in which Medwin detects word-for-word parallels, especially in regard to the characterization of Juan. Byron's interest in the text is no mystery. Casti's poem had likewise focused on the exploits of Don Juan who, upon meeting his rival Don Ignazio in hell, "undertook to recount his adventures to his former companion" ("Cast of Casti" 34). From this, Medwin proposes, "it is probably that Byron took the idea of giving this narration in his *Don Juan*" (34), noting that Byron had stated that he meant to finish the poem with his hero in hell. While Byron's obligations to Casti are, of course, significant for understanding his literary objectives in the poem more generally, Medwin's focus in the essay on the satirical nature of both *Don Juan* and *La Diavolessa* is of particular interest because his remarks make clear, as we have seen on other occasions, that for early nineteenth-century readers satirical objectives did not preclude charges of plagiarism.

Medwin's "Cast of Casti" was prompted by the recent publication of an unexpurgated edition of *Don Juan*, and his essay begins by reviewing the contradictory critical statements made in the periodical press about the poem's satirical intentions. Alternatively characterizing Byron's poem as at once "a *satire* on decency" and "innocent of *satire*" ("Cast of Casti" 30), Medwin intended to resolve the matter by restoring *Don Juan* to its appropriate context: the tradition of the Italian burlesque and, particularly, the ribald satires of Casti. Byron himself had indicated that the poem should be understood as the successor to satirical works such as John Hookham Frere's *Whistlecraft* (1817–18) and the "half-serious rhyme[s]" ("Cast of Casti" 31) of Luigi Pulci, and, while Medwin confirms these texts as influential models, he argues that Byron had neglected studiously any mention of his primary source for the poem because the correspondences with Casti's *Novelle* were so extensive. Throughout, Medwin suggests that Byron was determined that the poems should languish in obscurity and that his obligations should pass unremarked by his critics, and he calls attention to Byron's efforts at "mystification" (32) in regard to his sources. Yet, while Medwin castigates Byron and his "slip-shod Muse" (35) for these plagiarisms, he likewise asserts that the poem is a satire, in a tradition of satires. Casti's poetry was, as Peter Vassallo has observed, itself composed in the Italian mock-epic tradition of the *rifacimenti* (refashionings) and "his *ottava rima* satires [narrate] earlier stories told by Casti's more famous literary predecessors" (*Italian Literary Influence* 46). Texts composed as *rifacimenti* characteristically employed the language, imagery, and versification of their predecessors for the purposes of political or literary combat, and works such as Mary Shelley's *Lives of the Most Eminent Literary and Scientific Men of Italy* (1835) suggest that the tradition was receiving renewed attention in Britain during the Italian revival of the 1820s and 1830s.[32] Medwin surely must have understood the broader context of the Italian epic romance, for he could not have appreciated Casti without it, and to this degree his review essay is somewhat disingenuous: read as a *rifacimento* of

Casti, *Don Juan*'s appropriations were themselves part of the poem's satirical intent and consonant with one of the literary traditions that Byron actively engaged. The Romantic-period anxiety surrounding questions of plagiarism and literary property was culturally specific to Britain in important ways, and the internationalism of the second-generation post-Napoleonic writers inevitably exacerbated the larger conflict represented by the Wordsworth-Byron antagonism. However, the reception of *Don Juan* in the periodical press and the rhetoric of Medwin's review, as well as his efforts to renew this controversy with the 1835 publication of *Some Rejected Stanzas of "Don Juan,"* demonstrate that satirical objectives frequently were not considered relevant to discussions of plagiarism. Much like Wordsworth's claims earlier in the century that Peter Bayley had simultaneously plagiarized and satirized his poems, Byron's obligations were evaluated in the context of a critical climate that devalued comic literature and the license with literary property upon which it depended.

Finally, Byron's plagiarisms were also the subject of discussion in the memorials of the poet published by Lady Blessington from July 1832 to December 1833 in the *New Monthly Magazine*. These recollections, reprinted in 1834 under the title *A Journal of the Conversations of Lord Byron*, recorded additional information on Byron's literary obligations, and Blessington's account emphasized both the persistence of Romantic-period categories of improvement and unconscious appropriation and Byron's investment in the aesthetic elements of the charge of plagiarism. Reflecting upon Byron's heavy use of source materials in *The Deformed Transformed* (1822), Blessington observed that, in regard to "the unacknowledged, but visible, resemblances" with other texts,

It was possible that he [was] unconscious of the plagiary of ideas that he has committed, for his reading is so desultory that he seizes thoughts which, in passing through the alembic of his mind, become so embellished as to lose all identity with the original crude embryo he had adopted. . . . He told me that he rarely ever read a page that did not give rise to chains of thought, the first idea serving as the original link on which the others were formed.[33]

Blessington's commentary is similar to the account of Romantic-period plagiarism, and of Coleridge's debts particularly, that Thomas DeQuincey had offered in his nearly contemporaneous essay for *Tait's Magazine*. Byron's debts are justified by Blessington on grounds that mobilize several elements of the early nineteenth-century discourse on literary property, ranging from the suggestion that the borrowings may have been unconscious (and, therefore, legitimate) to the implication that Byron has, regardless, improved upon his materials by purifying or distilling "the original crude embryo" from which he drew. Even the language of association recalls Coleridge, whose appropriations in *Biographia Literaria* became the subject of controversy in 1834. The most important element of Blessington's account, however, is the emphasis she places on the unique nature of Byron's intellectual and creative experience, an experience that the poet had represented not as personal but as characteristic of the poetic mind in composition. For, as Blessington reports, Byron had asked:

[W]ho is the author that is not, intentionally or unintentionally, a plagiarist? Many more, I am persuaded, are the latter than the former; for if one has read much, it is difficult, if not impossible, to avoid adopting, not only the thoughts, but the expressions of others, which, after they have been some time stored in our minds, appear to us to come forth ready formed, like Minerva from the brain of Jupiter. . . . To be perfectly original . . . one should think much and read little; and this is impossible, as one must have read much before one learns to think. . . . But after one has laid in a tolerable stock of materials for thinking, I should think the best plan would be to give the mind time to digest . . . by which we make the knowledge acquired our own; and on this foundation we may let our originality (if we have any) build a superstructure[.] (330)

Returning to the questions of originality that had occupied his earliest periodical critics, Byron articulates a model of authorship that posits appropriation, adoption, digestion, and even plagiarism as the conditions of invention and self-expression. The literary tradition and popular print culture become the necessary foundations upon which all subsequent works rest, and, as authors cannot reasonably be expected to write in complete ignorance of the past, the question of originality depends upon assimilation. For Byron, the texts of one's predecessors and one's contemporaries become not the Wordsworthian private estates but the cultural superstructure upon which public works are built. At the root of the animosity played out in the periodical reviews between those aligned either with Wordsworth or with Byron was more than simple matters of attribution and citation. Originality, identity, consciousness, and power were all at stake, and Romantic-period plagiarism and the controversies it occasioned became the arena in which many of the period's most vital aesthetic judgments were contested.

I have argued in this chapter that for Byron those aesthetic judgments focused particularly on questions of voice and on the role of authorial subjectivity in lyric texts. Throughout his works, Byron maintained that originality was a function of poetic-narrative mastery and domination, and his readiness to borrow from the works of his contemporaries suggests how competitive early nineteenth-century literary culture could be and perhaps explains some part of the intense criticism that his appropriations generated in the periodical press. Of all the familiar Romantic-period writers, Byron's plagiarisms were the most celebrated and occasioned the most sustained public controversy during his lifetime, not because his obligations were, objectively speaking, the most extensive but, rather, because his celebrity and aristocratic persona coincided with a moment in British cultural history when the professional status of the author was emerging as culturally dominant. In the decade after the 1814 Copyright Act, literary works were increasingly evaluated in contexts informed by legal and economic arguments, and writers whose income depended upon their literary or critical productions resented, perhaps particularly, Byron's appropriations and their feudal overtones.[34] At the same time, his poems were deeply engaged with aspects of the literary tradition that most complicated Romantic-period attitudes toward authorship and appropriation, including popular historical genres and satire.

Monstrosities Strung into an Epic: Travel Writing and the Defense of "Modern" Poetry

This chapter focuses primarily on Percy Bysshe Shelley's relationship to plagiarism and issues of literary property, and his inclusion in this study perhaps merits some particular attention because Shelley's borrowings, unlike those of his contemporaries, were not the subject of sustained public controversy. He did borrow, often extensively, from the language of other writers, and the possibility of being accused of illegitimate appropriation was a source of concern for him as a writer, especially in the later years of his career. However, while scholars have identified and occasionally labeled as plagiarisms his borrowings in texts such as the juvenile *Original Poetry* (1810) or his early Gothic novels, the term was not applied to these debts during the Romantic period, and, to the extent that he avoided being charged with plagiarism even in a hostile periodical review climate, Shelley is an example of an early nineteenth-century writer who successfully negotiated contemporary attitudes toward literary property. Yet, the prefaces through which he contextualized his poems for the reading public frequently discussed the problem of plagiarism and demonstrate that Percy Bysshe Shelley understood clearly the aesthetic judgments that were central to the charge. Mary Shelley demonstrates this same familiarity in her critical defense of "modern" verse, in which she argues, as we have seen repeatedly in the course of this study, that successful appropriation during the Romantic period largely depended on the author's ability to maintain lyric mastery over his or her borrowed materials.

Travel Writing and Plagiarism in the Romantic Period

Although Percy Bysshe Shelley borrowed on occasion from a range of sources that included classical texts, contemporary poetry, and popular print-culture materials, he was particularly concerned that he would be charged with plagiarism from travel writing. Several of his works were indebted to exploration literature, and, as we have seen, borrowings from the genre sometimes occasioned charges of plagiarism in the periodical press because there was not a critical consensus regarding the authored status of these texts. There were numerous instances in which Romantic-period writers appropriated from travel materials, ranging from Byron's debts to Miss Tully in *Don Juan* to Coleridge's debts to Shevlocke in the *Rime of the Ancient Mariner*, and the reemployment of travel sources in literary contexts was widespread throughout the late eighteenth and early nineteenth centuries. Charles Norton Coe has documented over twenty travel texts from which William Wordsworth borrowed without citation in his poems, including the voyages of Bartram, Coxe, Hakluyt, and Barrow. In his *Road to Xanadu*, John Livingston Lowes identified dozens of exploration accounts to which Coleridge was indebted and argued that some of the most memorable lines from poems as justly famous as "Kubla Khan" had their sources in the language of contemporary travelers. The oriental tales of Robert Southey and Thomas Moore relied heavily upon traveler's accounts of the Levant, and Mary Shelley's novel *Lodore* (1835) drew from descriptions of North American voyages and emigration.[1] In fact, appropriation from travel material accounts for the majority of what modern readers might consider plagiarisms in the Romantic period, and some of the public accusations made against authors in the early nineteenth century, including Coleridge and Byron, detailed their debts to exploration accounts.

However, while Shelley was sensible to be concerned about his own appropriations from travel writing and about the potential controversy that they might occasion in the periodical press, borrowing from exploration accounts was viewed somewhat differently from obligations to other sorts of material during the period. Travel writing, like other commercial popular-print genres, represented a more complicated category of intellectual property than works written in self-consciously literary styles, and, as we have seen, it occupied an ambiguous relationship to categories of ownership and invention. Poised between the claims of scientific or historical documentation and the strategies of romance, these texts undermined conventional distinctions between fact and fiction and, in doing so, complicated their own relationship to intellectual property. Eighteenth-century legal decisions surrounding copyright had determined that facts, discoveries, and other knowledge of the historical, scientific, or natural sort were only entitled to limited protection as private property; works of creative invention, on the other hand, whether literary or mechanical, had broader claims.[2] As late as the end of the nineteenth century, commentators on plagiarism still distinguished specifically between borrowings from these different types of texts.[3] But to which category did early nineteenth-century travel writing belong?

As a mixed genre, travel writing had an indeterminate literary status. These texts presented themselves, on the one hand, as implicitly authorless material knowledge, as objective, truthful, and even scientific records of the facts of geography and cultural difference. On the other hand, emphasizing the personal experiences, insights, and emotional responses of an individual narrator and employing the stock devices of romance and epic traditions, they clearly exploited literary strategies. At stake in this contrast was the nature of history and the individual's relationship to it, and this disjunction between representations of history-as-objective-fact and representations of history-as-subjective-experience accounts, more than any other element, for the particular interest that Romantic-period writers had in borrowing from these texts. The mixed nature of the travel narrative mirrored in important respects the representational issues these authors, and especially Shelley, were interested in negotiating: the ratio between the external world and the internal psychological experience of it.

Because plagiarism from travel writing was at once authorized and complicated by the representational claims of the genre and by its relationship to different categories of intellectual property, borrowing from these texts occasioned particular benefits and particular risks for early nineteenth-century writers, both of which were directly tied to the contemporary discourse on plagiarism. The chief benefit of appropriating materials from travel sources for reemployment in literary contexts was their familiarity. It is difficult to underestimate the degree to which contemporary readers were familiar with travel texts. The genre was not only popular but also culturally pervasive. Its popularity cut across even the otherwise restrictive categories of class and gender in ways that few other types of writing in the period demonstrate. Both aristocratic young men and merchant sailors had access to travel writing. Women authored some of the most broadly circulated works in the genre, and the publication of travel memoirs, unlike the publication of other types of materials, was not considered as indecorous or injurious to a genteel woman's reputation.[4] Travel narratives were also the focus of intense cultural engagement. Readers could recognize the precise textual details of landscapes drawn from accounts by Montagu, Cook, Parry, Radcliffe, Wollstonecraft, and later Byron, who lamented to his mother that his descriptions of Constantinople were scarcely worth recording since "you have read fifty descriptions by sundry travelers" (*BLJ* 1:244).[5] The familiarity of travel writing, of course, meant that writers were unlikely to be charged persuasively with culpable plagiarisms from the most important works of the genre. As we have seen, where the reader could be expected to recognize and to credit the original source, it was not necessary for an author to acknowledge the obligation more explicitly. Moreover, many readers in the Romantic period did not consider travel writing a literary production at all, so that appropriations from it were not likely to have been considered culpable regardless. However, while the familiarity of these texts had commercial benefits for writers, it also represented an aesthetic risk. Readers and, more importantly, reviewers were likely to recognize appropriations from travel writing and, therefore, to evaluate a text according to the standards of early nineteenth-century aesthetic plagiarism. Literary borrowings represented an implicit claim for narrative or lyric mastery, and reviewers appear to have delighted in evaluating them.

"Modern" Poetry and Textual Appropriation: Thomas Love Peacock and Mary Shelley

Perhaps the most immediate critical context for understanding the attitude in the Shelley-Byron circle toward appropriations, and particularly toward appropriations from travel materials, is the exchange that occurred between Thomas Love Peacock and Mary Shelley from 1820 to 1823. Scholars of the Romantic period are, of course, familiar with the ways in which Peacock's polemical essay "The Four Ages of Poetry" (1820) galvanized Percy Bysshe Shelley and prompted him to write what has been considered a formative statement of Romantic aesthetics, "The Defence of Poetry or, Remarks Suggested by an Essay Entitled 'The Four Ages of Poetry'" (1821). What has been less frequently recognized is the extent either to which Peacock's attack on contemporary writers identifies patterns of unassimilated borrowing from travel materials as a central literary defect or to which Mary Shelley's brief review essay "Giovanni Villani" (1823) offers a defense of "modern" verse that answers Peacock by proposing lyric mastery as its most important aesthetic objective.

In "The Four Ages of Poetry," Peacock's central critique of Romantic-period poetry (what he calls "modern" poetry) is its tendency to borrow unsuccessfully and injudiciously from works of travel writing, which he characterized as explicitly historical materials. This representation of travel writing as a subliterary genre is significant because it lays the foundation for Peacock's subsequent claims about the exclusive relationship to the past embodied by contemporary poetry, and the context of the implied argument emerges out of the early nineteenth-century debate surrounding the category of history. Throughout the late eighteenth century and into the Romantic period, history had been generally understood along the lines articulated by William Godwin in his essay "Of History and Romance" (1797). Godwin had represented history as a genre not unlike what many travel writers did in practice; it blended information and invention, simultaneously communicating the facts of the past with imagined insight into the experience of them. However, the early nineteenth century also saw the rise of "modern" Utilitarian attitudes toward historical writing, an attitude reflected in contemporary works such as James Mill's *The History of British India* (1817).[6] In fact, Peacock's admiration for Mill, with whom he worked at the India House Examiner's Office, particularly motivated him to write "The Four Ages of Poetry," and, as Javeed Majeed has observed, Peacock's essay "resembled Mill's argument" in important respects.[7] Mill's argument, in particular, was that the proper function of history was progressive rather than reflective, and Peacock's thesis in "The Four Ages of Poetry" asserted that the work of the historian-philosopher was to advance the progress of human culture by providing a critical perspective from which to evaluate and transcend the past. In contrast, the poet's relationship to history was degenerative. By valorizing and even "romanticizing" the past, Peacock argued, the poet impedes the progress of civil culture by encouraging an admiration for archaic superstition, exotica, and outdated information. In short, he claims that "modern" history is useful, while "modern" poetry is dangerous, and he identifies literary Romanticism's infatuation with travel materials as symptomatic of its identification with regressive and irrational objectives.

From Peacock's perspective, the tendency of the modern poets to appropriate from exploration narratives is indicative of their sentimental attachments to the rude and barbaric artifacts of outdated knowledge, and he viewed travel writing as a primarily sentimental genre, preoccupied with presenting foreign manners and antique relics. In mounting his critique of contemporary verse in "The Four Ages of Poetry," he argues that the presence of these borrowed materials is evidence that the contemporary "poet is wallowing in the rubbish of departed ignorance and raking up the ashes of dead savages to find gee-gaws and rattles for the babies of the age."[8] This "rubbish" is specifically identified as having its source in travel writing, which poets borrow from and incorporate into their works. Describing the literary scene of his era, Peacock writes,

Lord Byron cruises for thieves and pirates on the shores of the Morea and among the Greek islands. Mr. Southey wades through ponderous volumes of travels and old chronicles, from which he carefully selected all that is false, useless, and absurd as being essentially poetical; and when he has a commonplace book full of monstrosities, strings them into an epic. . . . Mr. Moore presents us with a Persian, and Mr. Campbell with a Pennsylvanian tale, both formed on the same principle as Mr. Southey's epics, by extracting from a perfunctory and desultory perusal of a collection of voyages and travels, all that useful investigation would not seek for and that common sense would reject. ("The Four Ages" 128–29)

The claim here is that the assimilation of travel materials into works of modern poetry is a central defect. However, the criticism is both social and aesthetic. Not only do these borrowings render Romantic-period poems unfit for any "useful" social or progressive historical object, but they also undermine the aesthetic unity of the compositions. Peacock identifies careless and unassimilated appropriation as the compositional principle underlying what were, in fact, some of the most familiar poems of the early nineteenth century. The implication is that, having been extracted from travel narratives and then strung into an epic, the borrowed materials remain disparate and incoherent elements of the text. Indeed, the result is cast as monstrous: a work that is composed of parts that remain grotesquely and incongruously distinct.

While Peacock's social criticisms of poetry are part of a particular engagement with emerging notions of Utilitarian history in the second decade of the nineteenth century, the language of his aesthetic critique resonates with the rhetoric that had been characteristically associated with plagiarism and literary property since the late eighteenth century. Peacock's point in "The Four Ages of Poetry" is not to charge his literary contemporaries with culpable plagiarisms. Indeed, his matter-of-fact identification of travel materials as the overwhelming source of events and imagery in Romantic-period poetry suggests the extent to which these writers were understood by readers to have borrowed from recognizable popular representations. Peacock is, however, mobilizing the language of aesthetic plagiarism in this passage, a charge that depended upon issues of improvement, unity, and narrative or lyric mastery. This is most clearly evident in his emphasis on the unassimilated, monstrous, and chimerical nature of these hybrid texts.

The charge mirrors both Byron's complaints about "mixed" styles and Coleridge's characterization of "patchwork" plagiarisms. Peacock is proposing that modern poetry is fundamentally disjointed and, therefore, fundamentally flawed. These are texts from which no coherent unifying voice emerges. The authors have failed to assimilate fully their borrowed materials, and the resulting product is both socially useless and aesthetically grotesque.

Mary Shelley directly works to refute these claims in her essay "Giovanni Villani," in which she addresses literary Romanticism's investment in borrowing from travel writing and, particularly, from the epistolary accounts of women authors. Her essay, written in the context of the subsequently more famous debate between Peacock and Percy Bysshe Shelley, offers an alternative defense of "modern" poetry that directly engages the aesthetic issues surrounding borrowing and textual appropriation. Arguing that women's travel materials, in particular, demonstrate the unifying mastery of authorial subjectivity, Mary Shelley proposes that the incorporation of these texts into literary works guarantees the authenticity and cultural value of Romantic-period verse in fundamental ways.

Ostensibly a review of the fourteenth-century *Chronicle nelle quali si tratta dell'origine di Firenze, & di tutte e fatti & guerre state fatte da Fiorentini nella Italia* (Chronicles of Florence), Mary Shelley's argument in the "Giovanni Villani" essay corrects Peacock by claiming for Romantic-period poetry a unique form of textual unity that arises from its assimilation of travel materials and its projection of private subjectivity. Peacock had claimed in "The Four Ages of Poetry" that the habits of textual appropriation reflected in the poetry of writers such as Byron, Southey, Campbell, and Moore produced aesthetic monstrosities. Mary Shelley responds to these charges by demonstrating that Peacock's criticism is predicated upon his own misunderstanding of the objectives and particular accomplishments of modern literature. Her goal, she writes, is to discover for her readers "that which is beautiful even in [the] defects" that Peacock is identifying.[9] Her opening paragraphs of the essay summarize both Peacock's position and her response to it, and the verbal echoes in this passage indicate that she has his essay particularly in mind.[10] She writes:

Among the many accusations that have been made against modern writers by the exclusive lovers of ancient literature, none has been more frequently repeated than the want of art manifested in the conception of their work, and of unity in the conception. . . . [T]hey tell us, that such is the perfection of antiquity compared

with the monstrous distortions of modern times. These arguments and views . . .
have given rise to volumes concerning the Classic and the Romantic. (*NMS* 2: 128)

Here, Mary Shelley identifies Peacock's claims of monstrosity and compositional disunity as the central elements of his critique, and she classifies
"Greeky Peaky" (as he was known among his intimates) as a partisan and
polemical critic. The implication is that, as "exclusive lovers" of classical
literature, critics like Peacock are applying to "modern" Romantic-period
texts an irrelevant set of judgments.

The central claim that Mary Shelley disputes is Peacock's emphasis on
a certain form of textual coherence. In applying to contemporary poetry
the standards of classical or neoclassical "unity," Peacock is dismissing the
uniquely expressivist objectives of these "modern" works—and it is an aesthetic dismissal that is, once again, tied to issues of appropriation. Mary
Shelley's counterargument proposes for Romantic-period literature an alternative structural focus, one that privileges the unifying role of individual
subjectivity. Casting modern poetry as a literature of sensibility, she explains that the substance of critiques such as Peacock's concerns the inclina-
tion of authors, "particularly those of the present day," to incorporate their
own character into their compositions; they "introduce themselves, their
failings and opinions, into the midst of works" (*NMS* 2: 129). Shelley con-
cedes that, when poorly managed, the result can, indeed, be monstrous;
but, when successful, this insertion of authorial subjectivity into a contemporary text results in works of literature that are "incomparably beautiful"
(129). These "beautiful" works are texts in which the unique sensibilities of
the individual writer permeate the style and tone of the entire production.
The result is an organizing principle based on the expression of subjectivity.
Offering two examples of particularly successful texts, she explains the unifying effect this emphasis on the self can have. In these works, she writes,
"the individual feeling of the author imbues the whole subject with a particular hue. . . . Half the beauty of Lady Mary Montague's Letters consists
in the *I* that adorns them, and this *I*, this sensitive, imaginative, suffering,
enthusiastic pronoun, spreads an inexpressible charm over Mary Wollstonecraft's Letters from Norway" (130–31). By "imbu[ing]" the "whole"
work with a coherent and identifiable cast of mind, the Romantic-period
text succeeds or fails on the basis of the subjectivity that it develops. Although Shelley casts the emergence of this guiding voice in the genteel language of charm and adornment, at stake are the same questions of narrative
or lyric mastery and textual domination. Unity in an expressivist text de-

pends upon the author's ability to create a speaking self—an "I"—that both permeates and dominates the materials it employs.

By proposing a model of textual unity based on the development of voiced subjectivity, Mary Shelley is also able to address the Romantic-period writer's relationship to borrowed materials. In the context that she is proposing, a work is evaluated not on the novelty of its representations but on the unique and original expression of the self that controls them. The extent of an author's appropriations are less important than the degree to which he or she has assimilated them to the unifying voice of the text. This attitude, of course, is entirely in keeping with the literary property discourse of the Romantic period, in which assimilation and narrative or lyric mastery represented forms of textual improvement and transformation, and Mary Shelley's position resonates particularly with the attitude toward appropriation and literary achievement that Byron articulates in relation to *Childe Harold's Pilgrimage* and *Don Juan*.[11] In fact, her essay offers a clear critical summation of the aesthetic objectives tied to appropriation and literary borrowing in Romantic-period poetry, objectives ranging from the emphasis on voice and style that preoccupied Wordsworth and Coleridge to the questions of improvement and assimilation that concerned early nineteenth-century writers and their reviewers.

In the "Giovanni Villani" essay, however, Mary Shelley also explores the characteristically unspoken relationship between textual assimilation and gender, and she proposes that, in their borrowings from travel accounts, contemporary authors were drawn to appropriate especially from narratives written by women. These works are, she writes, "peculiar favourites" (130), and Shelley attributes this interest to the emphasis in women's writing both on the expression of sensibility and on "modern" forms of textual unity. These are works, in short, that achieve precisely the effects that Shelley proposes are central to Romantic-period aesthetics. She applauds Montagu and Wollstonecraft as particularly beautiful examples of voiced textual unity and identifies women's travel writing as a genre that was centrally concerned with modern authorial subjectivity. Montagu had made the same point, in fact, in the introduction to her *Letters . . . written during her Travels in Europe, Asia, and Africa* (1763), writing to contrast the objectives of women writers with those of their male contemporaries. Montagu had written that her book was made public with the intention that "[t]he world should see, to how much better purpose the LADIES travel than the LORDS; and that, whilst it is surfeited with *Male-Travels*, all in the same tone, and stuft with the same trifles; a lady has the skill to strike out a new path. . . . as her ladyship's penetration discovers the inmost follies of the heart" (iv-v). Mary Shelley reiterates this emphasis on the exploration and discovery of private sensibility in women's travel writing in order to explain why contemporary poets borrow with such frequency from these works. They are "often the peculiar favourites among men of imagination and sensibility [who] turn to the human heart as the undiscovered country. . . . The sight of land was not more welcome to Columbus, than are these traces of individual feeling, chequering their more formal works of art, to the voyagers in the noblest of terrae incognitae, the soul of man" (*NMS* 2: 130). Here, Shelley delineates clearly the relationship between women's travel narratives and Romantic-period literary productions. These works are attractive to "men of imagination" because they bear the "traces" of authentic authorial subjectivity, and appropriations from them can be detected in works of contemporary poetry. Not themselves having the properties of literature, these accounts "chequer . . . more formal works of art" and, as documentary texts, authenticate the psychological verisimilitude of the representations being crafted.

Mary Shelley's central point is that women's travel narratives demonstrate the principles of "modern" textual unity that Peacock had failed to appreciate in his critique of contemporary literature; indeed, she proposes that their assimilation into other texts is motivated by a recognition of the voice and persona that they develop. In articulating this claim in the "Giovanni Villani" essay, it is possible that Mary Shelley was responding to a point that Percy Bysshe Shelley made in his own response to Peacock. In "The Defence of Poetry," Percy Bysshe Shelley explicitly argues that the cultural value of poetry rests upon the author's ability to "assimilate" and to digest knowledge for his or her readers, using materials borrowed from contemporary sources, sources that presumably would have included travel writing. Peacock had argued that the productions of poetry were useless because they failed to produce new knowledge of the world. Percy Bysshe Shelley responded in "The Defence of Poetry" by proposing that:

We have more moral, political, and historical wisdom than we know how to reduce into practice; we have more scientific and economic knowledge than can be accommodated to the just distribution of the produce which it multiplies. The poetry in these systems of thought is concealed by the accumulation of facts and calculating processes. . . . The cultivation of poetry is never more to be desired than at periods when, from an excess of the selfish and calculating principle, the accumulation of the materials of external life exceeds the quantity of the power of assimilating them to the internal laws of nature. (*SPP* 293)

Society, Shelley observes, does not lack for facts and figures. What it lacks is the ability to imagine the relationship between what he calls the "materials of external life" and the "internal laws of nature." The result of this inability is a failure of understanding that leads to isolation, to individualism, and, because predicated upon a lack of self-reflection, to a collapse of moral judgment. The value of poetry lies in its characteristic "power of assimilating" knowledge and of demonstrating the ratio that connects the products of the mind to the operations of it. This emphasis, however, on the relationship between external sources and internal assimilation also recalls nineteenth-century attitudes toward the literary appropriation of borrowed materials, which were centrally concerned with evaluating a writer's powers of absorption, synthesis, and mastery. Throughout the course of this study, we have seen repeatedly that Romantic-period writers understood the legitimacy or illegitimacy of intellectual obligations in terms of subjectivity rather than in terms of linguistic correspondences. At stake was not the degree to which one's language corresponded with the language of one's predecessor, as had been the case earlier in the eighteenth century; far more important was the degree to which an author had, in Byron's terms, made the materials "his own." Improvement and assimilation of this sort might be accomplished through changes in context rather than content, particularly changes that reshaped the experience of tone or voice in a text. Percy Bysshe Shelley privileges a similar model of appropriation when he suggests that the poet assimilates the sources of cultural knowledge by demonstrating their effect upon and relationship to the operations of the individual mind, and, despite the familiar critical reiteration of Romanticism's investment in autogenous originality, he identifies the "power of assimilating" rather than ex nihilo invention as the highest objective of poetry.

Plagiarism and Shelley's Prefaces

Regardless of whether Percy Bysshe Shelley intended his discussion of the "power[s] of assimilating" in "The Defence of Poetry" as a response to the criticism of poetic "monstrosity" advanced by Peacock, the implications of this passage in "The Defence of Poetry"—that the highest aesthetic object of a poem is to assimilate material culture and to establish a ratio between the internal and external realms of experience—match very closely the arguments that Shelley did make directly about plagiarism in the prefaces that he published with his poems. As I have suggested, these critical reflections upon his poetry reveal a persistent concern regarding plagiarism and repeat the now-familiar considerations that were central to evaluations of the charge in early nineteenth-century British culture. The prefaces that Shelley published with several of his major poems allude to intellectual obligations to contemporary authors, and in these notices he attempts to forestall any implication that he has borrowed illegitimately by emphasizing an aesthetic engagement with metaphors of absorption, digestion, and appropriation. While Shelley was particularly concerned with the possibility of specific, unconscious plagiarisms being alleged in his works, his articulation of a common historical subjectivity or "spirit of the age" represents a more complicated account of the poet's relationship to his or her textual sources. Just as the infusion of tone and "spirit" could transform and effectively recreate a literary work, Shelley understood historical and cultural periods as products of a shared "spirit of the age," and he was particularly concerned with the poet's capacity to establish an assimilative ratio that was simultaneously individual and collective. Put another way, Shelley's anxieties concerning plagiarism stemmed from a philosophical concern about the extent to which consciousness was private at all.

Although Shelley borrowed from classical works in many of his poems, in the prefaces he maintained that the writer's obligation was to incorporate the materials of the present day into his or her works, and the prefaces demonstrate a persistent concern for charges of plagiarism from these sources. Shelley believed that texts were repositories of the states of mind and material conditions that produced them; however, he also argued that it was an error to imagine that mental operations and experiences were individual or that the writer's relationship to knowledge could be both productive and private. Instead, individual creative acts participate in and reflect a collective historical subjectivity or psychological experience. Because the task of the poet is to assimilate the "external" materials of knowledge into an "internal" understanding of human experience, it is his or her obligation to reveal the "poetry" hidden by systems of thought that shape experience and representation in the present. Shelley makes precisely this point in the preface that he published with *The Revolt of Islam* in 1818, and his remarks suggest that, like Coleridge, Shelley considered textual obligations as philosophical coincidences of a sort. Shelley explained to his readers:

I have avoided . . . the imitation of any contemporary style. But there must be a resemblance, which does not depend upon their own will, between all writers of any particular age. They cannot escape from subjection to a common influence. . . . In this view of things, Ford can no more be called the imitator of Shakespeare, than Shakespeare the imitator of Ford. There were perhaps few other points of resemblance between these two men, than that which the universal and inevitable influence of their age produced. And this is an influence which neither the meanest scribbler, not the sublimest genius of any era, can escape; and which I have not attempted to escape.[12]

Shelley asserts here that he has not deliberately imitated the writing of his contemporaries and has, in fact, attempted to avoid appropriating from other texts. Yet, he acknowledges that correspondences almost certainly exist. All writers of the same era are subject to "a common influence," which makes it meaningless to assert that Shakespeare borrowed from Ford or vice versa. Shelley considered textual influence as one of the unconscious and historical consequences of authorship, and, like Coleridge, he emphasizes the extent to which similarities can escaped the willed or conscious intentions of the writer.

This emphasis on the unconscious nature of literary appropriation is briefly reflected again in the preface to *The Cenci* (1819) and, more fully, in the preface to *Prometheus Unbound* (1820). Commenting on the *The Cenci*, Shelley writes that his debt to the poetry of Pedro Calderon de la Barca represents "the only plagiarism which I have intentionally committed in the whole piece" (*PWS* 130). He implies, of course, the possibility of other, unconscious obligations, a confession that could effectively forestall charges of culpable theft. Shelley's concern, however, was not for simply mobilizing in advance a public self-justification. In the preface to *Prometheus Unbound*, Shelley acknowledges his anxieties about charges of plagiarism but also offers his readers a model for understanding the central role of assimilation in poetic composition:

One word is due in candour to the degree in which the study of contemporary writings may have tinged my composition, for such has been a topic of censure with regard to poems far more popular, than mine. It is impossible that any one who inhabits the same age with such writers as those who stand in the foremost ranks of our own, can conscientiously assure himself that his language and tone of thought may not have been modified by the study of the productions of those extraordinary intellects. It is true, that, not the spirit of their genius, but the forms in which it has manifested itself, are due less to the peculiarities of their own minds than to the peculiarity of the moral and intellectual condition of the minds among which they have been produced. Thus a number of writers possess the form, whilst they want the spirit of those whom, it is alleged, they imitated. . . . As to imitation, poetry is a mimetic art. It creates, but it creates by combination and representation. Poetical abstractions are beautiful and new, not because the portions of which they are composed had no previous existence in the mind of man, or in nature, but because the whole produced by their combination has some intelligible and beautiful analogy with those sources of emotion and thought, and with the contemporary condition of them[.] (*PWS* 98–99)

Here is one of Shelley's most developed statements on the poet's relationship to the literary texts of his contemporaries, and his language reflects his familiarity with the rhetoric of Romantic-period plagiarism. Shelley is anxious to acknowledge that contemporary writings have "tinged" his composition, and his reference to the public censure of other poets for their appropriations almost certainly alludes, at least in part, to the attacks that Byron had suffered at the hands of his reviewers. At the same time, his emphasis on both "language" and "tone of thought" demonstrates how important issues of style and tone were in evaluating early nineteenth-century charges of plagiarism and textual identity; indeed, he draws a further distinction that casts textual "spirit" as a form of individual "genius" distinct from the external, material forms of language or genre through which it is communicated. Most importantly, however, Shelley's argument prefigures the point he makes in "The Defence of Poetry" about the "powers of assimilating": successful poetry does not create new information but instead discovers the "intelligible and beautiful analogy" between these "external" forms and the "internal" operations of the human mind, between the "spirit of the age" and individual consciousness. The function of poetry is to combine rather than to create, and many of its materials are both contemporary and textual. Despite Romanticism's familiar critical identification with the values of ex nihilo originality, Shelley proposes that the ability to appropriate and to illuminate the works of other writers is one of the period's central aesthetic judgments.

Assimilation and Textual Community in *Alastor*

While Shelley implies in the preface to *Prometheus Unbound* that his efforts to assimilate texts by other writers can be understood as an effort to articulate an "intelligible and beautiful analogy [between the] sources of emotion and thought, and with the contemporary condition of them," this textual process is most clearly modeled for readers in his early poem *Alastor* (1815).

Shelley not only borrowed extensively from travel writing in the process of composing *Alastor* but the poem's central narrative also portrays two writers, the Poet and the Narrator, both struggling to negotiate their textual influences. As an allegorical exploration of the poet's relationship to the literary tradition that he inhabits, *Alastor* both prefigures Shelley's claims about the powers of assimilation in "The Defence of Poetry" and reveals his anxieties about the consequences of failing to borrow appropriately, a failure that is finally cast in terms of a literary critique of Wordsworth.

During late August of 1815, the Shelleys, accompanied by Peacock and Claire Clairmont, undertook a short voyage, intending to travel by boat from Windsor to the source of the Thames. The immediate results of this ten-day river tour were an improvement in Percy Shelley's "delicate" health and the "commencement of several literary plans."[13] Foremost among these plans was the composition of *Alastor*, Shelley's exploration of the operations of the poetic mind and a work constructed as a textual engagement with various travel sources. Begun immediately upon Shelley's return from the Thames expedition, the poem describes, at one level, the course of his intellectual enthusiasm for travels and for exploration writing but also describes (to borrow Harold Bloom's familiar phrase) Shelley's anxiety of influence.[14] In *Alastor*, the Poet's frenzied expedition through the rivers of the Indian Caucasus toward the source of his vision can be considered in terms of Shelley's own voyage along the Thames and the subsequent reinvigoration of his poetic faculties. More importantly, the densely allusive landscapes through which both the Poet and the poem's Narrator pass in *Alastor* and their responses to this textual inheritance explore the writer's relationship to imaginative sources.

In his preface to the poem, Shelley wrote that *Alastor* was conceived as an allegory of the human mind and of the poet. "It represents," he wrote, "a youth . . . led forth by an imagination inflamed and purified" (*PWS* 41), who rejects the moral claims of sympathy. In consequence of his error, the "spirit of sweet human love" (l. 203) sends to the Poet's mind an *alastor* or avenging spirit, which appears to him in the image of a veiled maiden. The Poet has identified with the maiden in a way that he has failed to identify with the human community (she speaks to him in "the voice of his own soul" [l. 153]); her disappearance occasions his single-minded search for her in the second part of the narrative. However, because the maiden is a product of his own intellectual investments and is born out of the Poet's literary sources, the journey in search of the veiled maiden takes him through a series of landscapes that are recognizably drawn from the language of borrowed texts—texts largely composed of travel narratives and genres associated with them. Understood within the context of Shelley's subsequent reflections on the relationship between poetic composition and source materials, we might say that the Poet's experience dramatizes a failure of assimilation. He fails to establish the ratio between sources of material knowledge and the condition of the human community and remains, instead, enslaved both by his personal desires and by the texts that he has engaged. At one level, the Poet's failure of assimilation and his unfeeling solipsism are intended didactically and as an argument for the importance of sensibility and sympathy in the Romantic period. However, the assimilation at stake in the poem is also concrete and textual: the language of other contemporary writers shapes the geography of the poem, and, in what is also an allegory of Romantic-period plagiarism, Shelley describes in *Alastor* the consequences being possessed by one's literary and historical sources.

Shelley incorporates into *Alastor* landscapes that are appropriated from textual sources in travel literature, and it is likely that he intended for his readers to recognize his borrowings. Not only are some of his obligations to popular and well-known contemporary texts but the Poet's earliest travels in the poem are also represented as potentially textual encounters: as he wanders through Greece, Lebanon, and Ethopia and back in time, he is simultaneously fed at his couch by an Arab maiden (l. 73). The suggestion is that the Poet is engaging in the flights of an armchair traveler. Certainly, many Romantic-period readers would have recognized that the geography was drawn from exploration narratives, both classical and contemporary. Nearly all the landscapes through which the Poet travels have resonances with the language of published accounts. For example, early in the poem, the Poet purportedly wanders from home "to seek strange truths in undiscovered lands" (l. 77) but, as several scholars have observed, ends up in a landscape inhabited by imagery drawn from Southey's popular poem *Thalaba the Destroyer*, a work that imitated both the conventions and particular language of contemporary travel descriptions.[15] The Poet's adolescent voyages are narrated in language drawn from Constantin Volney's *The Ruins of Empire* (1787), while the visions of Cashmire and the veiled maiden allude to a complex web of textual appropriations drawn from oriental accounts by Sir William Jones, Lady Morgan, and Southey.[16]

The fact of Shelley's borrowings is simple enough, but his intentions in drawing from the language and imagery of travel writers are a more complicated matter. If he intended his readers to recognize the obligations, then to what end? The answer is not, I think, commercial expediency. Nor do I think Shelley would have claimed to appropriate unconsciously. The precise development of the textual borrowings in *Alastor* suggests that Shelley deployed them for thematic purposes and as a depiction of the poetic mind in the process of assimilation. In the poem, the Poet and the Narrator are drawn as figures who are invested in different textual traditions and who are each associated with a distinct set of travel materials. The itineraries that the Poet is credited with selecting for himself demonstrate a commitment to classical texts, and the language used to describe the travels that he imaginatively undertakes early in the poem (ll. 106–28) are indebted to sources on the ancient world. As Frederic Colwell has argued, even the Poet's subsequent Asian itinerary, although described by the Narrator and through the lens of his more contemporary textual sources, is "ultimately derived from Shelley's study of the travels and conquests of Alexander the Great."[17] Meanwhile, as Nicholas Birns has noted, the Narrator's descriptions of the Poet's wanderings are consistently drawn from Romantic-period sources, primarily Jones, Morgan, and Southey. The result of these bifurcated investments is the development in the poem of two distinct characters, each engaged in negotiating the relationship between textual materials and their imaginative psychological absorption.

The Poet is the character in *Alastor* upon whom the narrative focuses, and his relationship to his travel sources and the error that results from his misplaced identification with them are the most fully developed allusions in the poem. His itinerary can be seen in two stages, both of which are drawn from classical travel texts and describe his efforts to recover the mental attitudes that gave birth to the geography of antiquity and, ultimately, to the veiled maiden of his reverie, and each itinerary is associated with a different set of textual sources. The Poet's initial youthful travel readings trace the history of human civilization, back through time, from Greece, to Lebanon, Jerusalem, and Babylon, to their source in Africa. His purpose here is the same accumulation of "moral, political, and historical wisdom" that Shelley later outlined in "The Defence of Poetry," and these texts reveal to him the "thrilling secrets of the birth of time" (l. 128), as represented primarily by Volney. Enamored of his private relationship to this knowledge, the Poet fails to recognize the Arab maiden or her passion for him, and leaves her and "Arabie" to extend his travels into Persia and the mountains of the Indian Caucasus. In the vale of Cashmire, he experiences the vision of the veiled maiden, and his search to recover her leads the Poet on his second itinerary, through the Caucasus, to the rock of Aornos, Bactria, Parthia, Nysa, and Choromasia, following the Oxus river into Hyrcanian and the Caspian Sea, in a voyage that, as Joseph Raban has observed, imitates precisely the itinerary of Alexander's Indian campaign, as it is represented in various classical travel sources, including Strabo's *Geography* and Quintus Curtius's *Vita Alexandrina*.[18]

Located at the rupture between these two itineraries, the vision of the veiled maiden is simultaneously an experience of assimilation and alienation that marks a transformation in the Poet's relationship to the material world and to his textual sources. At the same moment that she "fold[s] his frame in her dissolving arms" (l. 187), the landscape grows foreign, "cold," and "vacant" (ll. 193–95) to the Poet. Initially, the Poet could perceive the classical landscape of his youthful intellectual fancies as symbolic and sympathetic, in a way that the post-Alexandrian geography through which he pursues his vision is not. While in his mind "Dark Ætheopia in her desert hills / Conceals . . . / . . . . / The thrilling secrets of the birth of time" (ll. 115–28), the contemporary Choromasian shore that he experiences in his searches reflects a "blind earth, and heaven / That echoes not [his] thoughts" (ll. 289–90). A failure of identification with the material world (and, perhaps simultaneously, with his textual materials) is the initial consequence of his vision.

Knowledge, travels, and psychological identification emerge as central components of the Poet's visionary experience, and, if *Alastor* is read as an allegorical exploration of the Poet's failed effort to assimilate external knowledge into an understanding of human nature, then the point is that his particular error is qualitative. As Shelley's preface to *Alastor* explains, the poem essentially concerns a precise state of the human mind, in which the Poet attempts to move from the external world to internal relation. He has drunk "deep from the fountain of knowledge" (*PWS* 40) and is, at first, satisfied with knowing the "magnificence and beauty of the external world" (40), which the poem suggests he has garnered from various textual sources. The period eventually arrives when this no longer suffices; the Poet desires "intercourse with an intelligence similar to itself" (40), and he undertakes to reconcile this knowledge with the interiority of imaginative human experience. However, the ratio the Poet establishes between external and internal knowledge is fundamentally flawed, because he confuses self and community. He attempts to "exist without human sympathy" (40), imagining that the internal relation is private, so that "none feel with [him his] common nature" (40). While the intellect and imagination "have their respective requisitions on the sympathy of corresponding powers in other human beings" (40), the Poet attaches them to a "single image" that reflects only his own mind. The result is his inevitable failure as a poet and a failure to achieve the right *kind* of imaginative assimilation. Searching only for a private ratio between the self and the world, he perceives unsympathetic landscapes that become barren representations of his own failing poetic faculties.

If for Shelley the poetic task is to articulate the relationship between the operations of the (one) mind and its material productions, the *Alastor* Poet fails to find the proper ratio because he mistakes individualism for universal human nature. In this respect, the poem explores the dangers of unsuccessful assimilation, in which the Poet is limited by the apparently direct correspondence between materiality and his own intellectual powers. As a figure for his error, the illusory veiled maiden represents his investment in establishing a private ratio between the "real" world and the mind-in-creation: a ratio which, because private, is fundamentally opposed to poetry itself. In his subsequent wanderings, the Poet searches for the origins of his vision, which he rediscovers only with the realization that the material world is an expression of (collective) mental attitudes. Initially surrounded by a desolate and empty environment that images for him the alienation and solipsism of his intellectual disengagement from the human community, his isolation is complete.

Significantly, it is the Poet's passage through one of the mostly densely allusive sections of the poem (ll. 420–68) that finally returns him to a visionary state and leads him to the recognition of his error, and it is a place that is metaphorically and textually described by the Narrator in the language of Romantic Cashmire. Here, in the contemporary language of Morgan and Southey, the Narrator describes how the Poet is freed from his *alastor* with the recognition that the various features of this contemporary landscape also "have each their type in [him]" (l. 508). More importantly, the Poet articulates his awareness in this moment that the sympathetic landscape not only reflects his experience but also his mental attitudes. As an expression of the mind, the external world will function, he realizes, as the residence of his "living thoughts . . . when stretched / upon thy flowers [his] bloodless limbs shall waste" (ll. 512–13). Landscapes and other forms of materiality continue to represent the mental states out of which they were produced. Here are the beginnings of the ratio between external knowledge and the operations of the human mind, which Romantic poetry seeks to assimilate.

The Poet's success within *Alastor* is problematic, because he never establishes an analogy that connects this material knowledge with the human community he inhabits; in the end, "He lived, he died, he sung, in solitude" (l. 60). At the same time, however, his recognition that geography and the other forms of material knowledge are psychological representations of human imaginings permits a degree of sympathetic association that is not limited by temporal boundaries. If the Poet's journey through his textual sources produces any knowledge, it is simply his developing awareness that the material world reflects his mental attitudes, and the familiar language of exploration writing that Shelley deploys functions as a shorthand representation of psychological and cultural reality. Documented within travel accounts are the remnants of the states of mind that produced these cultures and their conflicts. While the Poet's engagement with his classical travel sources operates as a figure for his relationship to the constructions of material and historical knowledge, the "Shelleyean" Narrator's textual allusions to contemporary Romantic-period landscapes are employed, in contrast, to depict a more appropriate means of investigating the mental operations of his age. In an effort to find the analogy between the contemporary "materials" of Eastern geography and self-knowledge, the Narrator of *Alastor* attempts to picture the psychological experience of assimilation, and, to the extent that the result is poetry, he succeeds where the poem's Poet failed. Dramatizing the dangers of the wrong kind of textual appropriation, *Alastor* explores the central importance of borrowing and textual "sympathy" within Shelley's definitions of poetry.

While the Narrator is associated with the Shelleyean values articulated in the preface to the poem, the Poet and his errors are part of a pointed critique of Wordsworth. This poem about assimilation and the poet's relationship to the human community is also a text that engages directly with questions of Romantic-period aesthetics and with its literary combats. Poetic failure is, after all, the result of the Poet's inability to distinguish between universal and private models of assimilation, and in *Alastor* this error is linked with Wordsworthian sensibilities and, particularly, with the figure of the Wanderer in the first book of *The Excursion* (1814). Wordsworth had aligned the voice of the Wanderer with his poetic identity in his preface to *The Excursion*, and Shelley emphasized these associations in the introductory remarks that accompanied *Alastor*. Quoting a passage spoken by the Wanderer, Shelley called attention to Wordsworth's own distinction between "[t]he good [who] die first, / And those whose hearts are dry as summer's dust [and] burn to the socket!" (*PWS* 41), and his implication here is that the youthful Poet described in *Alastor*, despite his failings, "perish[ed] through . . . intensity and passion," unlike the ancient Wordsworthian

Wanderer (or, indeed, the aging Wordsworth), whose sympathies remained "aloof" and disciplined. While the *Alastor* Poet failed in his efforts at assimilation, his keen sensibilities and open heart rendered him unable to endure the isolation and solipsism that he created for himself. The same, Shelley suggests, is not true of other failed poets.

The allusions to Wordsworth resonate throughout *Alastor*, and textual borrowings from Wordsworth's language are evident in the opening and concluding passages of the poem. As Ratomir Rastic has observed, "Echoes of Wordsworth are heard throughout the poem. . . . The first fifty lines are an invocation . . . which is Promethean in manner but continues in a tone which is recognizably Wordsworthian" and which borrows from both *The Excursion* and "Tintern Abbey."[19] Likewise, the final lines of the poem ventriloquize Wordsworth, even while placing memorable borrowed phrases from his verse in quotations. The rhetorical point of these associations is to suggest that, like the *Alastor* Poet, Wordsworth's error was to see the landscape only as a reflection of the self. Yet, unlike the Poet, Wordsworth has felt deeply neither his error nor his isolation; he remains, as it were, enamored of his own private illusion of community. As a figuration of the Poet's error, the veiled maiden becomes an image for what Keats called the "egotistical" sublime and for Wordsworth's desire to establish an exclusive and private ratio between the individual mind and the productions of material reality and for his failure to assimilate knowledge into understanding. At the heart of Shelley's critique of Wordsworth, then, is the importance of assimilation and of the poet's relationship to the texts of his literary contemporaries. The implication is that Wordsworth's refusal to engage with the sources of the material conditions of his era represents a larger refusal of community and of the poet's cultural responsibilities. Lacking or perhaps simply rejecting the "powers of assimilating," Wordsworth remains alternately associated either with the external materials of life (as Coleridge characterized it, his "matter-of-fact[ness]") or with the private solipsism that results from the misguided identification with them. At the same time, drawing from the language of Wordsworth's verse, Shelley performs both a metaphorical and textually concrete assimilation of the elder poet's work, in which he undertakes to reveal the internal operations of the mind that it and the other contemporary texts of the era can and should reflect.

Thus, while Shelley often articulated anxiety over issues of borrowing and over potential charges of plagiarism, he remained invested in strategies of assimilation and in the central importance of this activity to the poetic effort. Perhaps because Shelley developed an abstract and philosophical po-

sition regarding the necessity of appropriating from the texts of other writers, he was particularly attentive to the ways in which his borrowed
materials were reemployed, and he was more likely than many of his contemporaries to alert his readers to correspondences. Yet, despite his success
in avoiding charges of plagiarism, Shelley is important for understanding
the constructions of literary property and attitudes toward borrowing during the period. Like Wordsworth, Byron, and Coleridge, he understood
matters of subjectivity and psychology—rather than matters of linguistic
uniqueness—as central to judgments of plagiarism and to the aesthetic objectives of Romantic verse.

Chapter 6
Poaching on the Literary Estate: Class, Improvement, and Enclosure

In an 1817 letter, William Wordsworth wrote to his correspondent Henry Crabb Robinson that Lord Byron "ha[d] been poaching on my Manor" in *Childe Harold's Pilgrimage* (*LWDW* 3: 394), and Wordsworth's metaphor merits further consideration for what it implies about the relationship among literary property, professional authorship, and social class. The class inversion Wordsworth's statement performs is striking: here the professional Wordsworth casts himself as the lord of the literary estate and charges the aristocratic Byron with crass appropriations that are figuratively beyond the pale. While Wordsworth intended his remark dismissively and even sardonically, it nevertheless encapsulates significant elements of Romantic-period attitudes toward plagiarism and the metaphorical nexus that defined its relationship to class privilege. As I have argued throughout this study, the rhetoric of plagiarism during the Romantic period frequently mirrored broader social and legal contexts, and Wordsworth's characterization of his poetical productions as a simultaneously landed and literary "estate" evokes a more general set of associations that operated in the early nineteenth century to connect intellectual property and real property.

It is not surprising that literary plagiarism during the Romantic period drew some of its characteristic metaphors from the cultural discourse surrounding real estate and, particularly, the enclosures of the late eighteenth century. Throughout the eighteenth century, associations between land ownership and literary production had been part of the public controversy regarding copyright, and intellectual property had been compared to real estate at least since Locke's second *Treatise on Government* at the end of the seventeenth century.[1] This controversy and many of its central metaphors had been recalled to public attention in 1814 with the passage of the Copyright Act, which confirmed *Donaldson v. Beckett*. At the same time, the status of real property and public rights of access to it were in transition during the eighteenth and early nineteenth centuries, owing in large part to the rise of parliamentary enclosure in Britain's rural areas. During the period, some four thousand private bills were passed authorizing the enclosure of hitherto common lands into personal estates, leading the government to standardize the process in the Inclosure Consolidation Act of 1801. In addition to ending the rights of common that had often sustained the rural poor, the enclosure of these areas had additional cultural implications. The period saw the consolidation of agricultural and timber-lands to the extent that, according to one estimate, "By 1800 perhaps as little as 15 percent of the land of England [remained] in the hands of small proprietors."[2] The addition of enclosed acreage to large estates in turn encouraged the fashion for aesthetic landscape parks, which spread throughout Britain from 1760 to 1840, giving rise to a new class of rural professionals such as gardeners and surveyors (Williamson and Bellamy 150).[3] Perhaps most importantly for the poor and for the yeomanry, enclosure led to increasingly restrictive laws regulating hunting, poaching, forage, and the destruction of grazing wildlife. In light of these intersecting social contexts, it was perhaps inevitable that debates surrounding literary ownership and the enclosures would mobilize a shared set of discursive strategies. At stake in each situation was, finally, the same concern: how to regulate and to restrict public access to newly constructed private property, intellectual or real.

Wordsworth's characterization of his literary property as a manor and of Byron's obligations as poaching directly engages the metaphors associating artistic productions with real estate and feudal privilege, and in doing so Wordsworth was reflecting a broader cultural attitude that connected writing with other forms of enclosure, improvement, and appropriation. This same parallel is seen frequently in contemporary texts dealing with landscape aesthetics and the picturesque effects of enclosure, a discourse in which Wordsworth, like many of his contemporaries, was particularly invested. Timothy Brownlow, for example, has observed this metaphorical nexus connecting the picturesque with the literary "estate" in the works of both the novelist Thomas Love Peacock and the garden designer Capability Brown. Writing to the author Hannah More, Brown had described his efforts to shape and to enclose the picturesque landscape in literary terms, comparing his alterations to punctuation.[4] Later, Peacock satirized Brown and his colleague Humphrey Repton using a similar metaphor, writing in his roman à clef, *Headlong Hall* (1816): "[Y]our improved places, as you call them . . . are nothing but big bowling-greens, like sheets of green paper, with a parcel of round clumps scattered over them like so many spots of ink, flicked at random out of a pen."[5] The language of landscape designers frequently cast modifications in terms of "appropriation" or "improvement," and topographical poetry of the eighteenth century employed conventions drawn from the surveying activities associated with the process of enclosure (Brownlow 17).

For Wordsworth, these metaphorical associations among literary ownership, real estate, and, ultimately, class privilege shaped his attitude toward plagiarism in characteristic ways. Thomas Pfau has argued in *Wordsworth's Profession: Form, Class, and the Logic of Early Romantic Cultural Production* that Wordsworth's primary investment as a writer was in the figurative "estate" represented by the tradition of the picturesque, and certainly these parallels between enclosure and landscape aesthetics support Pfau's reading, which proposes that "[f]or William Wordsworth to write and publish [was to] stake out his professional claims in the imaginary estate of the Picturesque . . . reproduc[ing] to a large extent the very historical mode of production."[6] I would like to explore more fully the particular reasons for and consequences of the estate metaphor as it influenced both Wordsworth's articulation of literary property and the charges of plagiarism related to his work. In the end, this metaphor cannot be disassociated from the idea of poetic labor and the category of "improvement" to which Wordsworth frequently returns, a category that was deeply complicated for Wordsworth and for other Romantic-period writers by the question of satire.

Poetical Labor in *The Lyrical Ballads*

Throughout his career, Wordsworth understood his poetic productions in terms of comparisons to working the land and to the landscape. As early as 1792, Wordsworth had associated his productions with a cottager's labors, writing to his fellow poet Matthew Williams, "The field of Letters is very extensive, and it is astonishing if we cannot find some little corner, which with a little tillage will produce us enough for the necessities, nay even the comforts, of life" (*LWDW* 1: 76). By 1817 he was confident enough of his status as a poet to declare his works a "Manor," but the prevailing metaphor remained the same: Wordsworth imagined his literary productions as an estate appropriated to private use by his mental labors. His concern for trespass against the literary property represented by *The Lyrical Ballads*

(1798) was particularly intense, and, as I suggest in Chapter 3, the volume's status as literary property is complicated by the vernacular rhetoric and the authors' engagement with the folk-ballad tradition. Wordsworth, however, most often treated the volume as a textual object within a traditional print culture and alleged plagiarisms from the volume on numerous occasions and at different points in his professional career, suggesting that, despite (or perhaps because of) the collaborative and jointly authored nature of the work, the ownership of these poems was an abiding concern.[7] The language that Wordsworth uses to bring charges of plagiarism against other writers reflects his own investment in developing the metaphor of the literary estate and testifies to how well known the standards of early nineteenth-century plagiarism were to his contemporaries, especially the standards of improvement and consciousness. At the same time, the satirical or otherwise critical nature of many of the texts in which Wordsworth locates these obligations also demonstrates the extent of the Romantic-period literary devaluation of satirical genres, which were frequently charged with aesthetic plagiarisms on the grounds that they did not improve upon their original texts.

The first example of plagiarism from *The Lyrical Ballads* engages directly this issue of satire. The Romantic-period attitude toward plagiarism was distinct from the eighteenth-century neoclassical attitude particularly in relation to the question of satire, and the renewed interest in charges of plagiarism in the 1770s and 1780s overlaps historically with the critical devaluation of the genre during those decades. Perhaps more importantly, as Steve Jones argues in *Satire and Romanticism*, "satire [emerges] as a negative standard for the construction of canonical Romanticism" (16), and this is certainly the case for Wordsworth.[8] As Jones observes, "Wordsworth implies an important definition of 'Poetry' . . . as the opposite of 'satire'" (15). In fact, Wordsworth viewed satire as failed poetry, and as a result he was particularly angered by the assimilation of his works into satirical texts. For Wordsworth this represented not just a theft but also the degeneration of his poetry. This concern was at the heart of his anger over Byron's "plagiarisms" in *Childe Harold's Pilgrimage* and *Don Juan*, and it was also Wordsworth's central complaint against Peter Bayley, whom Wordsworth accused of plagiarizing from *The Lyrical Ballads* in his satirical *Poems* (1803).

Wordsworth's outrage over the publication of Peter Bayley's collection suggests that satirical texts were not given additional license to borrow and were, in fact, held to a standard of improvement that all but demanded that they be judged as literary failures and aesthetic plagiarisms. Although Wordsworth recognized the intentions of Bayley's volume as satirical, he also charged the poet with plagiarism in a long letter to Thomas De-Quincey, dated 6 March 1804:

> I cannot forbear mentioning to you the way in which a wretched creature of the name Peter Bailey has lately treated the author of your favourite book, the "Lyrical Ballads." After pillaging them in a style of plagiarism, I believe unexampled in the history of modern literature, the wretch has had the baseness to write a long poem in ridicule of them, chiefly of *The Idiot Boy*; and, not content with this, in a note annexed to the same poem, has spoken of me, *by name*, as the *simplest*, i.e. the most contemptible of all the poets! The complicated baseness of this (for the plagiarisms are absolutely by wholesale) grieved me to the heart. . . . If this unhappy creature's volumes should ever fall your way, you will find the plagiarisms chiefly in two poems, one entitled *Evening in the Vale of Festiniog*, which is a wretched parody of *Tintern Abbey*, and the other *The Ivy Seat*, also *The Truest Fay*, and some others. (*LWDW* 1: 455)

Rather than viewing the borrowings as a function of Bayley's satirical intent, Wordsworth insists on identifying each as a separate form of abuse, and his recognition of the satire does not mitigate charges of plagiarism. Romantic-period satirists, of course, were generally understood to be innocent of culpable plagiarism insofar as their entire objective was to target familiar works; there is little cultural purchase in mocking a text that readers do not recognize, and Wordsworth assumes that his readers will understand Bayley's poems as conscious parodies of *The Lyrical Ballads*. However, because satire does not typically undertake the improvement of its subject as an objective, authors working in this genre were almost certain to fail to improve upon their borrowed materials and, hence, to commit aesthetic plagiarism. Just as Wordsworth had also charged Byron with "spoiling" "Tintern Abbey" in his transmission of it, his claim that Bayley has plagiarized is necessarily based on the judgment of improvement. In the terms proposed by Gérard Gennette in his study of satire in *Palimpsestes: La littérature au deuxieme degré*, we might say that Wordsworth and his contemporaries did not perceive a clear distinction between the hypertextual and the simply intertextual. While satire and parody, as hypertextual relations, assume a transformative and dialogical relationship between texts, plagiarism represents simply the least legitimate form of intertextual incorporation.[9] Wordsworth at any rate did not consider Bayley's poems to have transformed or "improved" upon his work despite the satirical objectives, and he evaluated these appropriations as he would have evaluated any unacknowledged literary obligations.

The already "complicated baseness" with which Wordsworth charges

Bayley is further obscured by the fact that Bayley's borrowings—although in Wordsworth's mind "wholesale"—are not word-for-word. These represent, instead, an example of borrowings in tone, style, and spirit. "Evening in the Vale of Festiniog" imitates the sentiment, meter, tone, and vocabulary of "Tintern Abbey" but not the poem's phrasing. There is no passage in "Tintern Abbey" corresponding to lines such as Bayley's

Then hie thee to the fields, and let the warmth
And vital spirit that is interfused
And poured into thy bosom by the taste
Of Nature, and her soul-subduing voice,
Thaw thy congealed affections. (ll. 213–17)

Yet, the lines are recognizably Wordsworthian. In terms of Romantic-period plagiarism, there was no significant distinction between Wordsworthian and Wordsworth's. Authorial voice and narrative mastery operated throughout the period as elements of intellectual property, and, where satire revealed the presence of a second author, it engaged in practices that were frequently derided as plagiarism. As Peter Murphy has observed in his analysis of James Hogg's later verse parodies of Wordsworth, two questions are at stake in contemporary evaluations of borrowings of this sort, namely, "Can voice be stolen, as Hogg perpetually denies and asserts? [And, in] written culture, what belongs to the self, and what to others?" (*Poetry* 133). Hogg's ambivalence and the discourse of Romantic-period plagiarism more generally attest to the complicated ways in which satire disrupted familiar attitudes toward literary property and plagiarism.

Wordsworth's concern with appropriation from *The Lyrical Ballads* was extended in the revised edition of the poems, published in 1815. In his "Essay Supplementary to the Preface," Wordsworth again directly addresses the issue of plagiarism, and he returns to the subject as part of a larger effort to call to public attention the tendency of popular poets to draw from their more obscure predecessors. In the "Essay Supplementary," Wordsworth is careful to emphasize the unconscious and, therefore, aesthetic nature of these appropriations, a gesture that places his discussion within a discourse of literary property that was familiar to contemporary readers.[10] Written in the context of his disappointed expectations regarding *The Excursion* (1814), another early poem about which he had particular appropriation anxieties, Wordsworth distinguishes in the "Essay Supplementary" between two classes of poetry: works that are popular but unworthy and those that languish in obscurity despite their merits. In the essay, he offers James Macpherson's *The Poems of Ossian* (1796) as an example of the former, writing:

In Macpherson's work. . . . every thing (that is not stolen) is [spurious.] Mr. Malcolm Laing has ably shown that the diction of this pretended translation is a motley assemblage from all quarters; but he is so fond of making out parallel passages as to call poor Macpherson to account for his *"ands"* and his *"buts!"* and he has weakened his argument by conducting it as if he thought that every striking resemblance was a *conscious* plagiarism. It is enough that there are coincidences too remarkable for its being probable or possible that they could arise in different minds without communication between them. Now as the Translators of the Bible, and Shakespeare, Milton, and Pope, could not be indebted to Macpherson, it follows that he must have owed his fine feathers of them. (*PWWW* 3: 77–78)

This passage is interesting in several respects. Wordsworth's reference to Macpherson's text as a translation (*albeit* a "pretended" one) suggests that, in respect to charges of plagiarism, works of translation were subject to the same standards of evaluation as any literary text. Wordsworth also develops in this passage an early version of the poaching metaphor that he would apply to Byron two years later, casting some poets as plucked and plundered game and others as likely to line their nests with the "feathers" of their neighbors. Perhaps most importantly, however, Wordsworth recalls the central elements of Romantic-period evaluations of appropriation by emphasizing throughout this commentary questions of coincidence and, especially, of consciousness, which David McCracken has argued was the critical factor for the poet in issues of plagiarism ("Human Wishes" 392). Wordsworth suggests that Macpherson cannot be held to account for "conscious plagiarism" or for a culpable theft, while asserting that a real obligation nevertheless exists. To Wordsworth's mind, Macpherson is guilty, of course, of aesthetic plagiarism, and the grounds once again return to the judgment of improvement: Wordsworth describes Macpherson's work as a "motley assemblage," recalling the unassimilated, "monstrous," or "patchwork" language used to describe unimproved texts.

Wordsworth's larger argument in the "Essay Supplementary" concerns the caprices of popular reception and "the slow progress of . . . fame" (*PWWW* 3: 71), and his point about plagiarism and imitation is that they can impede the processes through which great authors are recognized by the public. Wordsworth proposes that, because they must "creat[e] the taste by which [they are] to be enjoyed" (80), great authors are very often not appreciated during their own era. At the same time, many inferior writers enjoy a period of celebrity and immediate commercial success. The poems of Milton, he observes, languished in obscurity for several generations after their initial publication, and Shakespeare was eclipsed in his time by the popularity of Beaumont and Fletcher (70). The danger of plagiarism is that, when a lesser but popular writer borrows from an unrecognized genius, the public may become confused about the direction of influence and fail to credit the original author, and the slow process of fame may be retarded further or interrupted entirely. Wordsworth offers the discussion of Macpherson as an example. Macpherson had borrowed from Milton and Shakespeare, and, because these writers had finally gained the audience that their works merited, his obligations had been recognized. However, had the popular Macpherson been a historical contemporary of either writer, Wordsworth suspects that it is far less likely that the path of influence would have been apparent, and Macpherson might well have been credited with the originality that was, in fact, borrowed. Of course, Wordsworth's real concern here is not for Milton or Shakespeare. It is for the reception of *The Lyrical Ballads* and for his own reputation as an author. In the "Essay Supplementary," Wordsworth directly asserts his confidence in the aesthetic merits of *The Lyrical Ballads* and dismisses the negative critical reception the volume received from contemporary reading audiences. However, despite his expectations that *The Lyrical Ballads*, as one of those unrecognized works of genius, will in time enjoy the reputation and readership that it deserves, there is some anxiety for the present. Already Wordsworth perceived around him the influence of his poems on the literature of his time, but he found it reflected, without acknowledgment, in the works of his more popular literary contemporaries.

Wordsworth was concerned that the recognition of *The Lyrical Ballads* as original and its slow path to fame would be undermined by confusion regarding the direction of influence, and his anxiety in this regard undoubtedly owed something to the situation in which Coleridge found himself circa 1815. Although not printed as part of *The Lyrical Ballads*, *Christabel* had been composed during the initial period of collaboration that led to the jointly authored 1798 edition, and Coleridge had hoped to include the poem in the revised 1800 edition. In 1815 Coleridge finally was preparing the poem for publication in an independent volume, and, as we have seen, he anticipated that *Christabel's* influence on his literary contemporaries would be misunderstood as plagiarism on his part. Coleridge's dilemma and the critical reception of *Christabel* resonated privately with Wordsworth's fears regarding appropriation from his work, particularly by more celebrated colleagues. Wordsworth had foreseen trouble for Coleridge's poem as early as 1805, the year after he had discovered Bayley's plagiarisms from his works in *The Lyrical Ballads*, and his concerns were addressed specifically to the questions of originality and reception. Dorothy Wordsworth also had anticipated Coleridge's inevitable predicament in a letter written to Lady Beaumont on 27 October 1805:

The resemblance between certain parts of the Lay of the last Minstrel and Christabel must strike everyone acquainted with the two poems, and I fear it is to be accounted for by Mr Scotts having heard Christabel repeated more than once. I believe that he is entirely unconscious of the imitation. . . . We were struck with the resemblance yet we were both equally convinced from the frankness of Walter Scott's manner that it was an unconscious imitation. . . . For my part I do not think the Imitations are of so much importance, Coleridge's poem bearing upon its face so bold a character of originality, but my Brother and Sister think that the Lay being published first it will tarnish the freshness of Christabel and considerably injure the first effect of it. At any rate, this circumstance shews how cautious poets ought to be in lending their manuscripts, or even *reading* them to Authors. If they came refreshed out of the Imitator's brain it would not be so grievous, but they are in general like faded impressions, or as the wrong side of a piece of Tapestry to the right. (*LWDW* 1: 632–33)

These concerns that Scott's borrowings would "tarnish" the original effect of *Christabel* and "injure" its reputation presage the anxiety that Wordsworth came to have about the reception of *The Lyrical Ballads*. While Dorothy was confident that readers would recognize the merits of *Christabel*, William expected that the critical recognition of the poem would be delayed by the overshadowing presence of Scott and his imitations of it, and Dorothy testifies to the abiding perception in the Wordsworth household that imitation degrades the original text and harms its reputation. However, while the terms of the argument are cast as a matter of improvement, the stakes for Wordsworth in questions of plagiarism focused on the problem posed by the relative unfamiliarity of his work. As Wordsworth's friend and advocate Henry Taylor argued in his essay on the subject of plagiarism, where there was either improvement or familiarity there could be no harm to the original author; Wordsworth's concern was that improvements might harm him precisely because the poems had not received the critical or popular reception that they deserved.

At the same time, it is worth reiterating a point developed in the first chapter of this book and at other points in the course of my argument regarding the ways in which the term *originality* was understood to operate in the late eighteenth and early nineteenth centuries. Contemporary evidence and a careful reading of important proto-Romantic texts such as Edward Young's *Conjectures on Original Composition* reveal a distinction between obligations to general and particular elements of a literary work. Romantic-period writers and their critics did not, in fact, insist on the impossible goal of ex nihilo creation that has often been attributed to them, and originality in the early nineteenth century did not preclude the possibility of borrowings—even extensive ones. In his very fine study *Romantic Poets and the Culture of Posterity*, Andrew Bennett writes, "Romantic theories of poetry produce an absolute and non-negotiable opposition between writing which is original, new, revolutionary, writing which breaks with the past and appeals to the future, and writing which is conventional, derivative, a copy or simulation of earlier work, writing which has an immediate appeal and an in-built redundancy. The sign of the great poem, then, is originality" (3). While originality was indeed espoused as a sign of genius and aesthetic merit in the period, the opposition between invention and imitation is not nearly so absolute as the critical history of Romanticism has often assumed. Indeed, it was the subject of constant and often controversial negotiation, as writers attempted to distinguish between the universal elements of aesthetics and the individual qualities grounded in authorial personality or creativity.

Textual Enclosure in *The Excursion*

While Wordsworth's early concerns about the appropriation of his work centered on the critical legacy of *The Lyrical Ballads*, his 1815 "Essay Supplementary to the Preface" was also composed in the context of his disappointed expectations regarding the public reception of the poem that he considered his major accomplishment to date, *The Excursion* (1814). As a poem focused in large part on the relationship among landscape, class, and the poetic tradition, *The Excursion* engages at the level of metaphor many of the issues central to Wordsworth's attitude toward literary ownership and inheritance. Perhaps because of this emphasis, *The Excursion* was a poem about which Wordsworth had considerable appropriation anxieties. This is especially true for the first book of the poem, which was simultaneously the most densely intertextual section of his narrative and the portion that Wordsworth perceived as most openly plagiarized by other writers.

In 1829 Wordsworth charged his literary contemporary John Wilson with plagiarisms from book 1 of *The Excursion*, an accusation that reflects his persistent dismissal of conscious appropriations such as satire. Writing to Henry Crabb Robinson on 27 January, Wordsworth complained of Wilson, "He is a perverse Mortal,—not to say worse of him. Have you peeped into his Trials of Margaret Lyndsay—you will see to what extent he has played the Plagiarist—with the very tale of Margaret in the Excursion, which he abuses" (*LWDW* 5: 17). Wordsworth alludes here to Wilson's 1823 novel *The Trials of Margaret Lyndsay* and to the more recent "abuse" of *The Excursion* that Wilson had published in an article for *Blackwood's Magazine* in 1828.[11] The correspondences between Wordsworth's poem and Wilson's novel are no longer immediately apparent and are limited to similarities in the heroine's given name, her humble social origins, and her distress at the desertion of a husband. From a historical distance, it is sometimes difficult to determine whether Wilson had Wordsworth's poem in mind or not. Wordsworth, however, considered that he did, a perception encouraged by Wilson's subsequent negative commentary on *The Excursion*, which characterized the poem as irreligious. Wordsworth likely understood *The Trials of Margaret Lyndsay* as a narrative expansion upon the tale of Margaret, in which Wilson, with a gentle satire, corrected the religious and moral shortcomings of Wordsworth's poem, and Wordsworth understood the novel as a didactical attempt to engage with his work and to critique it. Readers, one must assume, were meant to recognize the connections between the two works and to compare their value critically. For Wordsworth, Wilson's engagement represented a conscious appropriation from his poetry, and he responded to it in much the same way that he had responded to Bayley's satirical rewriting of *The Lyrical Ballads*: by charging the author with baseness, perversity, and plagiarism.

What seemed perverse to Wordsworth was that a writer should borrow from a work as a mode of criticism, satirical or otherwise, and this was a perspective shaped by Romantic-period attitudes toward aesthetic plagiarism and particularly toward the category of improvement. Early nineteenth-century conventions held that, in evaluating questions of appropriation, a writer was free to imitate insofar as he or she had selected good models and had improved upon them. To select what one believed was a bad model and to debase it was madness, and the consequences were charges of aesthetic plagiarism and literary failure. Indeed, part of the perversity was that such works were not literary at all: to engage with the text of another writer for purposes that were simply satirical or didactic was to write criticism in the guise of art. Implied distinctions between aesthetic and critical categories were at the heart of both Wordsworth's charge of plagiarism in this instance and his irritation.

At the same time, Wordsworth also had particular reasons for being sensitive to appropriations from the first book of *The Excursion*. He had been similarly anxious about borrowings from *The Lyrical Ballads*. Not only did the publication of *The Excursion* in 1814 coincide roughly with the revised edition of *The Lyrical Ballads* in 1815 but the first book of *The Excursion*, completed independently in manuscript under the title "The Ruined Cottage," also had been composed in 1798, during the same annus mirabilis that marked the most productive period of his collaboration with Coleridge. By the late 1820s, the period of his charges against Wilson, Wordsworth's concern for the value and protection of his intellectual property and personal reputation as a poet had become intense, but his concern was not unconnected to the failed collaborative relationship that Wordsworth and Coleridge shared and which marked the origins of the poems associated with *The Lyrical Ballads* as a reciprocal effort at what Coleridge called ventriloquism—the throwing of one's voice into a corpus inhabited by the consciousness of another.

Wordsworth's investment in his literary possession of the first book of *The Excursion* may also stem from the poem's symbolic engagement with themes of landscape, class, ownership, and a literary tradition that is simultaneously vernacular and textual. That the first book of *The Excursion* addresses the relationship between the rural landscape and the social and economic distinctions of class is, of course, a truism. Like many of Wordsworth's early poems, including many published in *The Lyrical Ballads*, its central narrative focuses on the lives of cottagers and the common folk, whose experiences and vernacular expressions were closely tied to the local landscape and represent part of the common oral tradition that Wordsworth and Coleridge set out to reinvigorate (and to appropriate) in *The Lyrical Ballads*. Indeed, the first book of *The Excursion* develops a complex set of relations among rural figures, oral poetry, and the repossession of the landscape that parallel Wordsworth's reflections on literary property as a form of enclosure. Wordsworth's figure of the "Wanderer" is, after all, specifically characterized as one of the many "Poets that are sown / By Nature; men endowed with highest gifts, / The vision the faculty divine; / . . . . . / . . . [who] live out their time, / Husbanding that which they possess within" (ll. 77–90).[12] These lines evoke the common eighteenth-century figure of the natural genius, but Wordsworth also specifically compares poetic genius with the cultivation and "husbandry" of an agricultural landscape. Later this same metaphor is repeated and extended, and poetry is compared not simply to the cultivation of the landscape but also, in the description of the enclosed bower on the "Common" that was Margaret's cottage garden, to the possession and shaping of it. As the Wanderer explains, landscapes become sympathetic monuments to the human lives that inhabit them, and poetry is frequently an effort to recover the "bond of brotherhood" (ll. 486–87) that is broken by death. He reflects:

> . . . that which each man loved
> And prized in his peculiar nook of earth
> Dies with him, or is changed . . .
> . . . .
> The Poets, in their elegies and songs,
> Lamenting the departed, call the groves,
> They call upon the hills and streams to mourn,
> And senseless rocks; nor idly; for they speak;
> In these their invocations, with a voice
> Obedient to the strong creative power (ll. 471–80)

While the individual landscape of "peculiar nook[s]" fails to monumentalize the individual life, poetry's invocation of nature's own "strong creative power" functions as a means of preserving human presence in and possession of the natural world. Poetry, thus, becomes a way of possessing and marking off as private particular aspects of a landscape, and within the poem this enclosure is performed by the oral work of laboring-class figures such as the Wanderer and Margaret, who maintain a more intimate relationship to the natural world. Rhetorically, Wordsworth identifies his poetic voice with these rural-class figures, going so far as to claim in his introduction to *The Excursion* that he might have chosen the life of a peddler for himself, and the suggestion is that, at least at the level of metaphor, Wordsworth privileged the Wanderer's vernacular ability to enclose a part of the common landscape as private through the infusion of subjectivity.

If the possession of poetry becomes a symbolic possession of the landscape in book 1 of *The Excursion*, the narrative also performs a more literal appropriation of the tradition of landscape poetry that is classed in a different manner. As other critics have demonstrated, in the first book of *The Excursion* Wordsworth drew from several seventeenth- and eighteenth-century pastoral texts and often incorporated images or passages that were indebted to works such as Milton's *Paradise Lost* (1667) and "Il Pensoroso" (1633), Thomson's *The Seasons* (1744), and—despite Wordsworth's condemnation of Gray as a plagiarist—even the "Elegy Written in a Country Churchyard" (1751).[13] David Reid has noted the extended parallels between lines 432–68 of Thomson's *Summer* and lines 1–32 of the first book of *The Excursion*, and he has called to our attention examples of "Miltonisings" throughout the book.[14] The editorial endeavors of DeSelincourt, Darbishire, and Haydn have uncovered additional obligations to a wide range of landscape poets, and even Wordsworth's description of the Wanderer as an unsung rural poet (ll. 77–91), tutored by volumes of Milton's verse (l. 250), recalls, of course, the mute and inglorious Milton of Gray's "Elegy."[15] In short, Wordsworth's text performs the poetic possession of the monumentalized landscape and of the literary tradition.

This is not to suggest that Wordsworth was guilty of plagiarism in assimilating from the poetic tradition in *The Excursion*; contemporary charges were never made against him on account of these particular obligations. However, the densely allusive nature of the first book of *The Excursion* and the poem's metaphoric representations of poetry as a means of enclosing, demarcating, and preserving an imaginative landscape had class implications for the poet. As Tim Fulford argues in *Landscape, Liberty, and Authority*, this "absorption of past poetry aligned Wordsworth with the gentlemanly class" (159) associated with a consciously literary tradition.[16] In *Cultural Capital*, John Guillory goes further to suggest that the idea of a common, vernacular literary tradition functioned as part of a bourgeois ideology even for eighteenth-century locodescriptive poets such as Gray, and he reiterates John Barrell's observation that the "gentleman . . . was believe to be the only member of society who spoke a language universally intelligible; his usage was 'common' in the sense of being neither a local dialect nor infected by the terms of any particular art" (97, quoting Barrell 34). In *The Excursion*, as in *The Lyrical Ballads*, the poetic self-identification with the language of the "common man" is, then, a means of transforming the appropriation of a putatively vernacular peasant folk tradition into a marker of social ascendancy. Moreover, Wordsworth's emphasis in *The Excursion* on the oral mode of poetic transmission, figured by Margaret and the Wanderer and associated with Wordsworth's own aesthetic identification in the preface, may also represent a way of distancing himself from and presenting as common cultural property his borrowings in the poem from familiar pastoral verse. Oral materials did not have the same rights to literary property in a print culture as texts did, and, by casting his rural characters as peasant poets within the narrative, he allows them to perform the appropriation of a literary tradition that troubled him in regard to work authored in his own persona. In short, the relationship between the literary assimilation of a shared past in *The Excursion* and the complex social and cultural registers in which it signified likely informed Wordsworth's sensitivity to appropriation from the work.

While *The Excursion* dramatizes Wordsworth's engagement with property and poetic tradition, the work was subject to charges of plagiarism during the 1830s. Although the poem works closely with texts by Milton, Shakespeare, Gray, and Thomson, Wordsworth was not censured for his reliance upon these earlier writers, likely because they were so familiar to early nineteenth-century readers. Rather, Wordsworth was accused in the periodical press of having plagiarized from his literary contemporary and early advocate Walter Savage Landor. To a modern eye, the obligations are slight, and the charge initially appears capricious. However, Wordsworth's readers acknowledged his obligations as real, even while they defended his improvements, and these charges were understood as part and parcel of the sustained aesthetic attack on Wordsworth that had begun with the publication of *The Excursion* in 1814. The sensitivity of Wordsworth and his immediate circle to these allegations, coming just at the moment in the mid-1830s when his reputation as an author was beginning to seem secure, once again suggests that the stakes in matters of plagiarism were literary and critical.

Landor leveled charges of plagiarism against Wordsworth in a series of satirical works of criticism that he published during the 1830s and 1840s, and in bringing these accusations Landor was engaging Wordsworth in an open literary combat. While Landor had been an early supporter of Wordsworth, he was affronted by the arrogance that he perceived had accompanied Wordsworth's rise to public prominence. He was particularly outraged by reports that Wordsworth had denigrated at a public gathering the poetry of another of his early advocates, Robert Southey. Landor retorted by launching a critical attack upon Wordsworth, targeting the poet particularly in his *Satire upon Satirists* (1836) and castigating Wordsworth for failing to acknowledge his obligations to literary contemporaries. Constructed as an extended poetical satire on contemporary criticism, Grub Street, and the periodical reviews, the *Satire upon Satirists* pointedly advised Wordsworth to be less parsimonious in his judgment of other poets, and Landor engaged the rhetoric of class in order to convey his point about plagiarism and influence. Directly addressing the poet, Landor writes:

Now Wordsworth! lest we never meet again,
Write, on the prose-side tablet of thy brain,

A worldly counsel to a worldly mind,
And grow less captious if thou grow less kind.
Leave Moore, sad torturer of the virgin breast,
One lyre for beauty, one for the opprest:
Leave Campbell Wyoming's deserted farms
And Hohenlinden's trumpet-tongued alarms.
Permit us to be pleased, or even try to please,
. . . .
Tho' Southey's poetry to thee would seem
Not worth five shillings (such thy phrase) the ream,
Courage! good wary Wordsworth! and disburse
The whole amount from that prudential purse.
. . . .
We, who love order, yield our betters place
With duteous zeal, and, if we can, with grace.
Roderick, Kehama, Thalaba, belong
To mightier movers of majestick song.
To such as these we give, by just controul,
Not five shillings, but our heart and soul.
Try what it is to pierce the mails of men
In their proud moods . . . kings, patriots, heroes . . . and then
Back wilt thou run as if on Kalgarth-flat
A shower had caught thee in thy Sunday hat.
. . . .
Why every author on thy hearthstone burn?
Why every neighbor twicht and shov'd in turn?
. . . .
But, O true poet of the country! why
With goatskin glove an ancient friend defy? (ll. 244–312)[17]

Landor suggests that, in his literary combats, Wordsworth has not been
quite a gentleman, and he casts the poet as a decidedly middle-class figure
who has clumsily challenged to a duel both his literary "betters" and his
"ancient" supporter, Southey. While the satire operates by mocking Wordsworth's class pretensions and by reminding him of the patronage that he
has received, the critique is not, of course, primarily social. At stake are
literary values and questions of appropriation, influence, and obligation.
Landor had taken particular offense at Wordsworth's dismissive remarks
about Southey's poetry not being worth "five shillings a ream," and in the
Satire upon Satirists he reminds Wordsworth that he owes Southey a full
account. The implication is that Wordsworth had taken something without
paying for it, not because he is a thief but because he is thrifty—a charge
with additional class undertones.

One suspects, of course, that Landor defended the poetical reputations of Campbell, Moore, and Southey so vigorously in the *Satire upon Satirists* because he identified with them. Like Landor, these poets had enjoyed a measure of literary celebrity early in the nineteenth century but had not secured lasting status for their works. Wordsworth—whom Landor believed they had supported and championed during the lean years—was emerging during the 1830s as a major figure, and he remembered his friends, it seemed, only to disparage them. The note that Landor published along with this passage from the *Satire upon Satirists* makes the personal context clear. In it, Landor wrote that Wordsworth, apart from his dismissal of Southey,

has thought worse poetry, if not worth five shillings, nor thanks, nor acknowledgement, yet worth borrowing and putting on. The author of the *Gebir* [Landor] never lamented when he believed it lost, and never complained when he saw it neglected. [But] it would have been honester and more decorous if the writer of the following verses [Wordsworth] had mentioned from what bar he drew his wire. (*WWSL* 16: 309)

Landor charges Wordsworth with unacknowledged appropriations in *The Excursion* from his own oriental tale, published in 1798, and he offers his readers parallel text comparisons in which he has found it more expedient to italicize the words "certainly *not* imitated from *Gebir*" (310). In *Gebir*, Landor had presented his readers with the image of

. . . sinuous shells of pearly hue.
. . . .
Shake one and it awakens; then apply
Its polisht lips to your attentive ear,
And it remembers its august abodes,
And murmurs as the ocean murmurs there. (ll. 120–27)[18]

In *The Excursion*, Wordsworth had described

A curious child, *who dwelt upon a tract*
Of inland ground, applying to his ear
The *convolutions* of a smooth-lipped shell;
To which, *in silence hushed*, his very soul
Listened intensely; and his countenance soon
Brightened with joy; for murmuring from within
Were heard, *sonorous cadences!* Whereby,
To his belief, the monitor expressed
Mysterious union with its native sea.
(*The Excursion* 4: 1131–38; Landor's emphasis)

While observing that his poem has been neglected, Landor complains that "this passage has been the most admired of any" in *The Excursion*. Wordsworth's talent has been applauded, but the source of his imagery has not been noted, and, extending the class critique of Wordsworth, Landor characterizes this failure as indecorous. At the same time, Landor's charges in this instance also illustrate the disparity between Romantic-period perceptions of plagiarism and modern constructions of the charge. Whatever extensive correspondences Landor perceived between the two passages are no longer immediately apparent, although there are obvious thematic parallels and the two passages both employ the familiar image of the echoing seashell. Yet, subsequent critical responses to Landor's accusation, even from within the Wordsworth household, recognize the merits of his complaint.

While the *Satire upon Satirists* did not provoke a defense of Wordsworth in the periodical press, Landor's subsequent extension of this critical attack on the poet did. In December 1842, Landor published his "Imaginary Conversation, Southey and Porson" in *Blackwood's Edinburgh Magazine*, and in this piece he continued the literary combat with Wordsworth that he had initiated in the *Satire upon Satirists*. In the conversation, "Southey" attempts to defend Wordsworth, while "Porson" demonstrates the grammatical irregularities of his verse (e.g., "If there is a Wordsworth school, it is certainly not a grammar school" [697]), the irrelevance of his subjects, and the inaccuracies of his descriptions. Most importantly, Landor calls attention for a second time to Wordsworth's territorial nature and his disinclination to acknowledge the influence of others. "Nothing," "Porson" observes, "is more amusing than to see him [Wordsworth] raise his bristles and expose his tusk at every invader of his brushwood, every marauder of his hips and haws" (*WWSL* 16: 691). "Southey" responds by suggesting that this behavior is part of the universal English character and that "We all carry sticks . . . to cut down the heads of higher poppies" (691). To this "Porson" wittily rejoins: "A very high poppy, and surcharged with Lethean dew, is that before us" (691). The implication, of course, is that Wordsworth is a wild boar/bore, jealous of the intrusion of other poets into his terrain, which is little more than an overgrown and blasted autumnal garden. At the same time, he is charged with cutting down poppies in other gardens—and with forgetting from whence he has harvested his literary soporifics. The landscape metaphors used to describe literary trespasses of this sort indicate how common these associations were, but Landor's satire also suggests that Wordsworth was believed to be particularly sensitive to charges that compared him to the common foragers, gatherers, and beggars of his own poems.

Although intimates later suggested that the publication of Landor's satire in *Blackwood's* did not trouble Wordsworth, it infuriated his son-in-law, Edward Quillinan, who responded to the "Southey and Porson" dialogue with an imaginary conversation of his own. Published in *Blackwood's* in April 1843, under the title "Imaginary Conversation, Between Mr. Walter Savage Landor and [Christopher North] The Editor of Blackwood's Magazine," Quillinan's article engaged the question of plagiarism directly, referring to Landor's recent periodical review but also quoting from the *Satire upon Satirists* and accusing Landor of unacknowledged borrowings of his own. Quillinan's dialogue was intended as a defense of *The Excursion* in particular, and in the essay he begins the discussion of plagiarism by accusing Landor of the same indiscretion. Quillinan's argument reveals that the cumulative Romantic-period standards for evaluating and describing illegitimate appropriations remained operative into the 1840s. In the "Southey and Porson" conversation, Landor's "Southey" had defended Wordsworth from charges of constitutional weakness, remarking, "Diamonds sparkle the most brilliantly on heads stricken by the palsy" (693). Quillinan observes that these lines were taken from "the very poet you would disparage—Wordsworth," whose poem "Inscriptions supposed to be found in and near a Hermit's Cell" had been published in 1818 and had included the same image (ll. 14–15). "Landor" responds that it is a matter of "coincidence," to which "North" responds:

Both original, no doubt. . . . But how busy Wordsworth would be . . . if he were to set about reclaiming the thousands of ideas that have been pilfered from him. . . . He makes no stir about such larcenies. And what a coil have you made about that eternal sea-shell, which you say he stole from you, and which, we know, is the true and trivial cause of your hostility towards him! (533)

The emphasis on "coincidential" plagiarism echoes the attitudes that both Wordsworth and Coleridge expressed at different points in their literary careers, and the reference to the "sea-shell" directly engages Landor's charges of appropriation from *Gebir* in *The Excursion*. However, Quillinan also articulates what was a subject of private discussion in the Wordsworth circle: the sense that Wordsworth's influence on the writings of his contemporaries had not been duly acknowledged and that considerable liberties had been taken by contemporaries with his works. This same sentiment had rested at the center of Wordsworth's discussion of plagiarism in the "Essay

Supplementary to the Preface" in 1815, and Quillinan was particularly aggrieved that Wordsworth's reputation as a poet should be jeopardized by hostile criticism that was so unjustly motivated. However, Quillinan also takes Landor's charges seriously, and after presenting in dialogue the parallel passages of stanzas from *Gebir* and *The Excursion*, "North" acknowledges that "[t]here is certainly much resemblance between the two passages" and that the *Gebir* "very likely . . . suggested" (534) Wordsworth's image.

Yet, when "Landor" complains that "these lines have been the most admired of any in Mr. Wordsworth's great poem" (534), Quillinan reiterates his earlier defense of Wordsworth, while extending the discussion to also address the question of improvement. He writes:

> The author of the *Excursion* could afford to spare you a thousand finer passages, and he would seem none the poorer. As to the imputed plagiarism, Wordsworth would no doubt have avowed it had he been conscious that it was one, and [it is strange] that you should attach so much importance to the honour of having reminded him of a secret of conchology, known . . . to every boy or girl that ever found a shell on the sea shore, or was tall enough to reach one off the cottage parlour mantlepiece. . . . [But] it is in the application of the familiar image, that we recognize the master-hand of the poet. . . . There is a pearl within Wordsworth's shell, which is not to be found in your's, Mr. Landor. (534)

Understood within the context of the nineteenth-century rhetoric of plagiarism, Quillinan is invoking familiar language. Wordsworth, he grants, may have been responsible for unconscious plagiarism—but unconscious plagiarism by definition cannot carry with it the implication of moral culpability. At worst, Wordsworth could be charged with a "poetical plagiarism," but only if the borrowed text were unfamiliar or if he had failed to improve upon the original, and, as Quillinan insists, the improvement is manifest: Wordsworth has added to the shell "pearls" of philosophical insight, by which he has transformed an empty image into a jewel. Landor was, apparently, chastened by the rebuke, which is perhaps a sign of how effective claims of improvement could be; in his 1846 reprint of the dialogue, Landor not only removed the passage indebted to Wordsworth's "Inscriptions" but also softened much of the personal satire (*Complete Works* 159).

This embarrassment in regard to the "Southey and Porson" dialogue, however, did not prevent Landor from renewing his charges against Wordsworth (and adding some charges against Southey) in his 1853 "Imaginary Conversation between Archdeacon Hare and Walter Landor," in which he refutes Quillinan's claims for improvement. In the dialogue, Landor described the critical reception of the *Gebir,* in the following exchange:

Landor. Within [a] few months, a wholesale dealer in the brittle crockery of market criticism has pickt up some shards of it, and stuck them in his shelves. Among them is my *Sea-shell,* which Wordsworth clapt into his pouch. There it became incrusted with a compost of mucus and shingle; there is lost its "pearly hue within," and its memory of where it had abided.

Archdeacon Hare. But Wordsworth had the industry and skill to turn everything to some account.

Landor. Perfectly true. And he is indebted to me for more than the value of twenty *Shells:* he is indebted to me for praise. . . . Truly he owes me little. My shell may be among the prettiest on his mantelpiece, but a trifle it is at best. I often wish, in his longest poem [*The Excursion*], he had obtained an Inclosure-act. . . .

Archdeacon Hare. It is dangerous to break into a park where the paling is high, for it may be difficult to find the way out again, or to escape the penalty of transgression. You never before spoke a syllable about your *Shell.* (*WWSL* 6: 29–32)

Here is, undoubtedly, the most direct connection that we find in Romantic-era literary conversations linking the rhetoric of plagiarism with enclosure. While Landor's statement comes in the middle of the nineteenth century, it mirrors language that Henry Fielding had employed as early as the mid-eighteenth century, when he wrote in *Tom Jones* (1749) that the works of the classical tradition "may be considered as a rich Common, where every person who hath the smallest Tenement in *Parnassus* hath a free Right to fatten his Muse," and, as Wolfram Schmidgen reminds us in *Eighteenth-Century Fiction and the Law of Property* (2002), throughout much of the eighteenth century, "The manor [represented] a communal form in which the operation of uninterrupted time has integrated land and practice."[19] Just as Wordsworth had used the metaphor of commons and enclosure to describe plagiarism in 1817, when he accused Byron of "poaching on [his] Manor," Landor casts Wordsworth as having "clapt into his pouch" the productions of his poetic efforts. Directly refuting Quillinan's claims for improvement, Landor maintains that the pearly luster of his image has been destroyed by the "compost" with which it had been mixed. The clear suggestion is that Wordsworth has failed in his efforts at assimilation and at writing verse. Most importantly, however, Landor directly links *The Excursion* with issues of plagiarism and the Inclosure Acts. While part of the point is that the poem would have been better had it been enclosed and divided, Landor's implication is also that Wordsworth's appropriations in the poem were not strictly legal either. Later in the passage, this metaphor is developed further, with "Archdeacon Hare's" comparison of the literary work to a deer park, enclosed by paling, in which a poacher might be caught in his transgressions. Alluding again to the plundered seashell from the *Gebir*, the charge is that Wordsworth has been an interloper on the estate of another—a metaphor that he had himself applied to his literary contemporaries and to their appropriations.[20]

Wordsworth, Literary Gentility, and Copyright Reform

The metaphorical associations between plagiarism and enclosure that both Wordsworth and Landor employed to address issues of illegitimate appropriation have obvious class implications. It becomes increasingly clear that not only Wordsworth but also many of his contemporaries understood literary property as analogous to a landed estate. The emergence of this cultural attitude, which became particularly predominant in the 1830s and 1840s, reflects the return to the earlier eighteenth-century Lockean arguments regarding the nature of intellectual ownership and copyright. Wordsworth was, to a large extent, responsible for shaping this public discourse. Although he had been concerned about issues of literary ownership since at least 1804, during the late 1830s and early 1840s he was actively involved with parliamentary efforts to reform copyright and to define the author's right to his or her literary productions. This was also a period characterized by an active public discussion of the enclosures, and the time between the second General Inclosure Act of 1836 and the third General Act of 1845 coincides with the years during which Wordsworth was most actively engaged in working for copyright reform. Not surprisingly, the language that Wordsworth employed in these efforts continued to reflect his concerns with issues of class, nobility, and the enclosure of landed property.

One of the most curious features of Wordsworth's attitude toward literary property is that he associated plagiarism with both labor and nobility. His letter of 1792 had cast his poetic efforts as a form of "tillage," and his correspondence is replete with instances in which he characterizes creative efforts in terms of labor and workmanship. Yet, as Susan Eilenberg has argued, Wordsworth also understood literary property as "the ownership of tangible or tangibly valued goods" (ix) and, particularly, as real estate. The evolution of Wordsworth language from "tillage" of a field to the possession of a literary "Manor" reflects the complexities of his concerns about class, land ownership, law, and inheritance.

Mark Schoenfield observes that Wordsworth was, after all, the son and sibling of lawyers, and he occupied the delicate position in nineteenth-century culture of the landless professional classes.[21] While disdainful of entering into trade, Wordsworth was nevertheless required to have an occupation, and his representations of literature as labor reflect both the complexity and the reality of his position as what he might have called a "plain gentleman." Dorothy had applied this term to Walter Scott in 1826, when the poet was suffering financial disaster, writing: "How *could* it happen that he should have so entered into *trade* . . . he a Baronet! a literary man! a Lawyer? . . . No doubt Sir Walter, having retained his offices, will have a sufficient income for a plain gentleman; but does he retain his *Estates*?" (*LWDW* 4: 432). Like Wordsworth, Scott had begun his life with a modest income and a profession. As a result of the popularity of his poetry, however, Scott had risen to a baronetcy and had gained, in the process, landed estates. By entering into trade, Scott had jeopardized his position. These distinctions capture many of the central elements of class, as Wordsworth understood its construction. Perhaps most importantly, "Estates" symbolize both Scott's literary success and his rise into a more firmly genteel rank. This conjunction of literary fame and the possession of landed estates helps to explain why property became such an important symbolic nexus for Wordsworth. To some degree, he seems to have understood the possession of real estate as a measure of professional and poetic achievement, and it is probably not coincidental that the two literary contemporaries whose commercial popularity he most resented—Sir Walter Scott and Lord Byron—both enjoyed more privileged class positions. These associations can only have been exacerbated by Wordsworth's private history. Upon the death of their father, the Wordsworth children were deprived of a significant portion of their expected inheritance when James Lowther, the first Earl Lonsdale, refused to settle an outstanding debt, a fact that complicated William's and Dorothy's aspirations to purchase a family residence. Meanwhile, Wordsworth spent much of his life financially dependent upon the offices of the subsequent Lord Lonsdale, William Lowther, who arranged for Wordsworth one of his primary sources of income, the position as Stamp Distributor. In very concrete ways, Lonsdale's goodwill made it possible for Wordsworth to continue writing, despite the commercial failure of his work, and Lonsdale was, as Wordsworth wrote in 1842, his "honored Patron" (*LWDW* 7: 356) in the traditionally feudal sense of that title.

Bringing together as it does the issues of inheritance, ownership, and literary success, it is not surprising that class was a complex subject for Wordsworth. Of course, he aspired to the position of Sir Walter Scott. He desired both public recognition of his literary achievements and the financial and social security that came with *genteel* commercial success. The improbable marriage between the genteel and the commercial in matters of literary fame was particularly important, and the apparent contradiction reveals one of the risks of professional authorship for middle-class writers in the Romantic period. Failure to strike the right balance had implications of trade, a charge with concrete social consequences. Insofar as he associated the land ownership of the gentility and the nobility with literary success, Wordsworth was invested in improving his class position. However, the language that he employs to describe intellectual property and particularly plagiarism and copyright often masks a considerable resentment of the nobility. Frequently, this resentment was figured as a metaphorical version of his own disenfranchisement at the hands of the first Lord Lonsdale. Wordsworth not only viewed his literary productions as tangible property and as a form of real estate but he also understood his copyrights as an inheritance for his family. As early as 1819, he was concerned about the "duration of Copyright" (*LWDW* 3: 534), which he described in a letter to J. Forbes Mitchell as the "pecuniary emoluments which are the natural Inheritance of the posterity of Authors" (535). From his perspective, infringement upon his rights as author represented not only a figurative trespass on his property as a gentleman but a more concrete diminishment of his estate, a diminishment that in the case of Byron he compared to poaching. Plagiarism was one form of trespass, of course, but by the 1830s Wordsworth was also convinced that the statutes governing copyright jeopardized the income of the author and the inheritance of his family in more systematic ways.

Although Wordsworth had been interested in matters of copyright for several decades, his most active engagement with the legal and rhetorical constructions of literary property came in the 1830s, and his correspondence on these subjects reflects the class concerns that were central to him. Increasingly, Wordsworth's commentary demonstrates a desire to reconfigure the way in which class is assigned to authorship. On the one hand, Wordsworth casts himself as a member of the literary elite in terms that directly evoke social hierarchies; one the other hand, he welcomes the open castigation of the nobility. Perhaps most importantly, his discussions of copyright frequently address the issue of plagiarism as a particular form of appropriation, providing some of the mature Wordsworth's most illuminating statements on the charge and its associations with the landed estate.

Wordsworth spent considerable energy during the 1830s studying the legal and cultural history of British copyright, and his initial interest was apparently sparked in the late spring of 1830, when Dorothy reported to her nephew Christopher that there was discussion of Wordsworth not publishing further poetry during his lifetime. "A much better plan," she wrote, "would be to publish nothing new, and let the whole remain for the benefit of his Family after death" (*LWDW* 5: 229). By this strategy, his heirs would have the benefit of the sale of the copyright. However, Wordsworth also became increasingly anxious about the expiration of the copyright protections to his work. The matter is curious, since Wordsworth did not, in fact, typically hold the copyright to his published works: these had been sold to the booksellers and printers in exchange for an initial outright payment, as was customary in the Romantic period. Rather, his concern was that his works would enter the public domain and that neither he nor his family would have the benefit of selling the copyright to new editions of those works. In the summer of 1830, he queried both John Gardner and Walter Scott about the legalities of the matter, writing to Gardner in May:

I am told that, when an Author dies, such of his works as have been twice fourteen years before the Public are public property, and that his heirs have no pecuniary interest in anything he may leave behind. . . . I think it would be best, in order to secure some especial value to any collection of my Works that might be printed after my decease, to reserve a certain number of new pieces to be intermixed with that collection. (*LWDW* 5: 265)

Wordsworth's concerns here reflect his increasingly secure literary reputation. By 1830, he anticipated, at long last, a broader popular audience for his poems, but he saw that timing would be everything. If his works were to enter the public domain before that audience was secure, there would be no "pecuniary" rewards. By holding back some "new pieces" of work, he was hoping not only to ensure financial security for his family but also to sell those works at a higher price than he had typically received.

By 1836, Wordsworth's investment in issues of copyright had evolved from legal strategizing to passionate indignation, and, throughout the 1830s and 1840s, Wordsworth was intimately involved in parliamentary efforts to reform copyright law. He began by raising the matter with his friend

Thomas Noon Talfourd, whose position as a Member of Parliament placed him advantageously, and, by the autumn of 1836, Wordsworth, still "unpossessed of an accurate historical knowledge of the Subject" (*LWDW* 6: 322), had determined to study the matter in earnest. In 1837, encouraged by Wordsworth, Talfourd undertook to the presentation of a reform copyright bill to Parliament, with a first reading of the bill on 18 May 1837 and a second reading on 11 April 1838. Wordsworth was by then relatively expert in the legal arguments surrounding copyright, and he claimed to have written "scarcely less than 50 notes or Letters" advocating support of the bill, "many of them to members of Parliament" (*LWDW* 6: 553). While Wordsworth's involvement with the intricacies of copyright reform reveals a great deal about the intersection of legal and aesthetic categories in his work, copyright is not, of course, the subject of immediate inquiry here. Yet, Wordsworth's extensive correspondence on copyright is important for understanding his attitude toward plagiarism—not only because it reflects the discursive strategies he applied to literary property generally but because the problem of determining plagiarism was one of the arguments made by those opposed to the passage of Talfourd's copyright bill.

As part of his letter-writing campaign in 1838, Wordsworth had written to Sir Robert Peel, asking him to support Talfourd's copyright bill. In the spring, Peel wrote to Wordsworth an account of his objections to the new reform, and he raised patents and plagiarism as his two points of concern, writing, "If the rights of the author to such extended protection be admitted, can we refuse it in the case of Patents? . . . There are also the difficulties of determining what constitutes an original work, as distinguished from plagiarism" (*LWDW* 6: 568). Peel's first point, regarding patents, was a version of the familiar eighteenth-century argument concerning copyright and the cultural importance of freely circulating knowledge: if discoveries or inventions were subject to lengthy private protections, the progress of civilization and learning would be retarded. Meanwhile, Peel's second point, on the matter of plagiarism, was to question the degree to which an author was permitted to draw from either the literary tradition of his predecessors or the learning already gathered in those texts. On 3 May 1838, Wordsworth responded to Peel's letter, sending him an extract of Talfourd's recent *Times* article on patent law to address the first concern and explaining the issue of plagiarism himself. Here, Wordsworth responds to "the difficulty stated by you of determining what constitutes an original work, as distinguished from plagiarism," writing:

Dr. Arnold is now engaged in writing a *History of Rome*, in which I know that he will be greatly indebted to Niebuhr [*Römische Geschichte*, 3 vols., 1811–12], but I have no doubt of the subject being treated by him in such a manner that Niebuhr—had he been an Englishman, and written in English—would be found, were he alive, to complain, nor could any competent tribunal to which the case might be referred condemn the subsequent writer for having made an unfair or illegal use of his predecessor's labours. So would it always be with the successful labours of men of honour and great talent employed upon the same subjects; and it is only upon the productions of such authors that the proposed extension of term has any bearing. Mere drudges and dishonest writers are sometimes protected by the law as it now exists; but their works, if not cried down at once, soon die of themselves, and the plundered author seldom thinks it worth while to complain, or seek a remedy by law. (*LWDW* 5: 572)

In making this argument, Wordsworth returns to the categories of early nineteenth-century plagiarism in several characteristic ways. He marks, for example, the implied contrast between authors who have successfully assimilated the materials of their predecessors and those "mere drudges" who have inappropriately employed the texts, images, or knowledge of another. At the same time, Wordsworth's description in this passage echoes the language of the article "Recent Poetical Plagiarisms and Imitations" that his friend Henry Taylor had published in 1823, in which Taylor had argued that the harm in plagiarism was primarily aesthetic and typically short-lived. In characteristic fashion, Wordsworth continues to define writing in terms of labor, and he also suggests that the issues of translation and perhaps even national identity complicated charges of plagiarism. Most importantly, however, in seeking to define the standard of originality by which Romantic literary works were to be judged, Wordsworth calls attention to imitation, tradition, and the inevitability of borrowing. Dr. Arnold *will* make use of Niebuhr's work, and there *will* be correspondences, but Arnold, Wordsworth contends, will not fail to make the work his own through the application of labor and "great talent." By originality, Wordsworth does not mean ex nihilo invention but, as we have seen, something closer to the infusion of subjectivity or personal labor into a text.

Wordsworth's language in this letter to Peel is also classed in particular ways. Like Taylor, Wordsworth implies that plagiarism is something a gentleman would not do. "Men of honour" are contrasted with the bourgeois "drudges and dishonest writers," and this characterization echoes a predominant eighteenth-century attitude that cast plagiarism as "the Grub Street version of imitation."[22] Wordsworth had made a similar point about the classes of writers in his earlier correspondence with Peel on the subject of copyright. In a letter of 5 February 1835, Wordsworth had explained to Peel, "Had I followed Literature as a *Trade* it might, as to pecuniary circumstances, have been very different. [I have written in] common with the worthier and nobler class of writers, who write not with a view to instant profit, and immediate effect, but with a hope of being permanently beneficial to mankind" (*LWDW* 6: 21). Wordsworth's distinction in this passage mirrors the concerns that he had articulated as early as 1815 in the "Essay Supplementary to the Preface," where he also engaged directly the question of plagiarism. There, Wordsworth had argued that the best literary works often took the longest to be appreciated, precisely because they endeavored to create the taste by which they were read. Writing to Peel in 1835, Wordsworth places himself among those writers, and the contrast that he draws is deliberately cast in the language of social distinction. Returning to the anxieties about class that characterized Dorothy's description of Sir Walter Scott as both a literary success and a public figure, Wordsworth proclaims his own rejection of "Trade" and his identification with the "nobler class of writers" whose members have rejected the pursuit of immediate commercial profit. The pecuniary gains of his work have been of the genteel sort, less Grub Street than the harvest of an ancient literary estate. Meanwhile, we may also read in the passage a suggestion of Wordsworth's earlier critique of Lord Byron and the class inversion he evokes by charging the lord with "poaching" on his "Manor." Byron was chief among those writers who Wordsworth cited: a failed poet, undeserving of the commercial success he received. While Wordsworth's animosity toward Byron had a personal element, to be sure, this irritation must have been part of Wordsworth's larger resentments toward the aristocracy and their uncomplicated relationship to literary production. As a "plain gentleman," Wordsworth needed to negotiate the territory between literature as a trade and literature as a noble pursuit, something that was not true for Byron or for contemporaries such as Shelley or even Scott.

Even after Wordsworth's 1838 appeal, Peel remained unwilling to support Talfourd's bill, as written, and the obstacles that Peel had raised—including the issue of plagiarism—remained at the center of the debate until the final passage of a compromise version in the 1842 Literary Copyright Act. As late as 4 March 1842, Wordsworth was still writing letters on the subject of plagiarism as it related to copyright, including a letter addressed to Lord Mahon, whose amendments and revisions finally led to the act's passage. In achieving this final result, Wordsworth's activities during the late 1830s and early 1840s were particularly important. Throughout the period, he remained closely involved with copyright reform and worked tirelessly to bring what he understood as the plight of authors to public attention. One of his most interesting efforts is his sonnet "A Plea for Authors, May 1838," which he published later that year. In the poem, Wordsworth once again engages the issues of class that lay at the foundation of his concerns about literary ownership. The poem contends:

Failing impartial measure to dispense
To every suitor, Equity is lame;
And social Justice, stript of reverence
For natural rights, a mockery and a shame;
Law but a servile dupe of false pretence,
If, guarding grossest things from common claim
Now and for ever, She, to works that came
From mind and spirit, grudge a short-lived fence.
"What! lengthened privilege, a lineal tie,
For 'Books'!" Yes, heartless Ones, or be it proved
That 'tis a fault in Us to have lived and loved
Like others, with like temporal hopes to die;
No public harm that Genius from her course
Be turned; and streams of truth dried up, even at their source![23]

Wordsworth's argument in the poem is that the law is unjust because it denies authors their natural rights to intellectual property while granting that same privilege to those who possess even the "grossest" tangible effects, and he presents in quotations the voice of those opposing the present copyright bill. While the voice of the opposition calls attention to the implicit class issues involved in copyright reform and to the protection of literary productions as "lineal" property, in particular, the most salient feature of the poem is Wordsworth's characterization of artistic works as landscape and of copyright as a "short-lived fence." While Genius is a "stream" that must be allowed to run freely for the benefit of civilization, Wordsworth's implication is that its flow will not be impeded by the enclosure of a park paling. Here, Wordsworth returns to the metaphor connecting intellectual property with the enclosed landed estate that he had first employed when charging Byron with poetical poaching.

Wordsworth's repetition of landscape and class metaphors to describe his own investment in literary property and its appropriation in instances of plagiarism reflects both personal concerns and the larger context of Romantic-period culture. Certainly, metaphors associating intellectual property and real property were employed broadly in the eighteenth and nineteenth centuries, and it was natural that the language used after the 1780s, when charges of plagiarism were receiving particular public attention, should have reflected the discursive strategies associated with enclosure. Yet, Wordsworth also understood the matter more intimately. Throughout his career, he came to understand his poetry as both a gentleman's occupation and as a literary estate, and he perceived plagiarism from his work as a form of disinheritance—from the landscape, from property, and, through its associations with class privilege, even from literature itself.

Natural Genius and Poetic Property: Yearsley and Chatterton

While Wordsworth represented literature as a form of labor and cast plagiarism in terms of his own class anxieties, the charges of literary obligation made against actual laboring-class poets were a far different matter. As Bridget Keegan has observed, laboring-class poets were frequently accused of unacknowledged appropriations, and these "accusations of plagiarism reveal one aspect of the class-based politics surrounding claims for 'natural genius'" in the Romantic period.[24] For these writers—and there were several hundred working from 1770 to 1830—the metaphors associating poetry with the landscape and its enclosure also had implications and even consequences distinct from those experienced by Wordsworth as a "plain gentleman" or by the bourgeois writers of Grub Street. Laboring-class poets held a different relationship not only to the legal and rhetorical conventions governing literary influence but also to the tradition itself. Indeed, it is this celebrated absence of a formal relationship to the poetic tradition that seems to account for many of the charges of plagiarism brought against these writers, precisely because the correspondences between their works and those of their predecessors confirmed for the genteel reading public the genius of the native English literary tradition.

In the Romantic period, there are several instances of laboring-class poets being accused of appropriation from other sources, and in these cases the focus was often on the question of consciousness. Unconscious plagiarism was, after all, not a culpable failing according to the rhetorical construction operative during this period, but the dilemma was to determine how "unlettered" and impoverished poets had come to know the literary tradition of their predecessors. Where, in short, did they obtain access to these texts? While an obvious answer might have been to posit a vernacular transmission, something like what John Guillory argues became the case with Gray's "Elegy" during the nineteenth and twentieth centuries (87), contemporary commentators typically do not advance this argument. Instead, influences on laboring-class poets are represented in one of two ways: as an accidental exposure to traditional texts, resulting in an unconscious imitation, or, more often, as a fortuitous "coincidence" that confirms the natural genius of both writers. Both instances mobilize the familiar language of nineteenth-century plagiarism, while turning it to account for the authenticity of Britain's greatest historical poets.

Ann Yearsley is one of the most familiar examples of a laboring-class poet who was credited with accidental exposure to the texts of the literary tradition and whose obligations were described in unconscious terms. The suggestion that the works of other writers influenced Yearsley was first made by one of her most enthusiastic advocates, Hannah More, who was anxious to forestall charges of plagiarism or suspicion of class fraud in her introduction to Yearsley's *Poems on Several Occasions* (1786). In her "Prefatory Letter to Mrs. Montagu," More defended the employment of literary allusions in Yearsley's poetry by explaining the circumstances in which the unlettered poet might encounter the language of tradition:

When I expressed surprise at two or three classical allusions in one of her Poems and inquired how she came by them, she said she had taken them from little ordinary prints which hung in a shop-window. This hint may, perhaps, help to account for the manner in which the late untutored, and unhappy, but very sublime genius of this town [Chatterton], caught some of those ideas which diffuse through his writings a certain air of learning, the reality of which he did not possess. A great mind at once seizes and appropriates to itself whatever is new and striking[.][25]

More suggests that Yearsley had learned what she knew of literary history from shop windows, and her primary concern in making that point was to refute in advance any charges that she was attempting to pass off an educated person as an unlettered bard and natural genius. In light of the controversy that had surrounded Chatterton's forgeries in the Rowley poems, More was wise to be cautious. However, More's account of the relationship both poets held to the tradition also draws from the categories of literary property and plagiarism. Chatterton, if perhaps not quite a laboring-class poet, was, as the son of an impoverished schoolmaster, distinctly lower middle class in his social origins, and like Yearsley his learning (or the appearance of it) was represented as a matter of accident. Yet, it was also a matter of appropriation. For, as More explains, Chatterton had appropriated to himself the materials around him, some of which were textual.

More's point is that appropriations of this sort are an inevitable part of the creative process, and the distinction that she implicitly draws is between the run-of-the-mill poet and the "sublime genius." While all poets borrow, the "genius" transforms his or her materials by fully assimilating them. Here we recognize the language of plagiarism and particularly the category of improvement that was so often applied to judgments of obligation. More argues that both Yearsley and Chatterton, as simultaneously sublime and unlettered poets, reveal the natural operations of poetic genius in its engagement with the literary tradition.

Several years later, in her verse epistle "To Mr. ***, an Unlettered Poet, on Genius Unimproved" (1787), Yearsley addressed this same issue of the laboring-class poet's relationship to traditions of learning and literature, and in the poem she casts the uneducated writer's relationship to nature in terms of improvement. However, she also returns to the metaphors of landscape enclosure that characterized Wordsworth's attitude toward plagiarism and its class dynamics. Drawing from eighteenth-century conventions of the natural genius, Yearsley's poem argues that, while the "unlettered" writer has greater independence, for such a person the traditional subjects of poetry represent an unimproved landscape that he or she must appropriate through intellectual labors. She writes:

> . . . estranged
> From Science and old Wisdom's classic lore,
> I've patient trod the wild entangled path
> Of unimproved idea. Dauntless thought
> I eager seized, no formal rule e'er awed;
> No precedent controlled; no custom fixed
> My independent spirit: . . . (ll. 34–40)

While Yearsley describes the unlettered poet's estrangement from "old Wisdom," the predominant metaphor in this passage is the comparison she draws between laboring-class poetic efforts and the process of improving a rural landscape. The language recalls the descriptions of landscape gardening, surveying, and enclosure that appear in locodescriptive poems of the late eighteenth century. The extension of this metaphor implies, of course, additional class dynamics: the laboring-class poet is represented not as a laborer at all but as a rural professional whose very independence from "rule" and "custom" qualifies him or her to create a more sublime and unmannered literary landscape.

Laboring-Class Ownership: Clare and Enclosure

In "To Mr. ***, an Unlettered Poet, on Genius Unimproved," Yearsley rejects the value of custom and tradition, just as, in her "Prefatory Letter," More is anxious to assure readers of Yearsley's natural genius. Other laboring-class writers, however, were more invested in locating their work in relation to the tradition of belles-lettres, an effort that was also likely to lead to charges of plagiarism. Among these writers, the intellectual obligations of the rural poet John Clare, the "Northamptonshire Peasant," were the most widely circulated in the Romantic-era periodical press. At the same time, Clare was also an author who—like Wordsworth and Yearsley—drew parallels between his writing and the cultural contexts of enclosure and landscape improvement. As John Goodridge and Kelsey Thorton have observed, Clare's very "initiation into literature involve[d] a literal and metaphoric trespass" into the enclosed grounds of Burghley Park, where Clare had been apprenticed as a gardener.[26] Likewise, Margaret Russett has argued that "Clare came to voice by consciously poaching on other literary properties" ("Like Wedding Gowns" 1), especially the works of celebrated contemporaries such as Wordsworth and Byron. And, of course, many of Clare's most familiar poems directly address the subject of enclosure and its effects on the rural poor.

While Clare's engagement with enclosure was one of the central themes in his poetry from 1814 to 1825, the public reception of his work focused primarily on questions of native genius and plagiarism. His first volume of poetry, *Poems Descriptive of Rural Life and Scenery* (1820), was an immediate popular success, running to four editions in the first year, and the critical introduction to the book, which emphasized Clare's peasant origins and his early love for the landscape poetry of Thomson, cast the young writer as a natural and otherwise unlettered genius. While this representation fueled Clare's celebrity, it also cast down the gauntlet for the periodical press, and within a month of the volume's release Clare had been publicly charged with plagiarism, primarily from seventeenth- and eighteenth-century landscape poets and from vernacular writers such as Scott and Burns. The public discourse surrounding these literary debts is finally more interesting than the obligations themselves, and, although several of these authors were in Clare's small library, his borrowings, as is so often the case with Romantic poets, were predominantly stylistic and thematic rather than closely textual. The controversy surrounding his plagiarisms, however, engaged with some of the issues central to early nineteenth-century attitudes toward literary property and genius.

Early reviews of Clare's *Poems Descriptive of Rural Life and Scenery* charged the poet with plagiarism, and by the 11 February 1820 edition of the *Morning Post* an anonymous contributor wrote to defend Claire's originality on the grounds that he was a natural genius, thus setting the standard by which the poet's productions were evaluated. In a letter posted to the paper under the title "A Well-Wisher to Merit," this contributor (perhaps Markham Sherwill) discounted the claims that Clare had inappropriately imitated literary predecessors:

Clare has been accused of plagiarism, which, in a few words, I will endeavour to shew is a very unjust and false opinion. In a letter I received from him *after* the publication of his first edition, he writes "When your letter arrived, I was reading Scott's 'Lady of the Lake', the first of that great Poet's work I ever saw". In several other letters, he repeatedly writes, I have *heard* of such and such works, but they are far beyond my capacity. In short, Sir, I know what his library consisted of at the time. . . . and he certainly had not more than eight or ten volumes, and those decidedly not of a character from which a natural genius like Clare would ever attempt to transcribe one idea. He owes no debt to any dead or living author. . . . [and we should] support the native genius of Britain, and of an unlettered Peasant[.][27]

Clare's advocate claims to know the content of the poet's library and dismisses the suggestion that Clare might have borrowed from his literary predecessors by emphasizing the natural qualities both of his poetry and of his genius. However, while the defense attempts to preserve the image of Clare as unlettered and naïve, it also has the effect of marking an aesthetic distinction between categories of poetry. Clare's library, the reviewer writes, contains works that are, presumably, written in a stylized manner that a natural poet would not "attempt to transcribe." This was an observation repeated by an author for *The Eclectic Review* the following month, who wrote that a line from John Cunningham's verse was "the extent of [Clare's] obligations" and that it "is, indeed, remarkable, that Clare's style should be so free of the vices of that school of poetry, to which his scanty reading appears to have been confined" (M. Storey 89).[28] Clare's supposed reading had been primarily in the elaborate and allusive landscape poetry of writers such as Gray, Goldsmith, Cowper, Pope, and Crabbe, and the suggestion was that his verse was not only independent of his sources but also represented an original counterpoint to his predecessors. At stake is the characterization not only of Clare but also of a particular type of naturalistic, spontaneous, and direct poetry as authentically and "natively" English, precisely the type of poetry that we have historically come to identify as characteristically Romantic. The critical investment in celebrating Clare's accomplishment primarily concerned the way that he functioned to guarantee as "authentic" and natural the familiar—but largely rhetorical—Romantic-period self-representations of originality, solitary genius, and national voice.

Although vigorously defended in the periodical reviews by writers who were invested in celebrating the aesthetics of natural genius, Clare was privately anxious about charges of plagiarism. As early as 1818 he had written a prefatory note to his poems, in which he anticipated these allegations. This note introduced his work as "Trifles . . . nothing but the simple productions of an Unlettered Rustic. . . . continually overburthend & depressed by hard labour. . . . It is hoped the unnoticed Imitation should any occur (being unknown to the author) will not be deem'd as Plagiarism. . . . the small catalogue [of books] he has seen might easily be enumerated a Thompson & a Milton" (M. Storey 29). Unfamiliar with the literary tradition and with the writer's relationship to it, Clare's concern for overstepping the boundaries of imitation led him to acknowledge, much as Matthew Lewis had done, the possibility of unconscious plagiarisms. After the public controversy in the periodical reviews, Clare continued to assert the unconscious nature of his obligations, but his correspondence marks an evolving understanding of his claims to originality as a writer. In May 1820, Clare was reading James Beattie's *The Minstrel* (1771), and he wrote to his correspondent C. H. Townsend with his concerns over plagiarism: "as far as I have read many thoughts occur which are in my 'Peasant Boy' I [do not] doubt the world will think them plagiarisms, therefore I must alter or cut them out altogether, but nature is the same here at Helpstone as it is elsewhere" (M. Storey 125). Townsend responded in September by emphasizing precisely this last point, writing: "It does not surprise me, that there should be coincidences . . . since you both copied from nature. . . . Do not alter one line from this fear. . . . Every original mind (and such is yours) will ever treat even a hacknied subject in an original manner" (M. Storey 125). In negotiating this point, both Clare and Townsend were assimilating the representations of natural genius, but they were also reflecting the contemporary understanding of originality as an expression tinctured and, therefore, necessarily "improved" by the mind and subject of the writer. Indeed, on this point, Townsend's assertion that Clare must feel empowered to borrow from nature and to still consider his work original reiterates the early and abiding distinction that Young had drawn between appropriate (universal) and inappropriate (particular) borrowings.

Perhaps most importantly, Clare, like Wordsworth, understood his particular relationship to intellectual property and the literary tradition in terms of class and enclosure. While Wordsworth had styled himself lord of his literary estate and had protested as a gentleman the invasion of his property by poachers and thieves, Clare compared Parnassus itself to an enclosed pleasure ground, perhaps metaphorically extending the associations of poetic awakening and private trespass represented by his hours stolen for reading in Burghley Park. In a letter to Allan Cunningham dated 9 September 1824, Clare addressed directly the issues of class and ownership that he negotiated as a writer:

Titles and distinction of pride have long ago been stript of their dignity by the levellers of genius; at least they have been convinced that the one is not a certain copyright or inheritance of the other. I should suppose, friend Allan, that "The Ettrick Shepherd," "The Nithsdale Mason," and "The Northamptonshire Peasant," are looked up as intruders and stray cattle in the fields of the Muses.[29]

Written in response to Byron's dismissal of the "farmer poet" Robert Bloomfield, Clare's letter engages questions of class and authorship in a particular Romantic-period context. While the passage contends that the nobility cannot claim genius as their exclusive "copyright or inheritance," Clare's language nevertheless acknowledges that literary distinctions, like hereditary ones, are figured in a legal language of ownership. Most interestingly, Clare casts himself and his fellow laboring-class poets not as lords of the literary estate or even as yeoman possessed of tillage but as "stray cattle" in the enclosed fields of the Muses. As Eric Miller has argued, Clare's metaphor in this instance precisely reflects the historical conditions of enclosure and, particularly, of the Northampton Inclosure Act of 1809, which specifically provided for the exclusion of "Horses, Beasts, Asses, Sheep, Lambs, or other Cattle" (637) from private grounds. The implication is that Clare, as a peasant poet, is doubly disenfranchised, having been denied access not only to the titled estates of poets such as Byron but even to the rural commons and fields. In light of these associations, it is unsurprising that, like Wordsworth, Clare also came to equate literary success with the ownership, either metaphorically or literally, of landed property. In 1822, following the popular success of his *Poems Descriptive of a Rural Life and Scenery*, it had been Clare's impassioned desire to purchase with the money held in trust for him by his genteel patrons a small local estate that had come to the market as a result of the enclosures. When his concerned patrons refused him the funds, fearing that he would not be able to maintain the property properly, he was bitterly disappointed, and he cannot have misunderstood the role his class played in the decision to deny him ownership of his own literary estate.

Late in his career, while Clare was institutionalized in the High Beech asylum, these same dynamics emerged in his obsession with Byron and with the access to literary enfranchisement that he represented. Just as Wordsworth had particularly resented Byron's easy commercial success and his privileged relationship to public authorship, Clare also came to associate Byron with the tradition from which he had been excluded. During the 1840s, one of the results of his mental illness was, in fact, Clare's complete identification with Byron and with other historical figures that, as William D. Brewer has shown, Clare connected with Byron.[30] This identification led Clare to write, in his Byronic persona, additional cantos of *Child Harold* [*sic*] and *Don Juan*. Although these poems were not published during the Romantic period and, therefore, were never subject to contemporary charges of plagiarism, Clare's ventriloquism suggests that questions of style remained central to the understanding of literary ownership and entitlement well into the nineteenth century. As Margaret Russett has demonstrated in her article exploring the cultural capital that Byron's work represented for Clare, "despite vague thematic parallels and intermittent echoes of Byron's vocabulary, Clare's major debts [in these poems] consist in the title and the stanzaic form" ("Like Wedding Gowns" 6). As a conscious engagement with the literary tradition to which he was heir, Byron's poetry was rich with allusive references to the history of verse forms, and it was, above all, the style of educated poetry that Clare could not possess. Throughout contemporary reviews, Clare's work was celebrated for the "authentic" provincialisms and the natural speech it displayed, reflections of his social class and part of his curious appeal.

Seen collectively, the investments of Wordsworth, Yearsley, and Clare represent the complex class dynamics that emerged in the Romantic-period literary marketplace, dynamics that often associated the charges of plagiarism with the ownership, improvement, and enclosure of a metaphorical literary estate. While Wordsworth's negotiation of class issues operated symbolically, his concrete engagement with copyright and plagiarism nevertheless reflects his desire to control and to shape the critical reception of his work. Meanwhile, for Yearsley and Clare, charges of appropriation and anxieties about them demonstrate a more radical sense of exclusion from the literary tradition and from the landscape it so often described. As we have seen throughout these examples, Romantic plagiarism and the questions of entitlement that it raised shaped the literary marketplace and its aesthetic values in constitutive ways.

Afterword

[O]riginal expression was consecrated by the Romantic cult of the individual genius.

—Paul K. Saint-Amour, The Copywrights

For years now, I have been planning to write a book titled Romantic Betrayal. *This will not be an autobiography, but an exposé in the true sense: an attempt to reveal the ways in which. . . . we still contend with the legacy of the Romantics' efforts to codify the past. . . . This self-centered literary history leads not only to anachronistic errors . . . but also to blindness.*

—David A. Boruchoff, "The Poetry of History"

Throughout the course of this study, I have argued that writers of the British Romantic period were invested deeply in models of appropriation, assimilation, and narrative or lyric mastery over the text of another, despite their conventional critical association with the values of autogenous originality and with what Paul K. Saint-Amour calls, in a typical formulation, "the Romantic cult of the individual genius" (6). My approach has been to read the history of plagiarism in the late eighteenth and, especially, early nineteenth centuries for what it tells us about how these authors engaged with the processes of literary borrowing and how they described the particular elements that constituted illegitimate appropriation and, by extension, aesthetic failure. As we have seen, those elements are historically distinct. Plagiarism in the Romantic period focused on questions of style, tone, voice, and improvement and involved a series of complex negotiations that centered on the processes of interpretive judgment. The contemporary controversies surrounding the subject often were motivated by competitive claims among writers who were vying to articulate the standards of the "new" poetics of the early nineteenth century, standards that did not define "originality" as an exclusive function of the solitary genius working in isolation from other writers or from print culture.

The rhetoric of plagiarism offers what is essentially a negative articulation of the aesthetic values central to Romanticism—an account of where and why particular texts fail to meet the minimum standards necessary to be considered "literary" or the more rigorous standards sufficient to merit the highest critical judgment of "originality." From this cultural model for coming to judgment, we can also infer, albeit somewhat speculatively, a positive account of the particular textual strategies that were central to the creation of a successful literary production. Perhaps above all, what the historical record suggests is that these writers valued poems and novels that "improved" upon their textual and historical resources by borrowing correctly, at a moment in time when the possible models for legitimate appropriation were quite distinct from what either came before or after. For, as we have seen, in the earlier part of the eighteenth century and in the latter part of the nineteenth century, plagiarism focused intently on what Richard Terry has called "phraseological" parallels, while the Romantic writers were far more invested in exploring the ownership of style, something that their immediate predecessors also recognized as an element of literary property. For writers and critics in the early part of the eighteenth century, however, the appropriation of style was not alone sufficient to merit charges of plagiarism. For writers and critics after the second half of the nineteenth century, when the precedents for current international copyright law were being set, the property an author had in his or her text increasingly excluded style as a protected element at all. For the Romantics, however, style was central. Where an author controlled and developed a unique textual subjectivity that dominated his or her borrowed materials, extensive unacknowledged appropriations, even verbatim, were permitted. It was, as Coleridge famously observed, an "age of personality," perhaps especially when it came to questions of plagiarism.

The difficulty, of course, is in defining the elements of style. It is challenging even to offer a contemporary account of what precisely constitutes authorial voice, and the historical and cultural difference of two hundred years, more or less, makes articulating how Romantic-era writers understood the production of lyric or narrative subjectivity a complex undertaking and one that merits an extended study of its own. However, in the late eighteenth and early nineteenth centuries, several terms and textual elements were consistently used to describe style and its relationship to literary property. I have suggested that writers in the Romantic period were apparently at liberty to borrow, extensively and verbatim, from the works of other authors so long as they dominated their appropriated materials. This domination—the central element in a judgment of improvement—was understood as a matter of controlling what they called "spirit," a term that Coleridge specifically identified with "genius" in the *Biographia Literaria* and that is associated throughout the period with numerous sublinguistic elements of a literary work, including "style," "voice," "tone," and what Mary Shelley called the "individual feeling of the author" (*NMS* 2:130). The notion, likely indebted to the trope of the *genii loci*, was that the "genius" or "spirit" of a work needed to be both appropriate to the textual place that it inhabited and interfused throughout the materials, thus functioning as its primary unifying structure. Texts that achieved both appropriateness and unity of "spirit" met the highest standard of aesthetic judgment in the period (i.e., they were "original" poems), regardless of the extent of an author's textual obligations. This "spirit," insofar as it was identified with authorial personality (his or her unique poetic "voice," his or her textual "persona"), could be rhetorically coterminous with the historical author (Wordsworth and his perceived matter-of-factness) or fictional (the poet-narrator of *Don Juan* as a Byronic figure but not as Byron), but appropriateness seems to have depended largely on meeting a certain threshold of realism that was primarily psychological. Meeting this threshold often represented a particular obstacle to writers of satire, who were also disadvantaged by the extent to which satirical genres depended on alienation through participation—on speaking in a voice or style recognizable as simultaneously belonging and not belonging to the author being imitated, thus forestalling the possibility of complete textual mastery.

While acknowledging that *voice, style,* and *tone* are notoriously difficult terms to define, it also seems clear that, in the late eighteenth and early nineteenth centuries, style (creating tone, conveyed through voice) clearly included the use of distinctive metrical patterns or innovations, as well as characteristic diction, attitude toward a subject (e.g., what Keats identified as Wordsworth's "egotistical sublime," Byron's caricature of sincerity and pose of disaffected cosmopolitanism), and, presumably, the particular deployment of identifiable syntactical structures and verse forms (e.g., Clare's imitation of Byron's use of the Spenserian stanza, Wordsworth's prosaic use of blank verse). The successful assimilation of borrowed materials meant achieving a form of poetic individualism based on the projection of a unified authorial subjectivity and was predicated upon an author's ability to re-voice persuasively any passages—verbatim or otherwise—with their historical "origins" in another textual source. However, the absence of such seamless integration represented, to borrow a phrase from Henry Taylor, a "negation of improvement," and the resulting text was described as alternatively "patchwork," "monstrous," or merely an instance of "servile" imitation. As I have argued throughout the course of this study, these terms were synonymous with a judgment of literary failure. Scientific, documentary, and historical texts that performed a rhetorical erasure of voice, like oral or traditional texts that could not be attributed to the personality or identity of any individual author, often were not considered "literary" genres at all and were, therefore, particularly easy to appropriate successfully. Thus, in the context of Romantic-period literary and print culture, the rhetoric of plagiarism represented a means of articulating and encapsulating a set of aesthetic judgments that praised particular works as "original" but that did not depend upon an absence of borrowing or on the necessity of ex nihilo invention. Quite the contrary, it assumed a collaborative and even competitive relationship to other texts and valued strategies of domination, control, and assimilation.

In his essay "Romantic Lyric Voice: What Shall We Call the 'I'?," David Perkins offers a particularly nuanced discussion of how the production of subjectivity operates not only in the Romantic-period lyric but also in what he calls the Romantic "theory" of reading lyric poetry, as distinguished from Symbolist, Modernist, Structuralist, and Deconstructive constructions of authorial subjectivity.[1] Reading William Wordsworth's own interpretive account of his "failed" sonnet "With Ships the sea was sprinkled far and wide" (1807), along with critical commentaries on the River Duddon sonnet cycle published in *The British Critic* in 1822, Perkins teases out some of the central Romantic-period attitudes toward voice and persona. The "poetic self," he demonstrates, was understood as a "dramatic personage" (231) and functioned to create an *impression* of authorial subjectivity that invited readers to "reconstruct the sensory, psychological, emotional quality of the moment. . . . [and to] intuit meaning by sympathy, by participating imaginatively in an experience, an experience the textual signs cannot completely render" (232). What is critical in this reading is the emphasis on the extent to which sophisticated Romantic-period readers understood voice as an effect of language and as a function of stylistic and formal devices. As Perkins observes, "The concept of *artistic* illusion is central to the Romantic reading of lyric" (231, my emphasis).

The implications of this argument are important: the Romantic lyric is not, then, the spontaneous emotional self-expression of a unified consciousness. It is a series of rhetorical effects and poetic invitations and evasions intended to invite (and perhaps even to compel) the reader to call an imagined consciousness into being. Early nineteenth-century readers presumably praised as "original" those poems that most effectively engaged their imaginative sympathies—those poems that imposed their psychological effects most strongly and transformed the reader's consciousness into the site of poetic ventriloquism. Perkins suggests that it is because of the emphasis in the Romantic lyric on "psychological verisimilitude" that Wordsworth saw textual allusions and borrowings as "simply . . . irrelevant" (236) and that Coleridge saw them as illustrations of the individuality of the speaking persona. This distinction rather neatly summarizes the range of attitudes that Romantic-period writers had toward the appropriation of literary materials. However, Perkins is finally mistaken to suggest that Romantic readers "assume that intertextuality dissolves the individuality of the 'I'" (236). As I have argued throughout this study, there was a constitutive relationship between deficiencies in authorial subjectivity and charges of plagiarism. However, plagiarism was an evaluative judgment of the extent to which an author had unified his or her lyric "spirit" and had mastered his or her materials. It was the fragmentation of the "I" that created plagiarism and not the other way around. In fact, it was precisely the condition that we typically designate "intertextuality"—a determined *copresence* of textual traces and voiced authorial effects—that constituted aesthetic plagiarism in the Romantic period. The risk in the Romantic lyric was not in borrowing but in borrowing badly, in a fashion where the speaking subject and the imaginative invitation to the reader that the necessarily incomplete "I" represented were not sufficient to create the impression of controlling and unifying the textual and rhetorical origins of a poem.

The picture of late eighteenth- and early nineteenth-century verse that emerges is one that emphasizes the importance of a participatory readership and the aesthetic value of collaboration, assimilation, projection, and absorption. However, despite what I think is a reasonably articulate historical record on this subject, current analyses of intellectual property and plagiarism, in contexts ranging from postmodern literary theory to considerations of classroom practice, locate in the Romantic period the origins of a conservative cultural inheritance that defines authorship as solitary self-generation and solipsistic expressivism. There is, again in the words of Saint-Amour, a "near-invulnerable glamour of the self-generated, self-legislating Romantic artifact . . . [d]isserved not only from the more collective sources and modes of its own production but from the hypothetical nature of its originality" (8). Certainly, the self-representations of particular early nineteenth-century writers contributed to the articulation of the natural genius as an isolated and visionary figure. Far more frequently, however, their contests with each other and their reflections on those controversies reflect an active engagement in both collaborative and competitive textual interpenetration. Quite simply, the critical legacy of "Romantic" authorship does not square with what writers living in Britain during the late eighteenth and early nineteenth centuries did or with how they characterized their relationship to other writers and other texts.

In historicist criticism, this is familiar territory. In Jerome McGann's influential formulation, for example, part of the problem with "rethinking romanticism" in the 1990s was a critical reluctance to draw the "distinction between 'the romantic period' (that is, a particular historical epoch) and 'romanticism' (that is, a set of cultural/ideological formations that came to prominence during the romantic period)."[2] However, the historical difficulties are, in fact, even more complex than this: what is called Romanticism increasingly reflects a set of cultural/ideological formations that came to prominence *after* the Romantic period but have been ascribed to coming to prominence *during* it. Put another way, I have come to believe that the term *Romanticism* largely denotes in its conventional modern usage (and especially in discussions of contemporary American poetry and in current pedagogical theory) an aesthetic fantasy, the efficacy of which is affirmed by a determinedly nostalgic posture that posits its origins in the (distant, inescapable) history of the early nineteenth century—a history that often appears astonishingly similar to our own cultural horizons.[3] David Boruchoff's sense of Romanticism as a "betrayal" is emblematic of our present historical moment and of our relationship to the inheritance Romanticism represents, but this relationship is not a dialectical one. The dismay and even antagonism that Romanticism seems able to generate in our collective moment is less about history than it is about ourselves and our desire to construct a version of the past that never was what we want it to be but which we are invested in the impossible effort of renouncing all the same. By granting such cultural power to the distant, historical, and self-generated bogeyman that the "Romantic cult of the individual genius" represents, we fail to recognize that we are fighting our own demons, resisting and repressing our own commitments to ideas of American individualism, the autonomy of the self, genius, capitalism, the impossible ideals of autogenous originality, and the ownership of intellectual property. In the classroom, we hold our undergraduate students to higher standards of ex nihilo originality than those to which the Romantics ever held each other and attribute our own investments to the inescapable legacy of Romantic authorship. As I said at the outset of this book, our insistence on Romanticism as a model of autogenous originality tells us more about ourselves than it tells us about the specific aesthetic contests and objectives of writers working during the late eighteenth and early nineteenth centuries in Britain—writers who were often engaged in an aesthetic project that was far less solipsistic and far more interesting than we sometimes imagine.

Notes

Preface

1. Jerome McGann, *The Romantic Ideology: A Critical Investigation* (Chicago: University of Chicago Press, 1983).

2. Clifford Siskin, *The Historicity of Romantic Discourse* (Oxford: Oxford University Press, 1988), 3. For a more recent investigation into the disciplinary construction of Romanticism and its relationship to historicist criticism, see also James Chandler, *England in 1819: The Politics of Literary Culture and the Case of Romantic Historicism* (Chicago: University of Chicago Press, 1998).

3. Charles Altieri, "Can We Be Historical Ever? Some Hopes for a Dialectical Model of Historical Self-Consciousness," in *The Uses of Literary History*, ed. Marshall Brown (Durham, N.C.: Duke University Press, 1995), 219–32.

4. Roland Barthes, *Image, Music, Text*, trans. Stephen Heath (New York: Hill, 1977); Séan Burke, *The Death and Return of the Author: Criticism and Subjectivity in Barthes, Foucault and Derrida* (Edinburgh: Edinburgh University Press, 1992); Fiona Macmillan, "Copyright's Commodification of Creativity," *ICFAI Journal of Intellectual Property Rights* 2 (2003): 53–70.

5. James E. Porter, "Intertextuality and the Discourse of Community," *Rhetoric Review* 5 (1986): 34–47; Rebecca Moore Howard, *Standing in the Shadow of Giants: Plagiarists, Authors, Collaborators* (Stamford, Conn.: Ablex Publishing Corporation, 1999), 67, 76.

Chapter 1

1. See, for example, the subsequent discussion of works including [anonymous], "Lord Byron vindicated from alleged Plagiarism," *The Gentleman's Magazine* (1818); [anonymous], "Plagiarisms of Lord Byron Detected," *The Monthly Magazine* (1821); [anonymous], "The Plagiarisms of Lord Byron," *The Gentleman's Magazine* (1818); J. F. Ferrier, "The Plagiarisms of S. T. Coleridge," *Blackwood's Edinburgh Magazine* (1840); Thomas Medwin, "A Cast of Casti. By Lord Byron," *The New Anti-Jacobin* (1833); Thomas Medwin, *Some Rejected Stanzas of "Don Juan" with Byron's Own Curious Notes. The whole written in Double Rhyme, after Casti's manner, an Italian author from whom Byron is said to have plagiarized many of his beauties* (1845); Edward Quillinan, "Imaginary Conversation, Between Mr. Walter Savage Landor and the Editor of Blackwood's Magazine," *Blackwood's Edinburgh*

Magazine (1843); Henry Taylor, "Recent Poetical Plagiarisms and Imitations," *The London Magazine* (1823); and Thomas DeQuincey, "Samuel Taylor Coleridge: By the English Opium Eater," *Tait's Magazine* (1834–35).

2. A. C. Bradley, *A Commentary on Tennyson's "In Memoriam"* (Westport, Conn.: Greenwood Publishers, 1974), 71, qtd. in Alexander Lindey, *Plagiarism and Originality* (New York: Harpers, 1952), 88. Bradley's discussion of Tennyson's plagiarisms in poems written during the 1830s and 1840s proposes several instances in which borrowings may be considered legitimate, including familiarity, "coincidence," and "unconscious reproduction," all terms that operated (albeit with particular historical nuances) in the Romantic rhetoric of plagiarism until at least the late 1830s. Significantly, however, Bradley does not list improvement—the central aspect of earlier nineteenth-century attitudes toward the charge—as one of the possible legitimizing factors. By the latter part of the nineteenth century, improvement had become a less significant topic of critical investigation. The transition in attitudes toward plagiarism in the 1830s and 1840s is discussed at greater length in Chapter 6 of this study. On late nineteenth- and early twentieth-century British charges of literary plagiarism, see also Paul K. Saint-Amour, *The Copywrights: Intellectual Property and the Literary Imagination* (Ithaca, N.Y.: Cornell University Press, 2003).

3. Stuart P. Green, "Plagiarism, Norms, and the Limits of Theft Law: Some Observations on the Use of Criminal Sanctions in Enforcing Intellectual Property Rights," *Hastings Law Journal* 54 (November 2002): 200, 205.

4. *Napolitano v. Trustees of Princeton University* (N.J. App. Div. 1982), *Opinions of the New Jersey Courts* 453 A.2d 263: <http://lawlibrary.rutgers.edu>.

5. United States law currently recognizes mood and style as possible elements of a text subject to copyright protection if they do not constitute *scenes a faire* and are part of an extrinsic test determining a larger pattern of similarities, some of which *must* also include elements such as the sequence of events, character, dialogue, setting, place, and plot. As demonstrated in the case of *Dr. Seuss Enterprises v. Penguin Books* (924 F. Supp. 1559, 1562 [S.D. Cal. 1996]; affirmed 109 F.3d 1394 [9th Cir. 1997]) contemporary copyright law does not protect poetical style or the use of distinctive metrical devices as elements of authorial property; the case also engages some of the persistent problems posed by parody and assessments of "transformation."

6. Green, 179–80. For discussions of the morality of plagiarism, see also Lise Buranen and Alice M. Roy, eds., *Perspectives on Plagiarism and Intellectual Property in a Postmodern World* (Albany: State University of New York Press, 1999); Lisa Ede and Andrea Lunsford, "Crimes of Writing: Refiguring 'Proper' Discursive Practices," *Writing on the Edge* 11:2 (Spring/Summer 2000): 43–54; and Rebecca Moore Howard, "The Ethics of Plagiarism," in *The Ethics of Writing Instruction: Issues in Theory and Practice*, ed. Michael A. Pemberton (Stamford, Conn.: Ablex Publishing Corporation, 2000).

7. Barthes, *Image, Music, Text*; Michel Foucault, "The Author Function," in *Textual Strategies: Perspectives in Post-Structuralist Criticism*, ed. Josué V. Harari (Ithaca, N.Y.: Cornell University Press, 1979).

8. Rebecca Moore Howard, *Standing in the Shadow of Giants*; P. F. LaFollette, *Stealing into Print: Fraud, Plagiarism, and Misconduct in Scientific Publishing* (Berke-

ley: University of California Press, 1992); A. Lathrop, *Student Cheating and Plagiarism in the Internet Era: A Wake-Up Call* (Englewood, N.J.: Libraries Unlimited, 2000); and D. L. McCabe, L. K. Treveno, and K. D. Butterfield, "Cheating in Academic Institutions: A Decade of Research," *Ethics and Behavior* 11 (2001): 219–32.

9. Christopher Ricks, "Plagiarism," *Proceedings of the British Academy* 97 (1998): 149–68; and *Allusion to the Poets* (Oxford: Oxford University Press, 2002).

10. Paulina Kewes, ed. *Plagiarism in Early Modern England* (New York: Palgrave/Macmillan, 2002). Kewes likewise interrogates the historical conditions of Renaissance plagiarism in her *Authorship and Appropriation: Writing for the Stage in England, 1660–1710* (Oxford: Oxford University Press, 1998).

11. Romanticism is invoked, for example, by Rebecca Moore Howard, *Standing in the Shadow of Giants*, 67–76; see also Sherie Gradin, *Romancing Rhetorics: Social Expressivist Perspectives on the Teaching of Writing* (Portsmouth, N.H.: Boyton/Cook, 1995); and James A. Berlin, *Rhetoric and Reality: Writing Instruction in American Colleges, 1900–1985* (Carbondale: Southern Illinois University Press, 1987), 73.

12. Coleridge's plagiarisms were first discussed extensively by John Livingston Lowes, who offered a psychological and sympathetic approach in *The Road to Xanadu: A Study in the Ways of the Imagination* (Boston: Houghton Mifflin, 1927). The most detailed and important indictment of Coleridge was offered by Norman Fruman, whose *Coleridge: The Damaged Archangel* (New York: George Braziller, 1971) traced the critical history of the controversy from its origins in the periodical press of the 1830s to the academic contexts of the 1960s. Thomas McFarland's *Coleridge and the Pantheist Tradition* (Oxford: Oxford University Press, 1969) and Jerome Christensen's *Coleridge's Blessed Machine of Language* (Ithaca, N.Y.: Cornell University Press, 1981) defended the poet's borrowings, which Christensen argued constituted a conscious compositional method amounting to metanarrative. Jack Stillinger addressed the question of plagiarism from a poststructuralist perspective in *Multiple Authorship and the Myth of Solitary Genius* (Oxford: Oxford University Press, 1991), and Susan Eilbenberg offered an influential deconstructivist reading in *Strange Power of Speech: Wordsworth, Coleridge, and Literary Possession* (Oxford: Oxford University Press, 1992). Other important but brief discussions of Coleridge's plagiarisms, all cited by Fruman, include René Wellek's *A History of Modern Criticism, 1750–1950*, 2 vols. (New Haven, Conn.: Yale University Press, 1955); Joseph Warren Beach, "Coleridge's Borrowings from the German," *ELH* 9 (1942): 36–58; and G. N. G. Orsini, *Coleridge and German Idealism* (Carbondale: Southern Illinois University Press, 1969). See also Thomas Mallon, *Stolen Words: Forays into the Origins and Ravages of Plagiarism* (New York: Ticknor and Fields, 1989).

Apart from works addressing the appropriations of Coleridge, there have been relatively few studies addressing the subject of plagiarism in the Romantic period. Alina Clej touches upon the topic of plagiarism as "echoing" and subversion in *A Genealogy of the Modern Self: Thomas DeQuincey and the Intoxication of Writing* (Stanford, Calif.: Stanford University Press, 1995). Charles Coe's early work, *Wordsworth and the Literature of Travel* (New York: Bookman Associates, 1953), detailed Wordsworth's extensive debts to travel writing, and no subsequent scholarship has considered these borrowings in detail. Wordsworth's borrowings from eighteenth-century poetry, however, have been detailed by David McCracken in "Wordsworth on Human Wishes and Poetic Borrowing," *Modern Philology* 79:4 (May 1982): 386–99. McCracken offers a persuasive biographical analysis of Wordsworth's attitude toward plagiarism. The most important book-length studies of Wordsworth's relationship to his literary past include Edwin Stein's *Wordsworth's Art of Allusion* (University Park: Pennsylvania State University, 1988) and Lucy Newlyn's *Coleridge, Wordsworth, and the Language of Allusion* (Oxford: Oxford University Press, 1986). Newlyn's *Reading, Writing, and Romanticism: The Anxiety of Reception* (Oxford: Oxford University Press, 2000) extends her analysis. Margaret Russett's "Like 'Wedding Gowns or Money from the Mint': Clare's Borrowed Inheritance," in *Romanticism and the Law*, ed. Michael Macovski, *Romantic Circles Praxis Series* (University of Maryland, 1999; http://www.rc.umd.edu/praxis/law/russett/mruss.htm), considers Clare's plagiarisms from Byron.

13. These plagiarisms are discussed in detail throughout the course of this study; see citations in individual chapters.

14. Françoise Meltzer's *Hot Property: The Stakes and Claims of Literary Originality* (Chicago: University of Chicago Press, 1994) reads the textual debts of poets such as Paul Célan with an eye toward explicating the stakes in charges of plagiarism. More recently, Marilyn Randall has extended Meltzer's discussion in her admirable study *Pragmatic Plagiarism: Authorship, Profit, and Power* (Toronto: University of Toronto Press, 2001), in which she examines "the sociocultural conditions of the production of plagiarism as a negative—or positive—aesthetic category" (xi) and argues for an understanding of the ways in which allegations of plagiarism can be reduced to pragmatic issues of power and dominance. However, Randall explicitly states that defining plagiarism is not her project (16), and she does not account for the historical instability of the term. Indeed, she dismisses the problem: "Historical descriptions and definitions generally present a rather small and surprisingly stable range of elements to be considered" (15). Although I agree that charges of plagiarism frequently can be traced back to issues of dominance and competition, I take as my thesis the opposite claim: that plagiarism, at least during the Romantic period, did signify something distinct, surprising, and historically specific.

15. Wordsworth, *The Poetical Works of William Wordsworth*, ed. Ernest DeSelincourt and Helen Darbishire, 5 vols. (Oxford: Clarendon Press, 1949), 3: 82, 80.

16. Coleridge, *[The Selected Works of] Samuel Taylor Coleridge*, ed. H. J. Jackson (Oxford: Oxford University Press, 1985), 194.

17. Edward Young, *Conjectures on Original Composition in a Letter to [Samuel Richardson] the Author of Sir Charles Grandison* (London: A. Millar and R. and J. Dodsley, 1759), 94–95. As Brean Hammond has demonstrated, this emphasis on Young is probably misplaced to the extent that originality was the subject of significant discussion in theatrical contexts during the 1670s. See Kewes, ed., *Plagiarism in Early Modern England*, 48; and Brean Hammond, *Professional Imaginative Writing in England, 1670–1740* (Oxford: Clarendon Press, 1997).

18. A similar point is made by Richard Terry, who observes, "It would be wrong to see Young's essay as roundly hostile towards literary imitation; rather he tries to distinguish a technique of imitation . . . that could be seen as consistent

with invention of creativity." See Terry, "'In Pleasing Memory of All He Stole': Plagiarism and Literary Detraction, 1747–1785," in Kewes, ed., *Plagiarism in Early Modern England*, 181–200, 194.

19. Percy Bysshe Shelley, *Shelley's Poetry and Prose*, ed. Donald H. Reiman and Sharon B. Powers (New York: W. W. Norton, 1977), 499.

20. Mark Rose, *Authors and Owners: The Invention of Copyright* (Cambridge, Mass.: Harvard University Press, 1993); Lionel Bently and Brad Sherman, *The Making of Modern Intellectual Property Law: The British Experience, 1760–1911* (Cambridge: Cambridge University Press, 1999); Martha Woodmansee and Peter Jaszi, eds., *The Construction of Authorship: Textual Appropriation in Law and Literature* (Durham, N.C.: Duke University Press, 1994). The language that Rose employs to distinguish these two arguments is found in Romantic-period texts such as Thomas Hodgskin, *The Natural and Artificial Right of Property Contrasted* (London: B. Steil, 1832; rpt. Clifton: Augustus M. Kelley, 1973).

21. John Locke, *Two Treatises of Government*, ed. Peter H. Nidditch (Oxford: Oxford University Press, 1975).

22. Summarizing Rose, *Authors and Owners*.

23. *The Guardian* 30, 15 April 1713.

24. In Kewes, ed., *Plagiarism in Early Modern England*, 181–200.

25. These charges were brought against Milton by William Lauder in a series of articles published in *The Gentleman's Magazine* beginning in 1747; Lauder claimed to have uncovered plagiarisms in *Paradise Lost* (1667) from Hugo Grolius's *Adamus Exul* (1601), Andrew Ramsey's *Poemata Sacra* (1633), and J. Masen's *Sarcolis* (1654). The accusations prompted immediate controversy, and most contemporary reviewers, including Samuel Johnson, vigorously defended Milton. For more on the Lauder controversy, see Terry, "In Pleasing Memory," and Thomas Mallon, *Stolen Words*.

26. Richard Hurd, *Q. Horatii Flacci Epistola ad Augustum. With an English commentary and notes. To which is added a discourse concerning poetical imitation* (1751), qtd. in Terry, "In Pleasing Memory," 188.

27. William Warburton, *A Letter from an Author to a Member of Parliament Concerning Literary Property* (London: John and Paul Knapton, 1747). Rpt. *Horace Walpole's Political Tracts, 1747–1748, with Two by William Warburton on Literary Property, 1747 and 1762*, ed. Stephen Parks (New York: Garland, 1974); *Tonson v. Collins* cited in *English Reports: Full Reprints*, ed. Alexander Wood Repton, 176 vols. (London: W. Green and Sons, 1900–1932), 96: 169.

28. W. Enfield, *Observations on Literary Property* (London: Johnson, 1774). Rpt. *The Literary Property Debate: Eight Tracts, 1774–1775*, ed. Stephen Parks (New York: Garland, 1974), qtd. in Sherman and Bently, *The Making of Modern Intellectual Property Law*, 33; Francis Hargrave, *An Argument in Defence of Literary Property* (London: Otridge, 1774), 6–7.

29. Henry Fielding, *Tom Jones, A Foundling*, ed. Fredson Bowers (New York: Modern Library, 1994); Tobias Smollett, "Habakkuk Hilding, Justice and Chapman," *The Covent-Garden Journal*, 15 January 1752.

30. Thomas Lockwood, *Post-Augustan Satire: Charles Churchill and Satirical Poetry, 1750–1800* (Seattle: University of Washington Press, 1979). Lockwood notes

that "the Romantics . . . felt that satiric poems, and more particularly the poems of Pope, were not the best place to look for the definitions of poetry" and that authors of satire ran the "risk of being considered less than truly a poet" (168, 172). In *Towards a Literature of Knowledge* (Oxford: Oxford University Press, 1989), Jerome McGann has argued that satire was antithetical to fundamental aspects of the Romantic aesthetic (39).

31. Stephen Jones, *Satire and Romanticism* (New York: St. Martin's Press, 2002); and Gary Dyer, *British Satire and the Politics of Style, 1789–1832* (Cambridge: Cambridge University Press, 1997). Satire and its relationship to Romantic-period plagiarism are discussed in Chapter 6 of this study.

32. Edmund Burke, "Tristram Shandy," *The Annual Register* 3 (1760): 247.

33. John C. Ferriar, *Illustrations of Sterne, with Other Essays and Verses* (London: Cadell and Davies, 1798). Walter Scott, "Laurence Sterne," *Ballantyne's Novelists Library*, 8 vols. (London: Hurst, Robinson, and Company, 1821); rpt. in *The Miscellaneous Prose Works of Sir Walter Scott*, 30 vols. (Edinburgh: A. and C. Black, 1870), 3: 291–92.

34. Peter Bayley, *Poems* (London: William Millar, 1803). These plagiarisms are discussed in greater detail in Chapter 6.

35. *The Letters of William and Dorothy Wordsworth*, ed. Ernest DeSelincourt, rev. Mary Moore and Alan G. Hill, 7 vols. (Oxford: Clarendon Press, 1970), 1: 455.

36. In his *British Satire and the Politics of Style*, Dyer discusses the relationship between style and Romantic satire more generally, arguing for three predominant "modes" in the period, the Juvenalian, Horatian, and "Radical" (41). While each of these modes was distinguished by elements of style, which for Dyer includes tone, verse forms, diction, and rhetorical positioning, the individuation of personal authorial style, as I discuss it here, was not a defining feature.

Chapter 2

1. Thomas DeQuincey, "Samuel Taylor Coleridge: By the English Opium Eater," *Tait's Magazine* (September, October, and November 1834 and January 1835), rpt. *The Collected Writings of Thomas DeQuincey*, ed. David Mason, 2 vols. (Edinburgh: Adam and Charles Black, 1854).

2. See Coleridge's note published with his "Lines on an Autumnal Evening" (1796); as Robert Morrison has observed (North American Society for Study of Romanticism listserv [NASSR-L], 28 June 2002), Coleridge's plagiarisms had also been previously cited by John Wilson, in an October 1823 installment of *Blackwood's* "*Noctes Ambrosianes*" series, in which Coleridge was characterized as "not only a plagiary, but . . . a *bone fide* most unconscientious thief" (14: 500).

3. DeQuincey's "bright particular star" is a sly reference to *All's Well That Ends Well*, 1, sc. 1.

4. For a complete discussion of the More and Cowley controversy, see Ellen Donkin, *Getting into the Act: Women Playwrights in London, 1776–1829* (New York: Routledge, 1995); Cowley alleges the plagiarisms in her preface to *Albina, Countess*

Raimond; A Tragedy, by Mrs. Cowley: As it is Performed at the Theatre-Royal in the Hay-Market (London: T. Spilsbury, 1779). The charges of plagiarism here engage both questions of consciousness and improvement.

5. Henry Taylor, "Recent Poetical Plagiarisms and Imitations," *The London Magazine* 8 (December 1823): 597–604.

6. Matthew Lewis, "Advertisement," *The Monk* (1796), ed. John Berryman (New York: Grove Press, 1952), 32; Anna Seward, letter of 30 January 1800 to Thomas Park, *The Letters of Anna Seward*, 6 vols. (London: John Murray, 1811), 5: 270.

7. Coleridge, *Notebooks of Samuel Taylor Coleridge*, ed. Kathleen Coburn, 5 vols. (New York: Bollingen Foundation, 1957), entry 1421 4.108, vol. 1, pt. 1, 1421.

8. Coleridge, *The Collected Letters of Samuel Taylor Coleridge*, ed. E. L. Griggs, 4 vols. (Oxford: Oxford University Press, 1959), 2: 489–90.

9. For more on the authorship of this doggerel verse, see Coburn on the notebook entry dated November 1801 (*NSTC* 1003) and *Samuel Taylor Coleridge: The Collected Works*, ed. Kathleen Coburn, 16 vols. (Princeton, N.J.: Princeton University Press, 2001), 16 [vol. 1, pt. 1], 482, n. 1.19.

10. Margaret Russett, "Meter, Identity, Voice: Untranslating *Christabel*," *Studies in English Literature* 43:4 (2003): 773–97.

11. E.g., Coleridge's definition of the poet in the *Biographia Literaria* as one who "diffuses a tone, and a spirit of unity, that blends and (as it were) fuses, each into each, by that synthetic and magical power . . . imagination" (*STC* 319). Other instances of Romantic-period writers associating style as an element of literary property and critical evaluation are discussed throughout this study; see particularly Chapter 3.

12. Edward Bostetter, *The Romantic Ventriloquists* (Seattle: University of Washington Press, 1963). The syntax that Bostetter discusses is at once the particularity of the poetic sentence and a larger cultural narrative of origins and ontology, which he contrasts with the Christian worldview that preceded the Enlightenment.

13. Dorothy Wordsworth, *The Journals of Dorothy Wordsworth*, ed. Mary Moorman (Oxford: Oxford University Press, 1971).

14. On the voluntary aspects of the trance and the history of mesmerism, animal magnetism, and the trance in the Romantic period, see Charles J. Rzepka, "Re-Collecting Spontaneous Overflows: Romantic Passions, the Sublime, and Mesmerism," in *Romantic Passions*, ed. Elizabeth Fay, *Romantic Circles Praxis Series* (University of Maryland, 2001; http://www.rc.umd.edu/praxis/passions/rzepka/rzp.html); Nigel Leask, "Shelley's 'Magnetic Ladies': Romantic Mesmerism and the Politics of the Body," in *Beyond Romanticism: New Approaches to Texts and Contexts*, ed. Stephen Copley and John Whale (London: Routledge, 1992), 53–78; and Adam Crabtree, *From Mesmer to Freud: Magnetic Sleep and the Roots of Psychological Healing* (New Haven, Conn.: Yale University Press, 1993).

15. A point also emphasized later in the poem, ll. 618–20, when Coleridge writes: "and more she [Christabel] could not say: / For what she knew she could not tell, / O'er-mastered by the mighty spell."

16. An additional suggestion to this effect is the implication that Geraldine is also operating unwillingly and unconsciously to that extent throughout the remain-

der of the narrative; Coleridge writes: "O Geraldine! One hour was thine— / Thou'st had thy will!" (ll. 305–6).

17. Alan Richardson, *British Romanticism and the Science of the Mind* (Cambridge: Cambridge University Press, 2001), 39.

18. See particularly chapters 5–8 and 12 of the *Biographia.*

19. John Michael Kooy, *Coleridge, Schiller, and Aesthetic Education* (London: Palgrave/Macmillan, 2002), 96.

20. Friedrich Schelling, *System of Transcendental Idealism* (1800), trans. Peter Heath (Charlottesville: University of Virginia Press, 1978).

21. Russett, "Untranslating *Christabel*," 772; Eilenberg, *Strange Powers of Speech*, ix, passim.

22. *Biographia Literaria. Second Edition Prepared for Publication in Part by the Late Henry Nelson Coleridge, Completed and Published by his Widow* (1847), rpt. *The Complete Works of Samuel Taylor Coleridge*, ed. W. G. T. Shedd (New York: Harpers, 1884).

23. Summarizing here Fruman's researches into the nineteenth- and early twentieth-century critical history. See J. F. Ferrier, "The Plagiarisms of S. T. Coleridge," *Blackwood's Edinburgh Magazine* 47 (1840): 287–99; and C. M. Ingleby, "On Some Points Connected with the Philosophy of Coleridge," *Transactions of the Royal Society of Literature of the United Kingdom* 9 (2nd ser.): 400.

24. Lowes, *The Road to Xanadu*; Adrien Bonjour, "Coleridge's 'Hymn Before Sunrise'" (Ph.D. diss. University of Lausanne, 1942).

25. Beach, "Coleridge's Borrowings from the German"; Wellek, *The History of Modern Criticism*); McFarland, *Coleridge and the Pantheist Tradition*; and Christensen, *Coleridge's Blessed Machine of Language*. In this earlier work, Christensen describes Coleridge's plagiarisms in the *Biographia* as part of a metatextual "marginal method" (96–117); this argument is less persuasive than the position he later develops in *Romanticism at the End of History* (2000), where he observes that "only a conception of the will as strongly involuntary . . . explains the scandal of Coleridge's ascribing to the will the primary act of 'self-duplication'. . . . the primary act of the will could be said to plagiarize the self" (35). This reflects precisely the complexities surrounding Coleridge's association of plagiarism with the disassociation of the will from the volition that I discuss above. Donald H. Reiman also addressed the issue of Coleridge's plagiarisms in the *Biographia* in "Coleridge and the Art of Equivocation," *Studies in Romanticism* 25 (Fall 1986): 325–50. Reiman argues that Coleridge's borrowings are part of a rhetorical effort in the *Biographia* to construction an ironic and characteristically neoclassical display of erudition at the expense of his critics. While my argument does not exclude the possibility of such an ironic stance on Coleridge's part, satirical borrowings of this sort were particularly prone to plagiarism charges in the period and for reasons having to do with the disintegration of voice—a textual element that Coleridge, as we have seen, particularly valued.

26. A point also made and further developed by Alan Sheridan in his preface to Jacques Lacan, *Écrits: A Selection*, trans. Alan Sheridan (New York: W.W. Norton, 1977).

27. The historical trajectory linking the early reflections on the unconscious developed by eighteenth-century philosophers such as Schelling and writers such as

Coleridge to the works of Barthes or Lacan is not merely suggestive, of course. Freud was deeply indebted to Schelling, drawing from him, for example, the definition of terms such as *Unheimlich* (The Uncanny), while Lacan famously claimed, "I am the one who has read Freud." Roland Barthes, *The Pleasure of the Text*, trans. Richard Miller (New York: Farrar, Straus and Giroux, 1986), 21–22.

Chapter 3

1. For an instance of a woman writer accusing a woman of plagiarism, see the charges of plagiarism brought by Anna Seward against Charlotte Smith, whose sonnets she characterized as "hackneyed scraps of dismality, which her memory furnished her from our various poets," qtd. in Pinch 61. *The Letters of Anna Seward*, 2: 287. The emphasis on the "hackneyed" and unassimilated nature of the borrowings invokes the Romantic emphasis on improvement, narrative mastery, and voice in charges of plagiarism. For further discussion of Seward's allegations against Smith, see Adela Pinch, *Strange Fits of Passion: Epistemologies of Emotion from Hume to Austen* (Stanford, Calif.: Stanford University Press, 1996). The charges of plagiarism brought by Hannah More against Hannah Cowley offer another instance of a woman accusing another woman of plagiarism; these allegations are discussed in Chapter 2 and, more extensively, by Donkin in *Getting into the Act*. On this topic, see also Betsy Bolton, *Women, Nationalism, and the Romantic Stage: Theatre and Politics in Britain, 1780–1800* (Cambridge: Cambridge University Press, 2001).

2. William Blackstone, *Commentaries on the Laws of England* (Oxford: Clarendon Press, 1765–69), 4: 15.

3. Caroline Norton, *The Sorrows of Rosalie: A Tale, with Other Poems* (London: J. Ebers, 1829). For further information on Norton as a late-Romantic poet, see Isobel Armstrong and Virginia Blain, eds., *Women's Poetry, Late Romantic to Late Victorian: Genre and Genre, 1830–1900* (Houndsmill: Macmillan, 1999).

4. Caroline Norton, *English Laws for Women in the Nineteenth Century* (London, 1854).

5. John Guillory, *Cultural Capital: The Problems of Literary Canon Formation* (Chicago: University of Chicago Press, 1993), 101, 129. For further information on the emergence of the literary and literature in eighteenth-century and Romantic-period culture, see particularly Trevor Ross, *Making of the English Literary Canon from the Middle Ages to the Late Eighteenth Century* (Montreal: McGill-Queen's Press, 1998). Ross examines the process of canon formation as a discourse in the late eighteenth century as a process of "communal self-identification" (17). Jacques Derrida develops the same point more generally, arguing, "Literarity is not a natural essence . . . of the text. It is the correlative of an intentional relation to the text, an intentional layer which integrates in itself . . . the more or less implicit consciousness of rules which are conventional or institutional—social in any case" (44). Works communicated through the oral or folkloric tradition, by virtue of their circuitous route of transmission and employment and their evolving historical contexts, lack precisely this degree of certain or definable authorial intention, and the

evade the "consciousness" of social rules by their diffuse circulation. See Derrida, *Acts of Literature*, ed. Derek Attridge (London: Routledge, 1992).

6. There is no historical evidence to suggest that the fact of translation had any particular bearing on the question of plagiarism in the Romantic period. Works in translation were judged according to the same standards that applied to the aesthetic evaluation of other works. Where improvement existed, a translation could not be said to constitute an aesthetic plagiarism, and, where improvement did not exist, the fact of translation did not protect an author from these charges. The allegations that Coleridge plagiarized from Schelling's *System des transcendentalen Idealismus* demonstrates how obvious this point is. Both Coleridge and Wordsworth additionally discuss plagiarism in contexts related to works in translation; see Coleridge's charges against Mackintosh (*CLSTC* 2: 675), discussed above, and Wordsworth's reflections in the "Essay Supplementary to the Preface" (*PWWW* 3: 75–78).

Theories of translation in the Romantic period are discussed more fully in several studies. See particularly Timothy Webb, *The Violet in the Crucible: Shelley and Translation* (Oxford: Oxford University Press, 1976); Lawrence Venuti, *The Translator's Invisibility* (New York: Routledge, 1995); Bruce Graver, *William Wordsworth: Translations of Chaucer and Virgil* (Ithaca, N.Y: Cornell University Press, 1998); Peter Mortenson, "Robbing *The Robbers*: Schiller, Xenophobia and the Politics of British Romantic Translation," *Literature and History* 11:1 (Spring 2002): 41–61; Ruriko Suzuki, "Translation in the 1790s: A Means of Creating a Like Existence and/or Restoring the Original," *Romanticism on the Net* 2 (May 1992): <http://www/ron/umontreal.ca>; and Jennifer Wallace, "Tyranny and Translation: Shelley's Unbinding of Prometheus," *Romanticism* 1:1 (1995): 15–33.

7. Bonjour, "Coleridge's 'Hymn before Sun-rise.'" See Fruman, *The Damaged Archangel*, 26–30. For further discussion of this topic, see E. L. Shaffer, "Coleridge's Swiss Voice: Friederike Brun and the Vale of Chamouni," in *Essays in Memory of Michael Parkinson and Janine Dakyns*, ed. Christopher Smith, et al. (Norwich: East Anglia University, 1996).

8. For a discussion of the textual relationship between Robinson's ode and "The Visions of the Maid of Orleans," see Timothy Fulford, "Mary Robinson and the Abyssinian Maid: Coleridge's Muses and Feminist Criticism," *Romanticism on the Net* 13 (February 1999): <http://www.ron.umontreal.ca>. Fulford argues that the placement was intended to "link Robinson with a French maid" in order to associate her suffering with the contemporary political events in France.

9. Mary Robinson, *Mary Robinson: Selected Poems*, ed. Judith Pascoe (Peterborough: Broadview Literary Texts, 2000), 324, n. 1.

10. Coleridge, *The Complete Poetical Works of Samuel Taylor Coleridge*, ed. E. H. Coleridge, 2 vols. (Oxford: Oxford University Press, 1912), 1: 353, n. 1. According to J. C. C. Mays, "A Stranger Minstrel" was also composed during November of 1800; see Coleridge, *The Collected Works* vol. 16, pt. 2, 650. As a comparison of variants reveals, Coleridge responded not to the original version of the ode that Robinson published in the *Morning Post* but to her subsequent (and almost immediate) revision, later published posthumously in the 1806 edition of her poetry, which contained references to herself as a "stranger" and a "minstrel."

11. Coleridge, *Unpublished Letters of Samuel Taylor Coleridge,* ed. E. L. Griggs, 2 vols. (London: Constable, 1910), 1: 87. Letter dated 5 January 1798.

12. Peter Manning, *Reading Romantics: Texts and Contexts* (Oxford: Oxford University Press, 1990), 153.

13. On the matter of Dorothy Wordsworth's legal status as feme sole, it is worth recollecting that she and William were symbolically invested in casting their relationship as a version of marriage and, implicitly, of coverture. The exchange of the wedding ring between the siblings on the morning of William Wordsworth's marriage to Mary Hutchinson, described in Dorothy's journal entry for 4 October 1802, is particularly suggestive. Dorothy likely considered her property as part of the collective household property under these terms. See Dorothy Wordsworth, *Grasmere Journals,* ed. Pamela Woof (Oxford: Oxford University Press, 1991).

14. *[The Selected Works of] William Wordsworth,* ed. Stephen Gill (Oxford: Oxford University Press, 1984).

15. Dorothy Wordsworth, *Journals,* 109.

16. I discuss the circulation of Williams's journal at greater length in my essays "'A mixture of all the styles': Nationalism, Colonialism, and Plagiarism in Shelley's Indian Circle," *European Romantic Review* 8:2 (Spring 1997): 155–68; and "'Sporting Sketches during a Short Stay in Hindustane': Bodleian MS Shelley adds. e. 21 and Travel Literature in the Shelley Circle," *Romanticism* 4:2 (Fall 1998): 174–88.

17. Mary Poovey, *The Proper Lady and the Woman Writer* (Los Angeles: University of California Press, 1984), 36, citing *The Lady of Letters in the Eighteenth Century,* ed. Robert Halsband and Irvin Ehrenprein (Los Angeles: University of California Press, 1969).

18. The collaborative contexts of Romantic authorship have been most fully explored in relationship to John Keats and his circle. See particularly Jeffrey N. Cox, "Keats in the Cockney School," *Romanticism* 2: 1 (1996): 27–39; and Nicholas Roe, *John Keats and the Culture of Dissent* (Oxford: Clarendon Press, 1997).

19. Susan M. Levin, *Dorothy Wordsworth and Romanticism* (New Brunswick, N.J.: Rutgers University Press, 1987), 219–20. Levin was the first to republish this poem in a modern edition, as part of her appendix (1) to *The Complete Poetry of Dorothy Wordsworth,* 175–237.

20. Levin, *Dorothy Wordsworth and Romanticism.*

21. Kenneth Neill Cameron, ed., *Shelley and His Circle, 1773–1822,* 6 vols. (Cambridge: Harvard University Press, 1961).

22. *The Poetical Repository of Fugitive Poetry for 1810–11* (London: F. C. and J. Rivington, 1814), 617; and *The British Critic* (April 1811): 408–09.

23. Shelley, *The Complete Poetry of Percy Bysshe Shelley,* ed. Neil Fraistat and Donald H. Reiman, 1 vol. to date (Baltimore: Johns Hopkins University Press, 2000).

24. Richard Garnett, ed., *Original Poetry by Victor and Cazire* (London: John Lane, 1898), x.

25. Fraistat and Reiman argue that Percy Bysshe Shelley must have been responsible for the borrowing, rather than Elizabeth Shelley, on the basis that they believe the poem to have been copied from memory and that Percy Bysshe Shelley

was "more likely than Elizabeth Shelley to have admired *Tales of Terror* enough to memorize 'The Black Canon'" (158).

26. Thomas Jefferson Hogg, *The Life of Percy Bysshe Shelley*, 4 vols. (London: Edward Moxon, 1858), 262.

27. For further discussion of these celebrated cases, see Percy Fitzgerald, *A Famous Forgery: Being the Story of "the Unfortunate" Doctor Dodd* (London: Chapman and Hall, 1865); William Henry Ireland, *The Confessions of William-Henry Ireland: Containing the Particulars of his Fabrication of the Shakespeare Manuscripts* (London: T. Goddard, 1805); Paul Baines, *The House of Forgery in Eighteenth-Century Britain* (Brookfield: Ashgate, 1999); Joseph Rosenblum, *Practice to Deceive: The Amazing Stories of Literary Forgery's Most Notorious Practitioners* (New Castle: Oak Knoll Press, 2000); and Nick Groom, *The Forger's Shadow: How Forgery Changed the Course of Literature* (London: Picador, 2002). Other discussions of Romantic-period forgeries include Ian Haywood, *The Making of History: A Study of the Forgeries of James Macpherson and Thomas Chatterton in Relation to Eighteenth-Century Ideas of History and Fiction* (Rutherford, N.J.: Fairleigh Dickinson University Press, 1986); and James Soderholm, *Multiple Authorship and the Myth of Solitary Genius* (Oxford: Oxford University Press, 1991).

28. Jack Lynch, "The Love of Truth: Johnson and Literary Fraud," American Society for Eighteenth-Century Studies (ASECS) conference presentation (1999), <http://andromeda.rutgers.edu/~jlynch/Papers/sjfraud.html>; Samuel Johnson, *The Yale Edition of the Works of Samuel Johnson*. 16 vols. (New Haven, Conn.: Yale University Press, 1958–90), 14: 196–97.

29. Nicola Z. Trott, "North of the Border: Cultural Crossing in the *Noctes Ambrosiane*." *Romanticism on the Net* 20 (November 2000): <http://www.ron.umontreal.ca>.

30. Thomas Medwin, *The Life of Percy Bysshe Shelley*, 2 vols. (London: Thomas Cautley Newby, 1847), 1: 62.

31. Chatterton, *The Complete Works of Thomas Chatterton*, ed. Donald S. Taylor, 2 vols. (Oxford: Clarendon Press, 1971), 1: 211.

32. E. J. Clery, *The Rise of Supernatural Fiction, 1762–1800* (Cambridge: Cambridge University Press, 1995), 142.

33. Louis F. Peck, *The Life of Matthew G. Lewis* (Cambridge, Mass.: Harvard University Press, 1961), 21.

34. Syndy Conger, *Matthew G. Lewis, Charles Robert Maturin and the Germans* (Salzburg: Universität Salzburg, 1977).

35. Ambrose Merton [William John Thoms], *Athenauem* 862 (22 August 1846).

36. Katie Trumpener, *Bardic Nationalism: The Romantic Novel and the British Empire* (Princeton, N.J.: Princeton University Press, 1997), 74–82, 75.

37. Penny Fielding, *Writing and Orality: Nationality, Culture, and Nineteenth-Century Scottish Fiction* (Oxford: Oxford University Press, 1996).

38. Peter Murphy, *Poetry as an Occupation and an Art in Britain, 1760–1830* (Cambridge: Cambridge University Press, 1993).

39. The beginnings of German Romanticism have likewise been located in the early researches of Jakob and Wilhelm Grimm and of Johann Gottfried von Herder,

whose collected fairy tales and whose *Stimmen der Volker in ihren Liedern* (Voices of the People in Their Songs) respectively set out to preserve the "authentic" records of a common national tradition (1773).

40. Wordsworth, *The Prose Works of William Wordsworth*, ed. W. J. B. Owen and J. W. Smyser, 3 vols. (Oxford: Clarendon Press, 1974).

41. These issues are discussed further in Chapters 4 and 5. William Godwin's essay "Of History and Romance" (1797), however, neatly encapsulates the changing attitude toward history. Godwin argues that the romance best fulfills the function of history because of its effect on the imagination and subjectivity of the reader. In making this argument, he narrows the division between the romance as a literary genre and history as an implicitly authorless or objective form of narration. See vol. 5 of Godwin, *The Political and Philosophical Writings of William Godwin*, ed. Mark Philp, et al., 7 vols. (London: Pickering and Chatto, 1993).

42. Nick Groom, *The Making of Percy's Reliques* (New York: Oxford University Press, 1999).

43. Andrew Bennett, *The Romantic Poets and the Culture of Posterity* (Cambridge: Cambridge University Press, 1999), 40.

Chapter 4

1. For further discussion of Wordsworth's relationship to Lockean ideas of property, see Chapter 5. Numerous recent works have noted the formative influence of Locke on discussions of authorship and intellectual property in the eighteenth century. See particularly Mark Rose, "The Author as Proprietor: *Donaldson v. Beckett* and the Genealogy of Modern Authorship," *Representations* 23 (Summer 1998): 51–85; Rose, *Authors and Owners*; and Woodmansee and Jaszi, *The Construction of Authorship*.

2. Byron's attitude toward personal identity and its relationship to cultural and intellectual productions, although not the subject of extended discussion here, can be considered as a somewhat belated dramatization of what Dror Wahrman has theorized as the *"ancien regime* of identity" in *The Making of the Modern Self: Identity and Culture in Eighteenth-Century England* (New Haven, Conn.: Yale University Press, 2004).

3. *The Gentleman's Magazine* (February 1818): 121.

4. *The Gentleman's Magazine* (May 1818): 389–90, 389.

5. *The Gentleman's Magazine* (March 1818): 390–91.

6. *Byron's Letters and Journals*, ed. Leslie A. Marchand, 12 vols. (Cambridge, Mass.: Harvard University Press, 1974); see also Galt's *Life of Byron* (1830), chap. 28.

7. In February of 1816, before the publication of plagiarism charges in *The Gentleman's Magazine*, Byron had also been concerned about resemblances between his *Parasina* (1816) and Walter Scott's *Marmion* (1808). In a letter of 3 February 1816, Byron wrote to John Murray, concerned that perhaps he should note the parallels, but he ultimately decided the correspondences did not warrant the gesture; see *Lord Byron, The Complete Poetical Works*, ed. Jerome J. McGann, 7 vols. (Oxford: Claren-

don Press, 1980), 5: 22. All quotations of Byron's poetry are from this edition, unless otherwise noted.

8. The additional obligations in this passage to Dorothy Wordsworth's journals are discussed in Chapter 3.

9. *Letters of the Wordsworth Family from 1787–1855*, ed. William Knight, 3 vols. (Boston: Ginn and Company, 1907), 2: 104.

10. William Knight, *The Life of William Wordsworth*, 3 vols. (Edinburgh: William Patterson, 1889), 3: 50. Recollection dated 27 October 1820.

11. *The London Magazine* 8 (December 1823): 597–604.

12. As Eilenberg notes in *Strange Powers of Speech*: "by plagiarizing successfully [a Romantic] plagiarist transcends his crime" (18); but if his borrowed "material remains unassimilated . . . the resulting work is a muddle, from which no coherent voice emerges" (150).

13. Philip Martin, *Byron: A Poet before his Public* (Cambridge: Cambridge University Press, 1982), 69, 70, 71.

14. Coleridge's effusion is borrowed from the work of Friederike Brun; see Chapter 2 for further discussion.

15. Two additional instances of plagiarism from Continental sources merit brief attention, although, as neither was the subject of contemporary discussion, they are not directly relevant to this study. In the late nineteenth century, F. Leveson Gower published a periodical essay in which he claimed that Byron "was not the author of *Werner*, but that it was written by my grandmother, [Georgiana] the Duchess of Devonshire" (243). While Byron had acknowledged when the drama was published in 1821 that the story was founded on the incidents described by Harriet Lee in her tale *Kreutzner; or, the Hungarian* (1801), Gower's contention was that Byron had plagiarized from an intermediary version of Lee's drama, written by the Duchess of Devonshire for private entertainment. Donald Bewley has recently announced the rediscovery (North American Society for the Study of Romanticism listserv, NASSR-L, 22 July 2003) of the Duchess of Devonshire's "lost" dramas and has uncovered preliminary evidence that suggests Byron probably did encounter her rewriting of the story, so the parallels among the three versions may again become the subject of scholarly interest. However, there is no evidence to suggest that Byron's contemporaries considered this an instance of plagiarism, and the example probably reveals more about the ways in which gender intersected with attitudes toward private subliterary genres than about anything else. Byron's failure to cite the Duchess's unpublished work and private entertainment, if that proves to be the case, is analogous to the appropriations from Dorothy Wordsworth's journals that I take up in Chapter 3. See F. Leveson-Gower, "Did Byron Write 'Werner'?" *The Nineteenth Century* (August 1899): 243–50.

Likewise, Nancy M. Goslee has uncovered Byron's obligations in *Prometheus* (1816) to the 1815 John Black translation of A. W. Schlegel's *Vorlesungen über Dramatische Kunst und Literatur* (Course of Lectures on Dramatic Art and Literature), observing that the analysis of Aeschylus's *Prometheus Unbound* "corresponds strikingly to Byron's poem" (20). While Goslee excuses Byron from charges of plagiarism on the ground of his dialectical engagement with the German text and while Romantic-period charges of plagiarism were not leveled against the poet on account of these obligations, her discovery, nevertheless, contributes to the context of Byron's intertextual relationship to Continental literature and German criticism. See her "Pure Stream from a Troubled Source: Byron, Schlegel and Prometheus," *The Byron Journal* 10 (1982): 20–36.

16. Peter Culkin, "Byron's Plagiarisms," *Notes and Queries* 3 (January 1863): 55–56; and Peter Vassallo, *Byron: The Italian Literary Influence* (New York: St. Martin's, 1984). Culkin demonstrates parallels between de Staël's *Corinne* (1, chap. 4) and the "Apostrophe to Ocean" stanzas of *Childe Harold* 4 (55). Vassallo details at length Byron's obligations to Italian literary contexts, including the inclusion of the Filicaia sonnet (20).

17. See the anonymous essay "Filicaja," *The Retrospective Review* 10:2 (1824): 317. I am grateful to Nora Crook for calling this review to my attention.

18. "Plagiarisms of Lord Byron detected," *The Monthly Magazine* 52 (August 1821): 19–22; 52 (September 1821): 105–9.

19. See, for example, his letter to Leigh Hunt dated 30 October 1815, in which Byron writes of Wordsworth's "pretension of accurate observation" and his factual errors in *The Excursion*, book 4; *BLJ* 4: 324–25.

20. Percy G. Adams, *Travelers and Travel Liars, 1660–1800* (Berkeley: University of California Press, 1962), 12; and Irena Grudzinska Gross, "Stendahl, Travel Writing, and Plagiarism," *Nineteenth-Century French Studies* 18 (Fall 1989): 233.

21. For further discussion of this copyright dispute, see Neil Fraistat, "A Scourge for the Laureate: William Benbow vs. Robert Southey," *The Wordsworth Circle* 19 (1988): 45–9; and Robert Southey, "Inquiry into the Copyright Act," *Quarterly Review* 21: 41 (January 1819): 196–213.

22. Thomas Medwin, *Conversations of Lord Byron* (1824), ed. Ernest R. Lovell, Jr. (Princeton, N.J.: Princeton University Press, 1966), 165.

23. Peter Cochran, "A Note on Some Sources for the Feast in *Don Juan*, Canto III," *Notes and Queries* 40: 238 (March 1993): 43–45, 44. See also his "Byron and 'Tully's Tripoli'," *The Byron Journal* 20 (1992): 77–88.

24. The etymology of *plagiarism* as signifying the unlawful kidnapping and illegitimate enslavement of a free person is noted by nearly all commentators on the history of intellectual property law and authorship but is best explored in *Pragmatic Plagiarism*, 63.

25. Debbie Lee, *Slavery and the Romantic Imagination* (Philadelphia: University of Pennsylvania Press, 2002).

26. On the concept of aping and its relationship to histories of slavery and colonialism, see particularly Henry Louis Gates, Jr., *Figures in Black* (Oxford: Oxford University Press, 1989), and *The Signifying Monkey: A Theory of African-American Literary Criticism* (New York: Oxford University Press, 1988); and Homi Bhabha, "Of Mimicry and Man: The Ambivalence of Colonial Discourse," *October* 31 (Spring 1984): 125–33.

27. The emphasis on the textual condition of orientalism is, of course, among the central claims made by Edward Said in *Orientalism* (New York: Random House, 1979). This insight is developed and extended in postcolonial studies, with particular attention to travel writing and the Romantic period, in works such as Sara Suleri, *The Rhetoric of British India* (Chicago: University of Chicago Press, 1992); David

Spurr, *The Rhetoric of Empire: Colonial Discourse in Journalism, Travel Writing, and Imperial Administration* (Durham, N.C.: Duke University Press, 1993); and Mary Louise Pratt, *Imperial Eyes: Travel Writing and Transculturation* (New York: Routledge, 1992).

28. Thomas Malthus, "Statements Respecting the East India College, with an Appeal to Facts," *The Quarterly Review* 17 (April 1817): 110.

29. Edward Trelawny, *The Adventures of a Younger Son*, ed. William St Clair (London: Oxford University Press, 1974), 260–61.

30. When informed in 1825 of Byron's "plagiarisms" from *Faust* in *Manfred*, Goethe simply wondered why the poet had not defended himself against such charges more vigorously, saying:

Lord Byron is great only as a poet; as soon as he reflects he is a child. He knows not how to hold himself against the stupid attacks . . . made upon himself by his own countrymen. He ought to have expressed himself more strongly against them. "What is there is mine," he should have said, "and whether I got it from a book or from life is of no consequence; the only point is whether I made a right use of it." Walter Scott used a scene from my *Egmont*, and he was entitled to do so; because he did it well he deserves praise. (Qtd. in Lindey, *Plagiarism and Originality*, [Westport, Conn.: Greenwood, 1974], 85)

Byron had, in fact, made precisely this argument to Murray regarding the charges of plagiarism in *Don Juan*. While Byron's charge that Goethe had imitated the styles of other writers in *Faust* has often been read (e.g., by Lindey) as bad faith, the failure to create a unified voice and, thereby, to improve upon borrowed source materials, as we have seen, functioned as a legitimate criticism that did not imply a censure of borrowing per se but only of borrowing badly. Although German attitudes toward plagiarism in the period are beyond the scope of this study, Goethe's statement suggests that narrative or lyric mastery functioned as a form of "right use" in Continental contexts as well.

31. Thomas Medwin, "A Cast of Casti. By Lord Byron," *The New Anti-Jacobin* 1 (April 1833): 30–35, 35–54.

32. As I have argued elsewhere, Mary Shelley's series of biographies, published as part of the renewed interest in Italian literature in Britain during the Romantic period, focused particular attention on the mock-epic romance and the tradition of the *rifacimento*; see *Mary Shelley's "Lives of the Most Eminent Scientific and Literary Men of Italy,"* ed. and intro. Tilar J. Mazzeo, vol. 1 of *Mary Shelley: Literary Lives and Uncollected Writings*, gen. ed. Nora Crook, 4 vols. (London: Pickering and Chatto, 2002).

33. Marguerite Gardiner, Lady Blessington, *A Journal of the Conversations of Lord Byron with the Countess of Blessington* (London: Richard Bentley, 1894).

34. The perception that Byron's literary appropriations were classed is discussed further in Chapter 6.

Chapter 5

1. Both Southey and Moore document their reliance on travel sources in the extensive notes appended to their poems; see particularly Robert Southey, *Thalaba*

the Destroyer (1801), *Madoc* (1805), and *The Curse of Kehama* (1810), rpt. *Robert Southey: Poetical Works, 1793–1810*, gen. ed. Lynda Pratt, 5 vols. (London: Pickering and Chatto, 2003); and Thomas Moore, *Lalla Rookh* (London: Longman, Hurst, and Rees, 1817). On Shelley's use of contemporary travel sources in her novel, see Mary Shelley, *Lodore*, ed. Lisa Vargo (Peterborough: Broadview, 1997); and Tilar J. Mazzeo, "The Impossibility of Being Anglo-American: The Rhetoric of Emigration and Transatlanticism in British Romantic Culture, 1791–1833," *European Romantic Review* 16:1 (January 2005): 61–81.

2. A subject explored more fully in several histories of intellectual property law, notably Rose and Woodmansee and Jaszi.

3. A late nineteenth-century American commentator, Brander Matthews, observes, for example, "Facts are the foundation of fiction, and the novelist and romancer, the dramatist and the poet, may make free with the labors of the traveller, the historian, the botanist, and the astronomer"; see *Pen and Ink: Papers on Subjects of More or Less Importance* (New York: Longman, Green, and Company, 1894), 33. This attitude toward the appropriation of travel writing and other historical or scientific forms existed as early as the seventeenth century; see Adams, *Travelers and Travel Liars, 1660–1800*.

4. The number of travel narratives published by socially prominent women confirms that it was a genre appropriate for female authorship. See particularly narratives such as Lady Mary Montagu, *Letters of the Right Honourable Lady M——y W——y M——e: Written during her Travels in Europe, Asia, and Africa, to Persons of Distinction, Men of Letters, &c in Different Parts of Europe* (Dublin: P. Wilson, 1763); and Ann Radcliffe, *A Journey made in the summer of 1794, through Holland and the western frontier of Germany, with a return down the Rhine: to which are added observations during a tour to the Lakes of Lancashire, Westmoreland, and Cumberland* (London: G. G. and J. Robinson, 1795).

5. See Montagu, *Letters . . . Written during her Travels in Europe*; James Cook, *A Journal of a voyage round the world, in His Majesty's ship Endeavour, in the years 1768, 1769, 1770, and 1771* (London: T. Becket and P. A. De Hondt, 1771); Sir William Edward Parry, *Journal of a voyage for the discovery . . . of a north-west passage from the Atlantic to the Pacific* (Edinburgh: A. Constable, 1821), and his *Journal of a second voyage for the discovery of a north-west passage from the Atlantic to the Pacific* (London: John Murray, 1824); Radcliffe, *A Journey made in the summer of 1794*; and Mary Wollstonecraft, *Letters written during a short residence in Sweden, Norway, and Denmark* (London: J. Johnson, 1796). On the familiarity of contemporary travel writing to Romantic-period audiences, see also Nigel Leask, "'Wandering through Elbis': Absorption and Containment in Romantic Exoticism," in *Romanticism and Colonialism: Writing and Empire, 1780–1830*, ed. Tim Fulford and Peter J. Kitson (Cambridge: Cambridge University Press, 1998); and Nigel Leask, *Curiosity and the Aesthetics of Travel Writing, 1770–1840* (Oxford: Oxford University Press, 2002).

6. James Mill, *The History of British India* (1817; rpt. London: Baldwin, Cradock, and Joy, 1826–48).

7. Javeed Majeed, *Ungoverned Imaginings: James Mill's "The History of British India" and Orientalism* (Oxford: Oxford University Press, 1992), 165.

8. Peacock, "The Four Ages of Poetry," in *Thomas Love Peacock: Memoirs of*

Shelley and Other Essays and Reviews, ed. Rupert Hart-Davis (London: Rupert-Hart Davis, 1970), 128.

9. Mary Shelley, *The Novels and Selected Works of Mary Shelley*, gen. ed. Nora Crook, 8 vols. (London: Pickering and Chatto, 1996), 2: 129.

10. Peacock's essay was published in the first and only issue of *Ollier's Literary Miscellany*, and Percy Bysshe Shelley intended to publish his response in the February/March 1821 volume, but the review failed before the essay appeared. After the poet's death in 1822, Mary Shelley again tried to publish "The Defence of Poetry" in the second volume of Leigh Hunt's fledgling periodical *The Liberal*, also without success, and she was only able to publish Shelley's piece in 1840, as part of a collected volume entitled *Essay, Letters from Abroad, Translations and Fragments*. However, in 1823 the conversation between Peacock and Shelley would have been very much in mind for Mary Shelley. Her essay "Giovanni Villani" was published in the fourth issue of *The Liberal* in 1823. Mary Shelley, *Essay, Letters from Abroad, Translations and Fragments* (London: Edward Moxon, 1840); and Mary Shelley, "Giovanni Villani," *The Liberal* 4 (1823): 281–97, rpt. vol. 2, *The Novels and Selected Works of Mary Shelley*, gen. ed. Nora Crook, 8 vols. (London, Pickering and Chatto, 1996).

11. Discussed in Chapter 4.

12. Shelley, *The Poetical Works of Percy Bysshe Shelley*, ed. Mary Shelley (London: Edward Moxon, 1840), 49–50.

13. Shelley, *The Letters of Percy Bysshe Shelley*, ed. Frederick L. Jones, 2 vols. (Oxford: Oxford University Press, 1964), 1: 432.

14. Harold Bloom, *The Anxiety of Influence: A Theory of Poetry* (New York: Oxford University Press, 1973).

15. E.g., *SPP* 72, n. 4; Shelley, *The Complete Poetical Works of Percy Bysshe Shelley*, ed. Neville Rogers, 4 vols. (Oxford: Oxford University Press, 1975), 338–39; and Southey, *Poetical Works*, 3: 331 ff.

16. Nicholas Birns, "Secrets of the Birth of Time: The Rhetoric of Cultural Origins in 'Alastor' and 'Mont Blanc'," *Studies in Romanticism* 32 (Fall 1993): 339–65; John Drew, *India and the Romantic Imagination* (Oxford: Oxford University Press, 1987), chap. 7.

17. Frederick S. Colwell, *The Rivermen: A Romantic Iconography of the River and the Source* (Montreal: McGill-Queen's University Press, 1989); quoted in Birns, "Secrets of the Birth of Time," 350.

18. Joseph Raban, *Shelley Revalued: Essays from the Greynog Conference* (Leicester: Leicester University Press, 1983).

19. Ratomir Rastic, "Shelley's First Major Lyrics and *Prometheus Unbound*," *Linguistics and Literature* 2:7 (2000): 69–86, 73.

Chapter 6

1. Locke's comparison of copyright and literary ownership with the appropriation of unoccupied land through the application of labor is further discussed, especially in eighteenth-century contexts, by Rose, *Authors and Owners*, and Woodmansee and Jaszi, *The Construction of Authorship*.

2. Tom Williamson and Liz Bellamy, *Property and Landscape: A Social History of Land Ownership and the English Countryside* (London: George Philip, 1987), 100.

3. The phrase "rural professional class" is borrowed from John Barrell, *The Idea of the Landscape and the Sense of Place, 1730–1840: An Approach to the Poetry of John Clare* (Cambridge: Cambridge University Press, 1972), 64.

4. Dorothy Stroud, *Capability Brown* (London: Faber and Faber, 1975), 201; qtd. in Timothy Brownlow, *John Clare and the Picturesque Landscape* (Oxford: Oxford University Press, 1983), 2.

5. Thomas Love Peacock, *Headlong Hall and Nightmare Abbey* (London: G. P. Putnam's Sons, 1887), 26.

6. Thomas Pfau, *Wordsworth's Profession: Form, Class, and the Logic of Early Romantic Cultural Production* (Stanford, Calif.: Stanford University Press, 1997).

7. Eilenberg discusses at length the competitive/collaborative relationship between Wordsworth and Coleridge and their formulation of joint authorship in *Strange Powers of Speech*.

8. For further discussion of the devaluation and persistence of satire in the Romantic period, see also Chapter 4.

9. Gérard Gennette, *Palimpsestes: La littérature au deuxieme degré* (Paris: Editions du Seuil, 1982). Gennette borrows his use of the term *intertextualité* from Julia Kristeva, *Sèméiôtikè: Recherches pour une sémanalyse* (Paris, Editions du Seuil, 1969), and he reemploys her description of intertextuality as the "coprésence entre deux ou plusiers textes" (the copresence of two or more texts) (qtd. in Gennette 8). Gennette identifies citation, allusion, and plagiarism as forms of intertextual relations that are distinguished from each other by their degree of cultural legitimacy (7–16), and these are contrasted with the transformative hypertextual relations of parody (performing a ludicrous function) and travesty (performing a satirical function) (37).

10. While Wordsworth demonstrates his familiarity with the Romantic-period standards of plagiarism in making his allegations against Bayley, other correspondence from within the household reconfirms how well acquainted both William and Dorothy were with the particular categories of evaluation that operated during the early nineteenth century. In her letter to Lady Beaumont, Dorothy emphasizes the questions of Scott's consciousness and maintains that Scott's intellectual obligations were unconscious and could not, therefore, be attributed to any pecuniary or morally culpable motives. This was a justification that William frequently used to account for the borrowings of several figures associated with his circle of correspondents, including Scott, Coleridge, and R. P. Gillies. At the same time, an 1816 letter by Wordsworth addressed to Gillies indicates that he too considered narrative mastery and the control of voiced subjectivity, what Byron called the "machinery" of his "own spirits," as one of the central elements in any charge of plagiarism. Wordsworth writes: "I am sorry you should have been rendered uneasy by charges of plagiarism. . . . I cannot deny that I have been frequently reminded of what I have written by your verses. . . . The resemblances are such as you probably are for the most part wholly unconscious of. . . . Your poems are sufficiently original, and tinctured enough, perhaps too exclusively, from your own mind" (*LWDW* 3: 343). Because unconscious, the correspondences between Gillies's verse and Wordsworth's

own are free from charges of culpable plagiarism. However, as works sufficiently "tinctured" with the mind and subjectivity of the author, the implication is that Gillies's poems are also free from the charges of aesthetic plagiarism, as Taylor delineated that category. Unlike the "motley assemblage" of Macpherson, Gillies is praised with having presented a unified—and, therefore, successful—lyric text.

11. John Wilson, "Sacred Poetry," *Blackwood's Edinburgh Magazine* 24:146 (December 1828): 917–38.

12. William Wordsworth, *The Excursion* (London: Longman, Hurst, Rees, Ormes, and Brown, 1814).

13. On Wordsworth's attitude toward the literary appropriations of Gray, see particularly McCracken, "Wordsworth on Human Wishes and Poetic Borrowings." See also Roy Flannagan, ed., *The Riverside Milton* (Boston: Houghton Mifflin, 1998); James Thomson, *The Seasons* (London: A. Millar, 1744); and Thomas Gray, *The Complete Poems of Thomas Gray: English, Latin, and Greek*, ed. Herbert W. Starr and J. R. Henrickson (Oxford: Clarendon Press, 1966; rpt. 1972).

14. David Reid, "Thomson and Wordsworth: A Debt with a Difference," *Scottish Literary Journal* 19:1 (May 1992): 5–17, 14.

15. Wordsworth, *William Wordsworth: The Poems*, ed. John O. Hayden, 2 vols. (New Haven, Conn.: Yale University Press, 1977); *Poetical Works*, ed. DeSelincourt and Darbishire.

16. Timothy Fulford, *Landscape, Liberty, Authority: Poetry, Criticism and Politics from Thomson to Wordsworth* (Cambridge: Cambridge University Press, 1996), 159.

17. Walter Savage Landor, *The Complete Works of Walter Savage Landor*, ed. Stephen Wheeler, 16 vols. (London: Chapman and Hall, 1936).

18. Walter Savage Landor, *The Gebir* (1797), ed. Jonathan Wordsworth (Oxford: Woodstock Books, 1993).

19. Fielding, *Tom Jones*, 620; Wolfram Schmidgen, *Eighteenth-Century Fiction and the Law of Property* (Cambridge: Cambridge University Press, 2002), 16.

20. The metaphor of the literary estate as an enclosed park may also echo Edward Young's *Conjectures on Original Composition*, in which, as Murphy observes, Young describes the poetic genius as the author able to leap over the paling that surrounds tradition and learning; see *Poetry as an Occupation and an Art*, 12.

21. Mark Schoenfield, *The Professional Wordsworth: Law, Labor, and the Poet's Contract* (Athens: University of Georgia Press, 1996).

22. Quoted in Laura J. Rosenthal, *Playwrights and Plagiarists in Early Modern England: Gender, Authorship, and Literary Property* (Ithaca, N.Y.: Cornell University Press, 1993), 13. In this fine study, Rosenthal offers a nuanced historical reading of how charges of plagiarism operated in the early modern period and in an era before the Statute of Anne.

23. William Wordsworth, *Last Poems*, ed. J. Curtis (Ithaca, N.Y.: Cornell University Press, 1999).

24. Bridget Keegan, "The Mean Unletter'd—female Bard of Aberdeen!: The Complexities of Christian Milne's *Simple Poems on Simple Subjects*," in *Scottish Women Poets of the Romantic Period*, ed. Nancy Kushigian and Stephen Behrendt (Chicago: Alexander Street Press, 2001), 3.

25. Ann Yearsley, *Poems on Several Occasions* (London: G. G. J. and J. Robinson, 1786), 8–9.

26. Quoted in Eric Miller, "Enclosure and Taxonomy in John Clare," *Studies in English Literature* 40:4 (Autumn 2000): 635–58; 637; John Goodridge and Kelsey Thorton, "John Clare: The Trespasser," in *John Clare in Context*, ed. Hugh Haughton, Adam Phillips, and Geoffrey Summerfield (Cambridge: Cambridge University Press, 1994), 87–129.

27. Mark Storey, ed., *Clare: The Critical Heritage* (London: Routledge and Kegan Paul, 1973), 83.

28. *The Eclectic Review* 13 (April 1820): 326–40.

29. Frederick Martin, *The Life of John Clare* (London: Macmillan and Company, 1865), 188–89.

30. William D. Brewer, "John Clare and Lord Byron," *John Clare Society Journal* 11 (July 1992): 43–57.

Afterword

1. David Perkins, "Romantic Lyric Voice: What Shall We Call the 'I'?," *Southern Review* 29:2 (Spring 1993): 225–39.

2. Jerome McGann, "Rethinking Romanticism," *ELH* 59:3 (Autumn 1992): 735.

3. On Romantic nostalgia in contemporary American poetry, see, particularly, Ira Sadoff, "Louise Glück and the Last Stage of Romanticism," *New England Review* 22:4 (Fall 2001): 81–92.

Bibliography

Abelove, Henry. "John Wesley's Plagiarism of Samuel Johnson and Its Contemporary Reception." *Huntington Library Quarterly* 59:1 (1997): 73–79.

Abrams, M. H. *The Mirror and the Lamp*. Oxford: Oxford University Press, 1953.

Adams, Percy. *Travel Literature and the Evolution of the Novel*. Lexington: University Press of Kentucky, 1983.

———. *Travelers and Travel Liars, 1660–1800*. Berkeley: University of California Press, 1962.

Altieri, Charles. "Can We Be Historical Ever? Some Hopes for a Dialectical Model of Historical Self-Consciousness." *The Uses of Literary History*. Ed. Marshall Brown. Durham, N.C.: Duke University Press, 1995.

Anonymous. "An Address to the Parliament of Great Britain, on the Claims of Authors to their Own Copyright." *The Pamphleteer: Respectfully Dedicated to Both Houses of Parliament* 3 (September 1813): 169–202.

———. "Article XI." *The Quarterly Review* 16 (1816–17): 225–79.

———. "Case of Walcot v. Walker; Southey v. Sherwood; Murray v. Benbow; and Lawrence v. Smith." *The Quarterly Review* 27 (1822): 123–38.

———. "Filicaja." *The Retrospective Review* 10:2 (1824): 317.

———. "Lord Byron vindicated from alleged Plagiarism." *The Gentleman's Magazine* 88 (May 1818): 390–91.

———. "Plagiarisms of Lord Byron Detected." *The Monthly Magazine* 52 (August 1821): 19–22; 52 (September 1821): 105–9.

———. "The Plagiarisms of Lord Byron." *The Gentleman's Magazine* 88 (February 1818): 121.

———. *Reasons for the Modification of the Act of Anne Respecting the Delivery of Books and Copyright*. London: Nichols, Son, and Bentley, 1813.

Armstrong, Isobel, and Virginia Blain, eds. *Women's Poetry, Late Romantic to Late Victorian: Genre and Genre, 1830–1900*. Houndsmill: Macmillan, 1999.

Baines, Paul. *The House of Forgery in Eighteenth-Century Britain*. Brookfield: Ashgate, 1999.

Barrell, John. *The Idea of the Landscape and the Sense of Place, 1730–1840: An Approach to the Poetry of John Clare*. Cambridge: Cambridge University Press, 1972.

Barthes, Roland. *Image, Music, Text*. Trans. Stephen Heath. New York: Hill, 1977.

———. *The Pleasure of the Text*. Trans. Richard Miller. New York: Farrar, Straus and Giroux, 1986.

———. *The Rustle of Language*. New York: Hill and Wang, 1986.

Bayley, Peter. *Poems*. London: William Millar, 1803.

Beach, Joseph W. "Coleridge's Borrowings from the German." *ELH* 9 (1942): 36–57.

Beattie, James. *The Minstrel; or, the Progress of Genius.* London: E. and C. Dilly, 1771.

Bennett, Andrew. *Romantic Poets and the Culture of Posterity.* Cambridge: Cambridge University Press, 1999.

Bently, Lionel, and Brad Sherman. *The Making of Modern Intellectual Property Law: The British Experience, 1760–1911.* Cambridge: Cambridge University Press, 1999.

Berlin, James A. *Rhetoric and Reality: Writing Instruction in American Colleges, 1900–1985.* Carbondale: Southern Illinois University Press, 1987.

Bhabha, Homi. "Of Mimicry and Man: The Ambivalence of Colonial Discourse" *October* 31 (Spring 1984): 125–33.

Birns, Nicholas. "Secrets of the Birth of Time: The Rhetoric of Cultural Origins in 'Alastor' and 'Mont Blanc'." *Studies in Romanticism* 32 (Fall 1993): 339–65.

Blackstone, William. *Commentaries on the Laws of England.* Oxford: Clarendon Press, 1765–69.

Blessington, Lady. [Marguerite Gardiner.] *A Journal of the Conversations of Lord Byron with the Countess Blessington.* London: Richard Bentley, 1894.

Bloom, Harold. *The Anxiety of Influence: A Theory of Poetry.* New York: Oxford University Press, 1973.

Bogen, Don. "Isn't It Romantic?" *Kenyon Review* 20: 3/4 (Summer/Fall 1998): 174–80.

Bolton, Betsy. *Women, Nationalism, and the Romantic Stage: Theatre and Politics in Britain, 1780–1800.* Cambridge: Cambridge University Press, 2001.

Bonjour, Adrien. "Coleridge's 'Hymn before Sun-rise.'" Ph.D. diss. University of Lausanne, 1942.

Bostetter, Edward. *The Romantic Ventriloquists.* Seattle: University of Washington Press, 1963.

Boswell, James. *The Life of Samuel Johnson, LL.D.* 4 vols. London: T. Cadell, 1822.

Bradley, A. C. *A Commentary on Tennyson's "In Memoriam."* New York: Macmillan, 1907.

Brewer, William D. "John Clare and Lord Byron." *John Clare Society Journal* 11 (July 1992): 43–56.

Brower, Ruben Arthur. *Alexander Pope: The Poetry of Allusion.* Oxford: Clarendon Press, 1959.

Brownlow, Timothy. *John Clare and the Picturesque Landscape.* Oxford: Oxford University Press, 1983.

Buranen, Lise, and Alice M. Roy, eds. *Perspectives on Plagiarism and Intellectual Property in a Postmodern World.* Albany: State University of New York Press, 1999.

Burke, Edmund. "Tristram Shandy." *The Annual Register* 3 (1760): 247.

Burke, Séan. *The Death and Return of the Author: Criticism and Subjectivity in Barthes, Foucault and Derrida.* Edinburgh: Edinburgh University Press, 1992.

Burton, Robert. *The Anatomy of Melancholy.* 2 vols. London: Thomas McLean, 1826.

Byron, Lord [George Gordon]. *Byron's Letters and Journals.* Ed. Leslie A. Marchand. 12 vols. Cambridge, Mass.: Harvard University Press, 1974.

————. *Lord Byron: The Complete Poetical Works.* Ed. Jerome J. McGann. 7 vols. Oxford: Clarendon Press, 1980.

————. *Works of Lord Byron.* Ed. Jeffrey D. Hoeper and E. H. Coleridge. London: Murray, 1904.

Cameron, Kenneth Neill. *The Young Shelley: Genesis of a Radical.* New York: Macmillan, 1950.

————, ed. *Shelley and His Circle, 1773–1822.* 6 vols. Cambridge, Mass.: Harvard University Press, 1961.

Chambers, E. K. *The History and Motives of Literary Forgeries.* Oxford: Clarendon Press, 1891.

Chandler, James. *England in 1819: The Politics of Literary Culture and the Case of Romantic Historicism.* Chicago: University of Chicago Press, 1998.

Chatterton, Thomas. *The Complete Works of Thomas Chatterton.* Ed. Donald S. Taylor. 2 vols. Oxford: Clarendon Press, 1971.

Cherry, J. L. *Life and Remains of John Clare.* London: Frederick Warne, 1873.

Christensen, Jerome. *Coleridge's Blessed Machine of Language.* Ithaca, N.Y.: Cornell University Press, 1981.

————. *Romanticism at the End of History.* Baltimore: Johns Hopkins University, 2000.

Clare, John. *John Clare: Journals, Essays, The Journey from Essex.* Ed. Anne Tibble. Manchester: Carcanet New Press, 1980.

————. *John Clare: Poems Chiefly from Manuscript.* London: Richard Cobden Sanderson, 1920.

————. *Later Poems of John Clare.* Ed. Eric Robinson and Geoffrey Summerfield. Manchester: Manchester University Press, 1964.

————. *Letters of John Clare.* Ed. Mark Storey. Oxford: Clarendon Press, 1985.

————. *Poems Descriptive of Rural Life and Scenery.* London: Taylor and Hessey, 1821.

————. *Poems of John Clare.* Ed. J. W. Tibble. 3 vols. London: J. M. Dent and Sons, 1935.

————. *Sketches in the Life of John Clare, Written By Himself.* Ed. Edmund Blunden. London: Richard Cobden Sanderson, 1931.

Clej, Alina. *A Genealogy of the Modern Self: Thomas DeQuincey and the Intoxication of Writing.* Stanford, Calif.: Stanford University Press, 1995.

Clery, E. J. *The Rise of Supernatural Fiction, 1762–1800.* Cambridge: Cambridge University Press, 1995.

Clifford, James L. "Johnson and Lauder." *Philological Quarterly* 54 (1975): 342–56.

Cochran, Peter. "A Note on Some Sources for the Feast in *Don Juan*, Canto III." *Notes and Queries* 40: 238 (March 1993): 43–45.

————. "Byron and 'Tully's Tripoli'." *The Byron Journal* 20 (1992): 77–88.

————. "*Don Juan*, Canto II: A Reconsideration of Some of Byron's Borrowings from his Shipwreck Sources." *The Byron Journal* 19 (1991): 141–45.

Coe, Charles Norton. *Wordsworth and the Literature of Travel.* New York: Bookman Associates, 1953.

Coleridge, Samuel Taylor. *Biographia Literaria. Second Edition Prepared for Publication in Part by the Late Henry Nelson Coleridge, Completed and Published by his Widow* (1847). Rpt. *The Complete Works of Samuel Taylor Coleridge*. Ed. W. G. T. Shedd. New York: Harpers, 1884.

———. *The Collected Letters of Samuel Taylor Coleridge*. Ed. E. L. Griggs. 4 vols. Oxford: Oxford University Press, 1959.

———. *The Collected Poetical Works of Samuel Taylor Coleridge*. 16 vols. Princeton, N.J.: Princeton University Press, 1969–2002.

———. *The Complete Poetical Works of Samuel Taylor Coleridge*. Ed. E. H. Coleridge. 2 vols. Oxford: Oxford University Press, 1912.

———. *Notebooks of Samuel Taylor Coleridge*. Ed. Kathleen Coburn. 5 vols. New York: Bollingen Foundation, 1957.

———. *Samuel Taylor Coleridge: The Collected Works*. Ed. Kathleen Coburn. 16 vols. Princeton, N.J.: Princeton University Press, 2001.

———. *[The Selected Works of] Samuel Taylor Coleridge*. Ed. H. J. Jackson. Oxford: Oxford University Press, 1985.

———. *Unpublished Letters of Samuel Taylor Coleridge*. Ed. E. L. Griggs. 2 vols. London: Constable, 1910.

Colwell, Frederick S. "Figures in a Promethean Landscape." *Keats-Shelley Journal* 45 (1996): 119–31.

———. *The Rivermen: A Romantic Iconography of the River and the Source*. Montreal: McGill-Queen's University Press, 1989.

Conger, Syndy. *Matthew G. Lewis, Charles Robert Maturin and the Germans*. Salzburg: Universität Salzburg, 1977.

Cook, James. *A Journal of a voyage round the world, in His Majesty's ship Endeavour, in the years 1768, 1769, 1770, and 1771*. London: T. Becket and P. A. De Hondt, 1771.

Cowley, Hannah. *Albina, Countess Raimond; A Tragedy, by Mrs. Cowley: As it is Performed at the Theatre-Royal in the Hay-Market*. London: T. Spilsbury, 1779.

Cox, Jeffrey N. "Keats in the Cockney School." *Romanticism* 2:1 (1996): 32–41.

Crabtree, Adam. *From Mesmer to Freud: Magnetic Sleep and the Roots of Psychological Healing*. New Haven, Conn.: Yale University Press, 1993.

Crossan, Greg. "Clare's Debts to the Poets in His Library." *The John Clare Society Journal* 10 (July 1991): 27–42.

Culkin, Peter. "Byron's Plagiarisms." *Notes and Queries* 3 (January 1863): 55–56.

Davies, Miles. *Athenae Britanicae; Or, the Critical News*. 6 vols. London: n.p., 1715.

DeQuincey, Thomas. "Samuel Taylor Coleridge: By the English Opium Eater." *Tait's Magazine* (September, October, and November 1834 and January 1835). Rpt. *The Collected Writings of Thomas DeQuincey*. Ed. David Mason. 2 vols. Edinburgh: Adam and Charles Black, 1854.

Derrida, Jacques. *Acts of Literature*. Ed. Derek Attridge. London: Routledge, 1992.

DeSelincourt, Ernest. *Dorothy Wordsworth*. Oxford: Clarendon Press, 1933.

Donkin, Ellen. *Getting into the Act: Women Playwrights in London, 1776–1829*. New York: Routledge, 1995.

Donovan, J. P. "Don Juan in Constantinople: Waiting and Watching." *The Byron Journal* 21 (1993): 14–29.

Drew, John. *India and the Romantic Imagination*. Oxford: Oxford University Press, 1987.

Dyer, Gary. *British Satire and the Politics of Style, 1789–1832*. Cambridge: Cambridge University Press, 1997.

Ede, Lisa, and Andrea Lunsford. "Crimes of Writing: Refiguring 'Proper' Discursive Practices." *Writing on the Edge* 11:2 (Spring/Summer 2000): 43–54.

———, eds. *Singular Texts/Plural Authors: Perspectives on Collaborative Writing*. Carbondale: Southern Illinois University Press, 1994.

Eilenberg, Susan. *Strange Power of Speech: Wordsworth, Coleridge, and Literary Possession*. Oxford: Oxford University Press, 1992.

Elton, Charles Abraham. "The Idler's Epistle to John Clare." *The London Magazine* 10 (August 1824): 143–45.

Enfield, W. *Observations on Literary Property*. London: Johnson, 1774. Rpt. *The Literary Property Debate: Eight Tracts, 1774–1775*. Ed. Stephen Parks. New York: Garland, 1974.

Feathers, John. *Publishing, Piracy, and Politics: An Historical Study of Copyright in Britain*. New York: Mansell, 1994.

Ferriar, John C. *Illustrations of Sterne, with Other Essays and Verses*. London: Cadell and Davies, 1798.

Ferrier, J. F. "The Plagiarisms of S. T. Coleridge." *Blackwood's Edinburgh Magazine* 47 (March 1840): 287–99.

Fielding, Henry. *Tom Jones, A Foundling*. Ed. Fredson Bowers. New York: Modern Library, 1994.

Fielding, Penny. *Writing and Orality: Nationality, Culture, and Nineteenth-Century Scottish Fiction*. Oxford: Oxford University Press, 1996.

Fitzgerald, Percy. *A Famous Forgery: Being the Story of "the Unfortunate" Doctor Dodd*. London: Chapman and Hall, 1865.

Flannagan, Roy, ed. *The Riverside Milton*. Boston: Houghton Mifflin, 1998.

Forsyth, Joseph. *Remarks on Antiquities, Arts, and Letters During an Excursion in Italy in the Years 1802 and 1803*. London: John Murray, 1816.

Foucault, Michel. "The Author Function." *Textual Strategies: Perspectives in Post-Structuralist Criticism*. Ed. Josué V. Harari. Ithaca, N.Y.: Cornell University Press, 1979.

Fraistat, Neil. "A Scourge for the Laureate: William Benbow vs. Robert Southey." *The Wordsworth Circle* 19 (1988): 45–49.

Fruman, Norman. *Coleridge, The Damaged Archangel*. New York: George Braziller, 1971.

Fulford, Timothy. *Landscape, Liberty, Authority: Poetry, Criticism and Politics from Thomson to Wordsworth*. Cambridge: Cambridge University Press, 1996.

———. "Mary Robinson and the Abyssinian Maid: Coleridge's Muses and Feminist Criticism." *Romanticism on the Net* 13 (February 1999): <http://www.ron.umontreal.ca>.

Galt, John. *The Life of Lord Byron*. London: H. Colburn and R. Bentley, 1830.

Gates, Henry Louis Jr. *Figures in Black*. Oxford: Oxford University Press, 1989.

———. *The Signifying Monkey: A Theory of African-American Literary Criticism*. New York: Oxford University Press, 1988.

Gennette, Gérard. *Palimpsestes: La littérature au deuxieme degré*. Paris: Editions du Seuil, 1982.

Godwin, William. *The Political and Philosophical Writings of William Godwin.* Ed. Mark Philp, et al. 7 vols. London: Pickering and Chatto, 1993.

Goodridge, John, and Kelsey Thornton. "John Clare: the Trespasser." *John Clare in Context.* Ed. Hugh Haughton, Adam Philips, and Geoffrey Summerfield. Cambridge: Cambridge University Press, 1994.

Goslee, Nancy M. "Pure Stream from a Troubled Source: Byron, Schlegel and Prometheus." *The Byron Journal* 10 (1982): 20–36.

Gower, F. Levenson. "Did Byron Write 'Werner'?" *The Nineteenth Century* (August 1899): 243–50.

Gradin, Sherie. *Romancing Rhetorics: Social Expressivist Perspectives on the Teaching of Writing.* Portsmouth, N.H.: Boyton/Cook, 1995.

Graver, Bruce. *William Wordsworth: Translations of Chaucer and Virgil.* Ithaca, N.Y.: Cornell University Press, 1998.

Gray, Thomas. *The Complete Poems of Thomas Gray: English, Latin, and Greek.* Ed. Herbert W. Starr and J. R. Henrickson. Oxford: Clarendon Press, 1966; rpt. 1972.

Green, Stuart P. "Plagiarism, Norms, and the Limits of Theft Law: Some Observations on the Use of Criminal Sanctions in Enforcing Intellectual Property Rights." *Hastings Law Journal* 54 (November 2002): 167–242.

Groom, Nick. *The Forger's Shadow: How Forgery Changed the Course of Literature.* London: Picador, 2002.

———. *The Making of Percy's Reliques.* New York: Oxford University Press, 1999.

Gross, Irena Grudzinska. "Stendahl, Travel Writing, and Plagiarism." *Nineteenth-Century French Studies* 18 (Fall 1989): 231–35.

Guillory, John. *Cultural Capital: The Problem of Literary Canon Formation.* Chicago: University of Chicago Press, 1993.

Halsband, Robert, and Irvin Ehrenprein, eds. *The Lady of Letters in the Eighteenth Century.* Los Angeles: University of California Press, 1969.

Hammond, Brean. *Professional Imaginative Writing in England, 1670–1740.* Oxford: Clarendon Press, 1997.

Hansard: The Parliamentary History of England from the Earliest Period to the Year 1803. London: Longman, 1803.

Hargrave, Francis. *An Argument in Defence of Literary Property.* London: Otridge, 1774.

Hatch, Gary Layne. "Adam Smith's Accusations of Plagiarism against Hugh Blair." *Eighteenth-Century Scotland* 8 (1994): 7–10.

Haywood, Ian. *The Making of History: A Study of the Forgeries of James Macpherson and Thomas Chatterton in Relation to Eighteenth-Century Ideas of History and Fiction.* Rutherford: Fairleigh Dickinson University Press, 1986.

Helsinger, Elizabeth. "Clare and the Place of the Peasant Poet." *Critical Inquiry* 13 (1987): 509–31.

Hobbes, Thomas. *Leviathan.* Ed. Richard Tuck. Cambridge: Cambridge University Press, 1991.

Hodgskin, Thomas. *The Natural and Artificial Right of Property Contrasted.* London: B. Steil, 1832. Rpt. Clifton: Augustus M. Kelley, 1973.

Hofkosh, Sonia. "A Woman's Profession: Sexual Difference and the Romance of Authorship." *Studies in Romanticism* 2 (Summer 1993): 245–72.

Hogg, James. *The Three Perils of Man: War, Women, and Witchcraft*. Ed. Douglas Gifford. Edinburgh: Scottish Academic Press, 1989.

Hogg, Thomas Jefferson. *Life of Percy Bysshe Shelley*. 4 vols. London: Edward Moxon, 1858.

Howard, Rebecca Moore. "The Ethics of Plagiarism." *The Ethics of Writing Instruction: Issues in Theory and Practice*. Ed. Michael A. Pemberton. Stamford, Conn.: Ablex Publishing Corporation, 2000.

———. *Standing in the Shadow of Giants: Plagiarists, Authors, Collaborators*. Stamford, Conn.: Ablex Publishing Corporation, 1999.

Howard, William. *John Clare*. Boston: Twayne Publishers, 1981.

Hunt, Leigh, ed. *The Liberal. Verse and Prose from the South*. London: John Hunt, 1822.

Hunter, Ian, and David Saunders. "Lessons from the 'Literatory': How to Historicize Authorship." *Critical Inquiry* 17: 3 (Spring 1991): 479–509.

Ingleby, C. M. "On Some Points Connected with the Philosophy of Coleridge." *Transactions of the Royal Society of Literature of the United Kingdom* 9, 2nd ser. (1870): 400.

Ireland, William Henry. *The Confessions of William-Henry Ireland: Containing the Particulars of his Fabrication of the Shakespeare Manuscripts*. London: T. Goddard, 1805.

Janowitz, Anne. *Lyric and Labour in the Romantic Tradition*. Cambridge: Cambridge University Press, 1998.

Johnson, Samuel. "Considerations on the Case of Dr. Trapp's Sermons abridged by Mr. Cave." *The Gentleman's Magazine* 57:2 (July 1787): 555–57.

———. *Yale Edition of the Works of Samuel Johnson*. 16 vols. New Haven, Conn.: Yale University Press, 1963.

Jones, Stephen. *Satire and Romanticism*. New York: St. Martin's Press, 2002.

Keegan, Bridget. "'The Mean Unletter'd—female Bard of Aberdeen!': The Complexities of Christian Milne's *Simple Poems on Simple Subjects*." *Scottish Women Poets of the Romantic Period*. Ed. Nancy Kushigian and Stephen Behrendt. Chicago: Alexander Street Press, 2001.

Kewes, Paulina. *Authorship and Appropriation: Writing for the Stage in England, 1660–1710*. Oxford: Oxford University Press, 1998.

———, ed. *Plagiarism in Early Modern England*. New York: Palgrave/Macmillan, 2002.

Kirschbaum, Leo. "Author's Copyright in England Before 1640." *Papers of the Bibliographical Society of America* 40 (1946): 43–80.

Knight, William. *The Life of William Wordsworth*. 3 vols. Edinburgh: William Patterson, 1889.

Kooy, John Michael. *Coleridge, Schiller, and Aesthetic Education*. London: Palgrave/Macmillan, 2002.

Kristeva, Julia. *Sèméiôtikè: Recherches pour une sémanalyse*. Paris: Editions du Seuil, 1969.

Lacan, Jacques. *Écrits: A Selection.* Trans. Alan Sheridan. New York: W. W. Norton, 1977.

LaFollette, P. F. *Stealing into Print: Fraud, Plagiarism, and Misconduct in Scientific Publishing.* Berkeley: University of California Press, 1992.

Landor, Walter Savage. *The Complete Works of Walter Savage Landor.* Ed. Stephen Wheeler. 16 vols. London: Chapman and Hall, 1936.

———. *The Gebir* (1797). Ed. Jonathan Wordsworth. Rpt. Oxford: Woodstock Books, 1993.

———. "Imaginary Conversation: Southey and Porson." *Blackwood's Edinburgh Magazine* 52:326 (December 1842): 687–715.

———. *Imaginary Conversations.* 2 vols. London: Taylor and Hessey, 1824.

———. *Letters and Other Unpublished Writings of Walter Savage Landor.* Ed. Stephen Wheeler. London: Richard Bentley and Son, 1897.

Lathrop, A. *Student Cheating and Plagiarism in the Internet Era: A Wake-Up Call.* Englewood, N.J.: Libraries Unlimited, 2000.

Leader, Zachary. *Revision and Romantic Authorship.* Oxford: Oxford University Press, 1996.

Leask, Nigel. *Curiosity and the Aesthetics of Travel Writing, 1770–1840.* Oxford: Oxford University Press, 2002.

———. "Shelley's 'Magnetic Ladies': Romantic Mesmerism and the Politics of the Body." *Beyond Romanticism: New Approaches to Texts and Contexts.* Ed. Stephen Copley and John Whale. London: Routledge, 1992.

———. "'Wandering through Elbis': Absorption and Containment in Romantic Exoticism." *Romanticism and Colonialism: Writing and Empire, 1780–1830.* Ed. Timothy Fulford and Peter J. Kitson. Cambridge: Cambridge University Press, 1998.

Lee, Debbie. *Slavery and the Romantic Imagination.* Philadelphia: University of Pennsylvania Press, 2002.

Levin, Susan M. *Dorothy Wordsworth and Romanticism.* New Brunswick, N.J.: Rutgers University Press, 1987.

Levinson, Marjorie. "Romantic Poetry: The State of the Art." *MLQ* 54:2 (June 1993): 183–214.

Lewis, Matthew. *The Monk.* Ed. John Berryman. New York: Grove Press, 1952.

———. *Tales of Terror with an Introductory Dialogue.* London: Bulmer and Co., 1801.

———. *Tales of Wonder; Written and Collected by M. G. Lewis.* 2 vols. London: W. Bulmer, 1801.

Lindey, Alexander. *Plagiarism and Originality.* Westport, Conn.: Greenwood Publishers, 1974.

Locke, John. *Two Treatises on Government.* Ed. Peter H. Nidditch. Oxford: Oxford University Press, 1975.

Lockwood, Thomas. *Post-Augustan Satire: Charles Churchill and Satirical Poetry, 1750–1800.* Seattle: University of Washington Press, 1979.

Lowes, John Livingston. *The Road to Xanadu: A Study in the Ways of the Imagination.* Boston: Houghton Mifflin, 1927.

Lynch, Jack. "The Love of Truth: Johnson and Literary Fraud." American Society for Eighteenth-Century Studies (ASECS) conference presentation (1999), <http://andromeda.rutgers.edu/~jlynch/Papers/sjfraud.html>.

Macmillan, Fiona. "Copyright's Commodification of Creativity." *ICFAI Journal of Intellectual Property Rights* 2 (2003): 53–70.

Macpherson, James. *The Poems of Ossian, Translated by James Macpherson.* 2 vols. London: A. Strahan and T. Cadell, 1796.

Majeed, Javeed. *Ungovered Imaginings: James Mill's "The History of British India" and Orientalism.* Oxford: Oxford University Press, 1992.

Mallon, Thomas. *Stolen Words: Forays into the Origins and Ravages of Plagiarism.* New York: Ticknor and Fields, 1989.

Malthus, Thomas. "Statements Respecting the East India College, with an Appeal to the Facts." *The Quarterly Review* 17 (April 1817): 107–54.

Manning, Peter. *Reading Romantics: Texts and Contexts.* Oxford: Oxford University Press, 1990.

Marcuse, Michael J. "The Lauder Controversy and the Jacobite Cause." *Studies in Burke and His Time* 18 (1977): 27–47.

Martin, Frederick. *The Life of John Clare.* London: Macmillan and Company, 1865.

Martin, Philip. "Authorial Identity and the Critical Act: John Clare and Lord Byron." *Questioning Romanticism.* Ed. John Beer. Baltimore: Johns Hopkins University Press, 1995.

———. *Byron: A Poet before His Public.* Cambridge: Cambridge University Press, 1982.

Matthews, Brander. *Pen and Ink: Papers on Subjects of More or Less Importance.* New York: Longman, Green, and Co., 1894.

Mazzeo, Tilar J. "The Impossibility of Being Anglo-American: The Rhetoric of Emigration and Transatlanticism in British Romantic Culture, 1791–1833." *European Romantic Review* 16:1 (January 2005): 61–81.

———. "'A mixture of all the styles': Nationalism, Colonialism, and Plagiarism in Shelley's Indian Circle." *European Romantic Review* 8:2 (Spring 1997): 155–68.

———. "'Sporting Sketches during a Short Stay in Hindustane': Bodleian MS Shelley adds.e.21 and Travel Literature in the Shelley Circle." *Romanticism* 4:2 (Fall 1998): 174–88.

McCabe, D. L., L. K. Treveno, and K. D. Butterfield. "Cheating in Academic Institutions: A Decade of Research." *Ethics and Behavior* 11 (2001): 219–32.

McCracken, David. "Wordsworth on Human Wishes and Poetic Borrowing." *Modern Philology* 79:4 (May 1982): 386–99.

———. *Wordsworth and the Lake District.* Oxford: Oxford University Press, 1984.

McFarland, Thomas. *Coleridge and the Pantheist Tradition.* Oxford: Oxford University Press, 1969.

McGann, Jerome. "Rethinking Romanticism." *ELH* 59:3 (Autumn 1992): 735–54.

———. *Towards a Literature of Knowledge.* Oxford: Oxford University Press, 1989.

———. *The Romantic Ideology: A Critical Investigation.* Chicago: University of Chicago Press, 1983.

Medwin, Thomas. "A Cast of Casti. By Lord Byron." *The New Anti-Jacobin* 1 (April 1833): 30–54.

————. *Conversations of Lord Byron.* Ed. Ernest R. Lovell, Jr. Princeton, N.J.: Princeton University Press, 1966.

————. "The Diavolessa, Translated; the Origins of Lord Byron's *Don Juan.*" *The New Anti-Jacobin: A Monthly Magazine* 1 (April 1833): 35–54.

————. *The Life of Percy Bysshe Shelley.* 2 vols. London: Thomas Cautley Newby, 1847.

————. *The Life of Percy Bysshe Shelley.* Ed. H. Buxton Forman. London: Oxford University Press, 1913.

————. *Some Rejected Stanzas of "Don Juan" with Byron's Own Curious Notes. The whole written in Double Rhyme, after Casti's manner, an Italian author from whom Byron is said to have plagiarized many of his beauties.* Great Totham: Charles Clark, 1845.

Meltzer, Françoise. *Hot Property: The Stakes and Claims of Literary Originality.* Chicago: University of Chicago Press, 1994.

Miller, Eric. "Enclosure and Taxonomy in John Clare." *Studies in English Literature* 40: 4 (Autumn 2000): 635–58.

Mill, James. *The History of British India.* 1817. Rpt. London: Baldwin, Cradock, and Joy, 1826–48.

Montagu, Mary Wortley. *Letters of the Right Honourable Lady M——y W——y M——e: Written during her Travels in Europe, Asian, and Africa, to Persons of Distinction, Men of Letters, &c in Different Parts of Europe.* Dublin: P. Wilson, 1763.

Moore, Jane. "Plagiarism with a Difference: Subjectivity in 'Kubla Khan' and *Letters Written during a Short Residence in Norway, Sweden, and Denmark.*" *Beyond Romanticism: New Approaches to Texts and Contexts, 1780–1832.* Ed. Stephen Coplet and John Whale. New York: Routledge, 1992.

Moore, Thomas. *Lalla Rookh.* London: Longman, Hurst, and Rees, 1817.

————. *Memoirs, Journal, and Correspondence of Thomas Moore.* London: Longman, 1853.

Morley, Edith J., ed. *Correspondence of Henry Crabb Robinson with the Wordsworth Circle.* 2 vols. Oxford: Clarendon Press, 1927.

Mortenson, Peter. "Robbing *The Robbers*: Schiller, Xenophobia and the Politics of British Romantic Translation." *Literature and History* 11:1 (Spring 2002): 41–61.

Murphy, Peter. "Impersonation and Authorship in Romantic Britain." *ELH* 59 (1992): 625–49.

————. *Poetry as an Occupation and an Art in Britain, 1760–1830.* Cambridge: Cambridge University Press, 1993.

Murray, J. Middleton. "Clare and Wordsworth." *Times Literary Supplement* 1179 (21 August 1924). Rpt. *Clare: The Critical Heritage.* Ed. Mark Storey. London: Routledge and Kegan Paul, 1973.

Napolitano v. Trustees of Princeton University (N.J. App. Div. 1982). *Opinions of the New Jersey Courts* 453 A.2d 263: <http://lawlibrary.rutgers.edu>.

Newlyn, Lucy. *Coleridge, Wordsworth, and the Language of Allusion.* Oxford: Oxford University Press, 1986.

————. *Reading, Writing, and Romanticism: The Anxiety of Reception.* Oxford: Oxford University Press, 2000.

Norton, Caroline. *English Laws for Women in the Nineteenth Century.* London: n.p., 1854.

————. *The Sorrows of Rosalie: A Tale, with Other Poems.* London: J. Ebers, 1829.

Noyes, Russell. *Wordsworth and the Art of Landscape.* Bloomington: Indiana University Press, 1968.

Orsini, G. N. G. "Coleridge and Schlegel Reconsidered." *Comparative Literature* 16 (1964): 101–2.

————. *Coleridge and German Idealism.* Carbondale: Southern Illinois University Press, 1969.

Parks, Stephen, ed. *English Publishing, the Struggle for Copyright, and the Freedom of the Press: Thirteen Tracts, 1666–1774.* New York: Garland, 1975.

————, ed. *The Great Property Debate: Eight Tracts, 1774–1775.* New York: Garland, 1974.

————, ed. *The Literary Property Debate: Seven Tracts, 1747–1773.* New York: Garland, 1974.

————, ed. *The Great Property Debate: Six Tracts, 1764–1774.* New York: Garland, 1975.

Parry, Edward William. *Journal of a second voyage for the discovery of a north-west passage from the Atlantic to the Pacific.* London: John Murray, 1824.

————. *Journal of a voyage for the discovery . . . of a north-west passage from the Atlantic to the Pacific.* Edinburgh: A. Constable, 1821.

Patterson, Lyman Ray. *Copyright in Historical Perspective.* Nashville, Tenn.: Vanderbilt University Press, 1988.

Peacock, Thomas Love. *Headlong Hall and Nightmare Abbey.* New York: G. P. Putnam's Sons, 1887.

————. *Memoirs of Shelley.* Ed. H. F. B. Brett-Smith. London: Henry Frowde, 1909.

————. *Thomas Love Peacock: Memoirs of Shelley and Other Essays and Reviews.* Ed. Rupert Hart-Davis. London: Rupert-Hart Davis, 1970.

Pearce, Lynn. "John Clare's 'Child Harold': A Polyphonic Reading." *Criticism* 31 (1989): 139–57.

Peck, Louis F. *The Life of Matthew G. Lewis.* Cambridge, Mass.: Harvard University Press, 1961.

Perkins, David. "Romantic Lyric Voice: What Shall We Call the 'I'?" *Southern Review* 29:2 (Spring 1993): 225–39.

Peterfreund, Stuart. "'In Free Homage and Generous Subjection': Miltonic Influence in *The Excursion.*" *The Wordsworth Circle* 9 (1978): 173–77.

Pfau, Thomas. *Form, Class, and the Logic of Early Romantic Cultural Production.* Stanford, Calif.: Stanford University Press, 1997.

Pinch, Adela. *Strange Fits of Passion: Epistemologies of Emotion from Hume to Austen.* Stanford, Calif.: Stanford University Press, 1996.

Poetical Repository of Fugitive Poetry for 1810–11. London: F. C. and J. Rivington, 1814.

Poovey, Mary. *The Proper Lady and the Woman Writer.* Los Angeles: University of California Press, 1984.

Porter, James E. "Intertextuality and the Discourse of Community." *Rhetoric Review* 5 (1986): 34–47.

Pratt, Mary Louise. *Imperial Eyes: Travel Writing and Transculturation.* New York: Routledge, 1992.

Quillinan, Edward. "Imaginary Conversation, Between Mr. Walter Savage Landor and the Editor of Blackwood's Magazine [Mr. Christopher North]." *Blackwood's Edinburgh Magazine* 53:330 (April 1843): 518–36.

Raban, Joseph, ed. *Shelley Revalued: Essays from the Greynog Conference.* Leicester: Leicester University Press, 1983.

Radcliffe, Ann. *A Journey made in the summer of 1794, through Holland and the western frontier of Germany, with a return down the Rhine: to which are added observations during a tour to the Lakes of Lancashire, Westmoreland, and Cumberland.* London: G. G. and J. Robinson, 1795.

Randall, Marilyn. "The Context of Decolonization and the Poetics of Plagiarism." *Comparative Literature East and West: Traditions and Trends.* Ed. Cornelia Moore and Raymond A. Moody. Honolulu: University of Hawaii Press, 1989.

———. *Pragmatic Plagiarism: Authorship, Profit, and Power.* Toronto: University of Toronto Press, 2001.

Ratomir, Rastic. "Shelley's First Major Lyrics and *Prometheus Unbound.*" *Linguistics and Literature* 2:7 (2000): 69–86.

Reid, David. "Thomson and Wordsworth: A Debt with a Difference." *Scottish Literary Journal* 19:1 (May 1992): 5–17.

Reiman, Donald H. "Coleridge and the Art of Equivocation." *Studies in Romanticism* 25 (Fall 1986): 325–50.

———. *Romantic Texts and Contexts.* Columbia: University of Missouri Press, 1987.

Repton, Alexander Wood, ed. *English Reports: Full Reprints.* 176 vols. London: W. Green and Sons, 1900–1932.

Richardson, Alan. *British Romanticism and the Science of the Mind.* Cambridge: Cambridge University Press, 2001.

Ricks, Christopher. *Allusion to the Poets.* Oxford: Oxford University Press, 2002.

———. "Plagiarism." *Proceedings of the British Academy* 97 (1998): 149–68.

Robinson, Mary. *Mary Robinson: Selected Poems.* Ed. Judith Pascoe. Peterborough: Broadview Literary Texts, 2000.

Roe, Nicholas. *John Keats and the Culture of Dissent.* Oxford: Clarendon Press, 1997.

Rose, Mark. "The Author as Proprietor: *Donaldson v. Beckett* and the Genealogy of Modern Authorship." *Representations* 23 (Summer 1998): 51–85.

———. *Authors and Owners: The Invention of Copyright.* Cambridge, Mass.: Harvard University Press, 1993.

Rosenblum, Joseph. *Practice to Deceive: The Amazing Stories of Literary Forgery's Most Notorious Practioners.* New Castle, Del.: Oak Knoll Press, 2000.

Rosenthal, Laura J. *Playwrights and Plagiarists in Early Modern England: Gender, Authorship, and Literary Property.* Ithaca, N.Y.: Cornell University Press, 1993.

Ross, Trevor. *Making of the English Literary Canon from the Middle Ages to the Late Eighteenth Century.* Montreal: McGill-Queen's Press, 1998.

Russett, Margaret. "Like 'Wedding Gowns or Money from the Mint': Clare's Borrowed Inheritance," *Romanticism and the Law: Romantic Circles Praxis Series.*

Ed. Michael Macovski. (University of Maryland, 1999; http://www.rc.umd
.edu/praxis/law/russett/mruss.htm).

———. "Meter, Identity, Voice: Untranslating *Christabel.*" *Studies in English Literature* 43:4 (2003): 773–97.

Rzepka, Charles J. "Re-Collecting Spontaneous Overflows: Romantic Passions, the Sublime, and Mesmerism," *Romantic Passions: Romantic Circles Praxis Series.* Ed. Elizabeth Fay. (University of Maryland, 2001; http://www.rc.umd.edu/ praxis/passions/rzepka/rzp.html).

Sadoff, Ira. "Louise Glück and the Last Stage of Romanticism." *New England Review* 22:4 (Fall 2001): 81–92.

Said, Edward. *Orientalism.* New York: Random House, 1979.

Saint-Amour, Paul K. *The Copywrights: Intellectual Property and the Literary Imagination.* Ithaca, N.Y.: Cornell University Press, 2003.

Schelling, Friedrich. *System of Transcendental Idealism.* Trans. Peter Heath. Charlottesville: University of Virginia Press, 1978.

Schmidgen, Wolfram. *Eighteenth-Century Fiction and the Law of Property.* Cambridge: Cambridge University Press, 2002.

Schoenfield, Mark. *The Professional Wordsworth: Law, Labor, and the Poet's Contract.* Athens: University of Georgia Press, 1996.

Scott, Walter. *Miscellaneous Prose Works of Sir Walter Scott.* 30 vols. Edinburgh: A. and C. Black, 1870.

———, ed. *Ballanytne's Novelist's Library.* 8 vols. London: Hurst, Robinson, and Company, 1821.

Seward, Ann. *The Letters of Anna Seward.* 6 vols. London: John Murray, 1811.

Shaffer, E. L. "Coleridge's Swiss Voice: Friederike Brun and the Vale of Chamouni." *Essays in Memory of Michael Parkinson and Janine Dakyns.* Ed. Christopher Smith, et al. Norwich: East Anglia University, 1996.

Shelley, Mary. *Essays, Letters from Abroad, Translations and Fragments.* London: Edward Moxon, 1840.

———. "Giovanni Villani." *The Liberal* 4 (1823): 281–97.

———. *Mary Shelley's "Lives of the Most Eminent Scientific and Literary Men of Italy."* Ed. Tilar J. Mazzeo. Vol. 1. *Mary Shelley: Literary Lives and Uncollected Writings.* Gen. ed. Nora Crook. 4 vols. London: Pickering and Chatto, 2002.

———. *Lodore.* Ed. Lisa Vargo. Peterborough: Broadview, 1997.

———. *Novels and Selected Works of Mary Shelley.* Gen. ed. Nora Crook. 8 vols. London: Pickering and Chatto, 1996.

Shelley, Percy Bysshe. *The Complete Poetical Works of Percy Bysshe Shelley.* Ed. Neville Rogers. 4 vols. Oxford: Oxford University Press, 1975.

———. *The Complete Poetry of Percy Bysshe Shelley.* Ed. Neil Fraistat and Donald H. Reiman. 1 vol. to date. Baltimore: Johns Hopkins University Press, 2000.

———. *The Letters of Percy Bysshe Shelley.* Ed. Frederick L. Jones. 2 vols. Oxford: Oxford University Press, 1964.

———. *Poetical Works of Percy Bysshe Shelley.* Ed. Mary Shelley. London: Edward Moxon, 1839.

———. *Shelley's Poetry and Prose.* Ed. Donald H. Reiman and Sharon B. Powers. New York: W.W. Norton, 1977.

———. *Original Poetry by Victor and Cazire*. [With Elizabeth Shelley.] Ed. Richard Garnett. London: John Lane, 1898.

Siskin, Clifford. *The Historicity of Romantic Discourse*. Oxford: Oxford University Press, 1988.

Smith, Brian Keith. "The Ballads of Friederike Brun." *Carleton Germanic Papers* 24 (1996): 37–55.

Smollett, Tobias. "Habakkuk Hilding, Justice and Chapman." *The Covent-Garden Journal* 2 (15 January 1752).

Soderholm, James. *Fantasy, Forgery, and the Byron Legend*. Lexington: University Press of Kentucky, 1996.

———. *Multiple Authorship and the Myth of Solitary Genius*. Oxford: Oxford University Press, 1991.

Southey, Robert. "Inquiry into the Copyright Act." *The Quarterly Review* 21:41 (January 1819): 196–213.

———. *Poetical Works, 1793–1810*. Gen. ed. Lynda Pratt. 5 vols. London: Pickering and Chatto, 2003.

Spurr, David. *The Rhetoric of Empire: Colonial Discourse in Journalism, Travel Writing, and Imperial Administration*. Durham, N.C.: Duke University Press, 1993.

Stein, Edwin. *Wordsworth's Art of Allusion*. University Park: Pennsylvania State University, 1988.

Stewart, Susan. *Crimes of Writing: Problems in the Containment of Representation*. Oxford: Oxford University Press, 1991.

Stillinger, Jack. *Multiple Authorship and the Myth of Solitary Genius*. Oxford: Oxford University Press, 1991.

Storey, Edward. *A Right to Song: The Life of John Clare*. London: Metheun, 1982.

Storey, Mark, ed. *John Clare: The Critical Heritage*. London: Routledge and Kegan Paul, 1973.

Strickland, Edward. "Boxer Byron: A Clare Obsession." *The Byron Journal* 17 (1989): 57–76.

Stroud, Dorothy. *Capability Brown*. London: Faber and Faber, 1975.

Suleri, Sara. *The Rhetoric of British India*. Chicago: University of Chicago Press, 1992.

Suzuki, Ruriko. "Translation in the 1790s: A Means of Creating a Like Existence and/or Restoring the Original." *Romanticism on the Net* 2 (May 1992): <http://ron.umontreal.ca>.

The Tatler. Ed. Donald F. Bond. 3 vols. Oxford: Oxford University Press, 1987.

Taylor, Henry. "Recent Poetical Plagiarisms and Imitations." *The London Magazine* 8 (December 1823): 597–604.

Thomson, James. *The Seasons*. London: A. Millar, 1744.

Timothy Webb. *The Violet in the Crucible: Shelley and Translation*. Oxford: Oxford University Press, 1976.

Trelawny, Edward. *The Adventures of a Younger Son*. Ed. William St. Clair. London: Oxford University Press, 1974.

Trott, Nicola Z. "North of the Border: Cultural Crossing in the *Noctes Ambrosiane*." *Romanticism on the Net* 20 (November 2000): <http://www.ron.umontreal.ca>.

Trumpener, Katie. *Bardic Nationalism: The Romantic Novel and the British Empire.* Princeton, N.J.: Princeton University Press, 1997.

Tully, James. *A Discourse on Property: John Locke and His Adversaries.* Oxford: Oxford University Press, 1980.

Tully, Richard, ed. *A Narrative of Ten Years' Residence at Tripoli in Africa; from the Original Correspondence in the Possession of the Late Richard Tully, Esq., the British Consul.* London: Henry Colburn, 1816.

Vassallo, Peter. *Byron: The Italian Literary Influence.* New York: St. Martin's Press, 1984.

Venuti, Lawrence. *The Translator's Invisibility.* New York: Routledge, 1995.

Verkoren, Lucas. *A Study of Shelley's "Defence of Poetry."* Netherlands: n.p., n.d.

Vincent, E. R. *Byron, Hobhouse and Foscolo.* Cambridge: Cambridge University Press, 1949.

Wahrman, Dror. *The Making of the Modern Self: Identity and Culture in Eighteenth-Century England.* New Haven, Conn.: Yale University Press, 2004.

Wallace, Jennifer. "Tyranny and Translation: Shelley's Unbinding of Prometheus." *Romanticism* 1:1 (1995): 15–33.

Warburton, William. *A Letter from an Author to a Member of Parliament Concerning Literary Property.* London: John and Paul Knapton, 1747. Rpt. *Horace Walpole's Political Tracts, 1747–1748, with Two by William Warburton on Literary Property, 1747 and 1762.* Ed. Stephen Parks. New York: Garland, 1974.

Webb, Timothy. *The Violet in the Crucible: Shelley and Translation.* Oxford: Oxford University Press, 1976.

Wellek. René. *The History of Modern Criticism: 1750–1950.* 2 vols. New Haven, Conn.: Yale University Press, 1955.

Williamson, Tom, and Liz Bellamy. *Property and Landscape: A Social History of Land Ownership and the English Countryside.* London: George Philip, 1987.

Wilson, John. "Sacred Poetry." *Blackwood's Edinburgh Magazine* 24:146 (December 1828): 917–38.

———. *The Trials of Margaret Lyndsay.* London: T. Cadell, 1823.

Wollstonecraft, Mary. *Letters written during a short residence in Sweden, Norway, and Denmark.* London: J. Johnson, 1796.

Woodmansee, Martha, and Peter Jaszi. *The Construction of Authorship: Textual Appropriation in Law and Literature.* Durham, N.C.: Duke University Press, 1994.

Wordsworth, Dorothy. *Grasmere Journals.* Ed. Pamela Woof. Oxford: Oxford University Press, 1991.

———. *The Journals of Dorothy Wordsworth.* Ed. Mary Moorman. Oxford: Oxford University Press, 1971.

———. *Poetry of Dorothy Wordsworth.* Ed. Hyman Eigerman. New York: Columbia University Press, 1940.

———. *Recollections of a tour made in Scotland, A.D. 1803.* Ed. J. C. Shairp. Edinburgh: Douglas, 1894.

Wordsworth, William. *The Excursion.* London: Longman, Hurst, Rees, Ormes, and Brown, 1814.

———. *Last Poems.* Ed. J. Curtis. Ithaca, N.Y.: Cornell University Press, 1999.

————. *Letters of the Wordsworth Family from 1787–1855.* Ed. William Knight. 3 vols. Boston: Ginn and Company, 1907.

————. *Letters of William and Dorothy Wordsworth.* Ed. Ernest DeSelincourt. Rev. Mary Moore and Alan G. Hill. 7 vols. Oxford: Clarendon Press, 1970.

————. *Poetical Works of William Wordsworth.* Ed. Ernest DeSelincourt and Helen Darbishire. 5 vols. Oxford: Clarendon Press, 1949.

————. *Prose Works of William Wordsworth.* Ed. W. J. B. Owen and Jane Worthington Smyser. 3 vols. Oxford: Clarendon Press, 1974.

————. *[The Selected Works of] William Wordsworth.* Ed. Stephen Gill. Oxford: Oxford University Press, 1984.

————. *William Wordsworth: The Poems.* Ed. John O. Hayden. 2 vols. New Haven, Conn.: Yale University Press, 1977.

Yearsley, Ann. *Poems on Several Occasions.* London: G. G. J. and J. Robinson, 1786.

Young, Edward. *Conjectures on Original Composition in a Letter to [Samuel Richardson] the Author of Sir Charles Grandison.* London: A. Millar and R. and J. Dodsley, 1759.

Index

Adams, Percy, 109
Addison, Joseph, 82
Altieri, Charles, xii
anonymous publication, 83, 109–11
Augustan literature, 12, 14. *See also* neoclassical aesthetics
authorship: assumptions regarding solitary genius, ix, xi, xiii, 6–7, 16, 30, 182, 186–88; commercial or professional, ix, xii, 54–62, 66, 75, 81, 85, 95–96, 123–24, 144, 166–75; poststructuralist theories of, xi, xiii, 1, 6–7, 147, 186–88; pre-Romantic constructions of, xiii, 1. *See also* gender

ballads, 49, 54, 70–85. *See also* Wordsworth, William
Barrell, John, 157
Barthes, Roland, 6, 47–48, 196–97 n.27
Bayley, Peter, 15–6, 103, 119, 147–49, 152, 207–8 n.10
Beach, Joseph Warren, 46
Beattie, James, 178
Beaumont, Francis, and John Fletcher, 151
Beckford, William, 108, 111, 116
Bennett, Andrew, 85, 153
Bently, Lionel, 11
Birns, Nicholas, 137
Blackstone, William, 51–53
Blessington, Marguerite Gardiner, countess of, 116, 119–21
Bloom, Harold (*The Anxiety of Influence*), 136
Bloomfield, Robert, 179
Bonjour, Adrien, 46, 56
Boruchoff, David, 182, 187
Bostetter, Edward, 30, 195 n.12
Bradley, A. C., 3, 190 n.2
Brewer, William, 180
Brown, Capability, 145
Brownlow, Timothy, 145–46
Brun, (Sophie Christiane) Friederike, 18–19, 45–46, 50, 55–57, 62

Burgher, Gottfried August, 75, 82
Burke, Edmund, 15
Burke, Séan, xiii
Burns, Robert, 176
Byron, George Gordon, lord: accused of plagiarism, x, xii, 2, 8, 41, 44, 73, 86, 106, 144–45, 147; concern with textual unity, 128, 130; conflict with William Wordsworth, 44, 86–87, 94–96, 106–7, 119, 144, 147; debts in *Childe Harold*, 94–107, 111, 144; debts to Coleridge, 91–94, 96–97, 100–101, 110, 116; debts to Continental literature, 104–7, 116–21, 202–3 n.15, 204 n.30; debts in *Deformed Transformed*, 119; debts in *Don Juan*, 43, 94, 107–13, 115–19; debts in oriental tales, 87–94; debts to travel writing, 50, 86, 90–91, 105, 107–13, 115–17, 123, 127–28; debts to William Wordsworth, 96, 100–101, 201–2 n.7; and empire, 112–16; investment in persona, 98–104, 111, 143, 201 n.2; and Lake School poets, 100–102; literary failure of, 98–104; literary property, attitude toward, 11, 87; originality, attitude toward, 112–16; peasant poets, attitude toward, 179–80; reputation as poet, 28, 54, 86–89, 176; resented by John Clare, 179–80; social class as factor, 121, 166; unconscious, attitude toward, 119–21

Calderon de la Barca, Pedro, 134
Campbell, Thomas, 127–28, 159–60, 196 n.25
Casti, Giambattista, 116–19
Chatterton, Thomas, 23, 72–73, 174–75
Christensen, Jerome, 47, 196 n.25
Clairmont, Claire, 136
Clare, John, x, 2, 8, 176–81, 184
class: related to charges of plagiarism, ix–x, 173–81; genteel or aristocratic contexts, 50, 66, 95–96, 121, 129, 144, 157; related to labor and social ascendancy, 146, 158–65, 173–81

Moore, Thomas, 91–92, 94, 105, 123, 127–28, 159–60, 204–5 n.1
Moorman, Mary, 65
More, Hannah, 8, 21, 145, 174–76, 194–95 n.4, 197 n.1
Morgan, Sydney, 137–38, 140
multiple-use property, 19–20, 84. *See also* enclosure
Murphy, Peter, 80–81, 149
Murray, John, 73, 108–11, 115, 201 n.7
Musäus, Johann Karl August, 77–79

nationalism, related to literature, 79, 84, 102, 113–15, 177–78
neoclassical aesthetics, 20, 129, 147. *See also* Augustan literature
new, in Romantic aesthetics. *See* novelty
New Historicism, xi
Newlyn, Lucy, 28–29
newspapers, attitude toward appropriation from, 54, 57–62
North, Christopher, 162–63
Norton, Caroline, 52–53
novelty, 9, 29–30, 153

oral circulation of texts: related to *Christabel*, 29–31, 91–92, 147; related to Gothic, 50, 75–85; related to other examples of plagiarism, x, 151–52, 155–58, 173–74. *See also* vernacular
oriental tales, 84–93
originality: and ideas of autogenous invention, ix, xiii, 5, 14, 22, 30, 90, 132, 182; modern characterization of, xiii, 5, 9–10; neoclassical attitudes toward, 10, 12–14, 117, 183, 192 n.17, 192–93 n.18; Romanticism associated with, ix, xi, xiii–xiv, 182; Romantic-period attitudes toward, xiv, 9–10, 16, 29–30, 86–90, 93, 117, 120, 152–53, 170, 178–79, 182–88

Parnell, Thomas, 88
parody, 15, 89, 104, 148, 190 n.5. *See also* satire
patchwork, used as critical complaint, 3, 21, 43, 128, 185
Peacock, Thomas Love, 125–31, 136, 145
Peck, Louis, 76–77
Peel, Robert, 169–71
Percy, Thomas, 82
Perkins, David, 185–86
Pfau, Thomas, 146

plagiarism: acknowledgment as factor in, 2–3, 107; aesthetic or poetical, x, 2–3, 20, 32, 41, 43, 65, 82, 88, 96–98, 127, 147, 163; aesthetic stakes in, xiv, 1–2, 4–5, 8, 46, 54–55, 73, 83, 87, 90–93, 97–98, 107, 116, 120, 130–32, 143; avowal, criteria for implicit, 2–3, 97, 106; coincidence as factor in, 24, 26, 38–41, 90, 92–93, 109, 133, 162, 174, 178, 190 n.2; as competition, 9, 28, 57, 185, 207 n.7; consciousness as factor in, 2–3, 17–24, 32, 34, 46, 63, 78–77, 83, 88–89, 93, 97, 117, 119, 133–34, 173–74, 190 n.2, 195 n.4; critical emphasis on, ix, xiii–xiv, 2, 6–8, 18, 20, 22, 42, 45–46, 190 n.6, 191–92 n.12; critical reluctance to historicize, xii–xiv, 1, 6–7, 45, 106–7, 192 n.14; criticism, as mode of, 9, 18, 28, 42, 45, 86, 112, 154–55; culpable, 2, 4, 7, 20, 32, 41, 45, 72, 83, 89, 97, 125, 148; described in Romantic period, 1–5, 8–9, 17, 19–24, 53–56, 63–64, 76, 88, 96–98, 182–85; etymology of, 110, 112, 203 n.24; familiarity of texts as factor in, 2–3, 19–24, 72, 122, 125, 158; improvement as factor in, 2–6, 19–23, 43–44, 56, 64–65, 83, 97–98, 107, 119, 130, 145, 152, 178, 190 n.2, 195 n.4; legal aspects of, 5–6, 10–14, 46, 49–50, 73; legal rhetoric associated with in Romantic period, 10–14, 16, 89–90, 94, 97, 110; literary failure, as implication of, 16, 20, 18, 44, 88, 97–104, 147; morality as factor in, xiv, 5–6, 8, 18, 20, 42, 45–46, 88, 190 n.6; neoclassical attitude toward, 7, 12–13; as passive imitation, 32, 34; persona as factor in, 97–104, 111, 129–32; and postmodernism, xiii, 5–7, 47; post-Romantic attitudes toward, 53, 162, 183, 190 n.2; psychological motives of assumed, x, 8, 46–48; real estate, compared to, 11, 144–47, 155; social class as factor in, 50, 66, 70, 144; textual unity as factor in, 3–4, 47, 129. *See also* copyright; gender; style, textual parallels
plot. *See* machinery
poetry, as privileged genre, xii, 9, 126, 131–35
Polwhele, Richard, 89
Pope, Alexander, 14, 88, 150, 177
Porter, James, xiii
Priestley, Joseph, 35
pseudonymous publication, 59
Pulci, Luigi, 118

Acknowledgments

In the course of this study I return repeatedly to questions of circulation, collaboration, and community, arguing that these values were central to the project of literary Romanticism, and, if my experience is any indication, the spirit of Romanticism is alive and well. Without the assistance of many colleagues and friends, this work would not have been possible, and I cannot properly recognize here the many voices that informed this project. There are several people, however, to whom I owe particular and substantial debts of gratitude. I am grateful to Sam Baker, Anna-Lisa Cox, Marilyn Gaull, Brean Hammond, Gary Handwerk, Nigel Leask, Carol Levin, Michael Macovski, Anne Mellor, Rob Mitchell, Mona Modiano, Margaret Russett, Dror Wahrman, the 2003–4 Newberry Library seminar participants, and my colleagues in the Department of English at Colby College for critiques, comments, and conversations that helped to shape the direction of this book in different ways. Among those colleagues at Colby, special thanks to Ira Sadoff and Adrian Blevins for fruitful exchanges about poetry and the inheritance of Romanticism. It is with great affection that I thank Jeff Cox, Michael Gamer, Greg Kucich, Dan White, and Paul Youngquist, along with Tim Fulford, for the many conversations that enriched this study and for the important personal friendships that make working in Romanticism such a pleasure. Noelle Baker and Roberta Maguire epitomized collegiality and many other virtues; along with Jérémie Fant and Jeremy and Paula Lowe, they provided intellectual sustenance and much more in lean times. I owe to Hazard Adams the enduring and very particular debt that all students owe to superb teachers. And, above all, my profound thanks and love to Thaine Stearns, for listening to it all with generosity and care and devotion and for always believing that everything was necessary.

This work could not have been completed without the financial generosity of several institutions. The Monticello Foundation Fellowship at the Newberry Library, the Andrew Mellon and Michael J. Connell Fellowships at the Huntington Library, the Keats-Shelley Association of America, and Pembroke College, University of Cambridge provided time and support at critical intervals. I am grateful to the staff of these institutions, as well as to the curators of the Pforzheimer Collection at the New York Public Library and to the staff of the University Library, Cambridge for their patience and expertise.

Portions of Chapter 2 first appeared in print in *European Romantic Review* as part of the 2003 North American Society for the Study of Romanticism (NASSR) conference proceedings, under the title "Coleridge, Plagiarism, and the Psychology of the Romantic Habit" (15:2 [June 2004]: 335–41); and a portion of Chapter 4 likewise appeared in *European Romantic Review* as part of the 1996 NASSR conference volume, under the title " 'A mixture of all the styles': Nationalism, Colonialism, and Plagiarism in Shelley's Indian Circle" (8:2 [Spring 1997]: 155–68). I am grateful to the journal for permission to republish.